Columbus and the Crisis of the West

ROBERT ROYAL

COLUMBUS

AND THE

CRISIS

OF THE

WEST

SOPHIA INSTITUTE PRESS
Manchester, New Hampshire

This book is a revised and expanded edition of *1492 and All That: Political Manipulations of History* (Washington, D.C.: Ethics and Public Policy Center, 1992). Chapter 7, revised for this edition, first appeared in the *Intercollegiate Review* (Spring 1998). The appendix is adapted from "Columbus and the Beginning of the World," *First Things* (May 1999).

Printed in the United States of America. All rights reserved.

Cover design by Perceptions Design Studio.

Cover images: Christopher Columbus (FNA30A) © IanDagnall Computing / Alamy Stock Photo; Waldseemüller map, Wikimedia Commons, public domain; decorative frame (27125491) © nodff / Shutterstock.com; texture (133936211) © sociologas / Shutterstock.com;

Sophia Institute Press
Box 5284, Manchester, NH 03108
1-800-888-9344

www.SophiaInstitute.com

Sophia Institute Press® is a registered trademark of Sophia Institute.

Paperback ISBN 978-1-64413-405-4
eBook ISBN 978-1-64413-406-1
Library of Congress Control Number: 2020944216

First printing

Venient annis
Saecula seris, quibus Oceanus
Vincula rerum laxent, et ingens
Pateat tellus, Typhisque novos
Detegat Orbes, nec sit terris
Ultima Thule.

—Seneca

The day was 4-Flower and the year 1-House.
They perished and all the mountains
    perished with them.
The water lasted fifty-two years
    and then their years ended.
We are now in the Sun 4-Movement
    and under this Sun
There will be earthquakes and famine,
    And we shall all be destroyed.

—Nahuatl Legend
of the Suns

Contents

Columbus and the Crisis of the West

Introduction to the 2020 Edition

Bartolomé de Las Casas, a Dominican friar active in the early years of the European missionary efforts in the Americas, earned the name *defensor de los Indios* (Defender of the Indians) because of his passionate diatribes against exploiters of native peoples in the New World. Along with other philosophers and theologians in Spain, Rome, and elsewhere in the Old Continent, he drew on classical and Christian traditions to argue that the newly encountered peoples were rational beings — human persons — who had rights and warranted respect on both secular and religious grounds. Naturally, his stance drew the ire of vested political and economic interests in Spain, which he stoutly resisted and rebutted. He also knew Christopher Columbus personally and, despite being highly critical of some of the things he did — though not the wild charges of which he typically stands accused today — spoke of his "sweetness and benignity." And Las Casas defended Columbus as well, against people who blamed him for the disorders and violence that occurred following the first contacts with indigenous peoples. The great explorer's missteps, he said, were the result of ignorance of divine law and misjudgments about how to proceed: "Truly. I would not dare blame the

Columbus and the Crisis of the West

admiral's intentions for I knew him well and I knew his intentions were good."[1]

During the riots that took place in America in mid-2020, several statues of Columbus were toppled. After a statue in Milwaukee fell, video circulated of people—mostly young white women—taking turns stomping on it. This was presumably because they regarded Columbus as the source of the displacement and killing of native peoples and subsequent slavery and racism in the Americas. Whatever the reason, however, it's quite certain that, unlike Las Casas, the mobs knew little or nothing about the person against whom they raged—or about other figures, including abolitionists, even the black activist Frederick Douglass, whose statues they toppled. And probably did not much care to know, because it has become self-evident to many people, insofar as there is any conceptual basis for such notions, that the whole history of Western exploration and expansion is nothing but a tale of exploitation, imperialism, and "white" supremacy. If you believe that, prior to any look at the facts—or any sense of the complexity of human history—then it also appears wrong to try to sort out the good and the bad present in this process, as in all things human. That amounts, on the radically critical view, to making excuses for genocide and racism.

It used to be possible to assume that any person who had graduated from high school (even grade school) would be familiar with at least a few facts about what happened in 1492. That this is no longer the case reflects failing educational institutions, to be sure, but also—it needs to be said—an anti-American, even an anti-Western and often anti-Christian, ideology that has arisen within the West itself: all the West, because, in 2020, mobs tore down statues in England, France, Belgium, Canada, Australia, and beyond.

---

[1] Bartolomé de las Casas, *History of the Indies*, trans. and ed. André Collard (New York: Harper & Row, 1971), 53.

Introduction to the 2020 Edition

This widespread unrest calls for careful attention. You don't need to believe that the French or communist revolutions, for example, were of unmixed benefit to the human race to take the trouble to know dates such as 1789 or 1917 and something about what they mean. Yet the year in which a far greater change came into the world—indeed, began the colossal process by which the various nations and continents truly *became* one global, interconnected *world*—has been taught for many years now as something to be ashamed of, even to denounce. In a saner mood, we might regard it as owing to the boldness and tenacity of Columbus, however little gratitude he now gets, that we today inhabit that *world*.

When the first edition of this book appeared, the contrary view was already starting to take hold. During the 1992 quincentenary of the first voyage by Columbus, which is examined in detail in these pages, many of us who had tried to think through what it meant—both good and bad—found it difficult to say anything positive about it in print, on television and radio, or even in academic settings. In the almost three decades since, scholars have done what they are meant to do: uncovered even more of the rich, sad, inspiring, frightening, appalling, glorious, and inglorious features of the Age of Exploration. But there exists something approaching a taboo about saying anything positive about Columbus or any of the other European explorers. People ready to condemn Columbus for every ill that has occurred on these shores, strangely, would never think of *crediting* him with the many indisputable goods that have been achieved as well, including the freedom to criticize past and present. And it would not be stretching things to say that the blanket rejection of Columbus has become a symbol for the uninformed repudiation of much of Western—and human—history.

The implications of that repudiation are legion. As historian Wilfred McClay has observed: "The pulling down of statues, as a form of symbolic murder, is congruent with the silencing of dissenting opinion, so prevalent a feature of campus life today. In my own academic field of history, it is entirely of a piece with the weaponizing of history, in which the past is regarded as nothing more than a malleable background for the concerns of the present, and not as an independent source of wisdom or insight or perspective." He adds:

> Those caught up in the moral frenzy of the moment ought to think twice, and more than twice, about jettisoning figures of the past who do not measure up perfectly to the standards of the present—a present, moreover, for which those past figures cannot reasonably be held responsible. For one thing, as the Scriptures warn us, the measure you use is the measure you will receive. Those who expect moral perfection of others can expect no mercy for themselves, either from their posterity or from the rebukes of their own inflamed consciences.[2]

Shakespeare's Hamlet had the old Christian wisdom and mere human decency exactly right: "Use every man after his desert, and who should 'scape whipping?"[3]

These truths take on even greater significance if we consider that what is at stake is not merely the historical evaluation of Columbus or Europe or "white privilege." It goes to the heart of what civilization means: given the universal evidence of human sinfulness and imperfection, we put ourselves in the position of preferring to have no cultural roots at all if we demand to allow into public spaces and permissible discourse only what we believe—on

---

[2]   Wilfred M. McClay, "Of Statues and Symbolic Murder," *First Things*, 26 June 2020, https://www.firstthings.com/web-exclusives/2020/06/of-statues-and-symbolic-murder.
[3]   William Shakespeare, *Hamlet* II, 2.

unclear grounds—is now the perfection of moral vision. One of the central things that this book seeks to demonstrate is that the radical critique of the West could not have happened without the very values—equality, human dignity, liberty—that spring from the Western tradition itself, and more specifically the Christian universalism that sees every human person, however imperfect, as a child of God, something that has existed in no other civilization.

Slavery, for example, has been a universal in human history from ancient Egypt and Mesopotamia to China, classical Greece and Rome, as well as Russia, the scattered kingdoms of Central Africa, the First Nations of Canada, various North American tribes, the great empires of the Mayan and Aztecs, the Ottoman Empire, and the antebellum American South. Chattel slavery—outright "ownership" of other human beings—which is often said to have been invented in the American South, can be dated back at least to the Code of Hammurabi (1750 B.C.) and ancient Egypt. It was almost entirely the work of "white" Christians such as Las Casas, beginning close to the time of the discovery of the Americas, and later British Quakers and Methodists drawing on biblical sources, that slavery was gradually eliminated in almost the entire world. Slavery still exists, of course. Something like forty million people are thought to be enslaved worldwide—but in places where a Christian sensibility is absent or inactive.

It disturbs some people to learn that slavery, genocide, imperialism, and even ritual human sacrifice and cannibalism were present in the Americas long before any European or other outsider ever set foot there. But they were.

Slavery was a part of Native American traditions, both before and after the arrival of Europeans. It was common in the large empires, as in empires on other continents. But it also existed in what is today Canada, particularly the Pacific Northwest, and almost everywhere. As late as the notorious Trail of Tears—the mid-nineteenth-century series of forced relocations of several tribes from the American Southeast to West of the Mississippi—there were black slaves, owned by Native Americans, among those making the trek. A 2018 Smithsonian Institution article, "How Native American Slaveholders Complicate the Trail of Tears Narrative," recalls how awful was that episode, in which at least four thousand died. But also explains:

> What you probably don't picture are Cherokee slaveholders, foremost among them Cherokee chief John Ross. What you probably don't picture are the numerous African-American slaves, Cherokee-owned, who made the brutal march themselves, or else were shipped en masse to what is now Oklahoma aboard cramped boats by their wealthy Indian masters. And what you may not know is that the federal policy of Indian removal, which ranged far beyond the Trail of Tears and the Cherokee, was not simply the vindictive scheme of Andrew Jackson, but rather a popularly endorsed, congressionally sanctioned campaign spanning the administrations of nine separate presidents.[4]

There was Native American genocide as well, even among groups for whom any decent person will today feel a great deal of sympathy. For instance, on July 4, 2020, controversy erupted over the American presidents represented on Mount Rushmore and even the U.S. government's ownership of the site. But the history of the place tells a melancholy tale. In 1776, the very year the

---

[4] Ryan P. Smith, "How Native American Slaveholders Complicate the Trail of Tears Narrative," *Smithsonian Magazine*, March 6, 2018, https://www.smithsonianmag.com/smithsonian-institution/how-native-american-slaveholders-complicate-trail-tears-narrative-180968339/.

American colonies declared their independence, the Lakota Sioux conquered the Black Hills, where Mount Rushmore is located. They wiped out the local Cheyenne, who held it previously; and the Cheyenne had taken it themselves from the Kiowa,[5] who took it from ... no doubt some other tribe. As one informed historian pointed out: "The Lakota-Sioux arrived in the West after being on the losing end of a war with other tribes in Minnesota in the late 1700s. Known as the Lakota, or simply the Sioux, they waged genocidal war on other tribes before they took over the Black Hills from the Cheyenne.... They did the exact same thing that the United States did to drive the Lakota out."[6]

It is very difficult to escape the network of human evils that have existed throughout history. The African American author Ta-Nehisi Coates wrote a highly influential book in 2015 on the history of racism and white supremacy, *Between the World and Me*, in the form of a kind of message to his son, Samori. The son was named after a late-nineteenth-century African leader, Samori Ture, a devout Muslim who fought French colonialism in West Africa—but also captured and sold black slaves to finance his empire building.[7] In so doing, he was carrying on a tradition—black Africans capturing and selling other black Africans as slaves to others—that predated the Atlantic slave trade by at least a thousand years and continues in various forms of human trafficking even today.

---

[5] "Westward Expansion of the Lakota," in "Sioux," Wikipedia, last modified July 27, 2020, https://en.wikipedia.org/wiki/Sioux#cite_note-cheyenne-53.

[6] Tom Correa, "The Last Tribe to Get the Black Hills," *The American Cowboy Chronicles* (blog), April 18, 2015, http://www.american-cowboychronicles.com/2015/04/the-last-tribe-to-get-black-hills.html.

[7] *New World Encyclopedia*, s.v. "Samory," https://www.newworldencyclopedia.org/entry/Samory.

Columbus and the Crisis of the West

To recall such things is not to excuse Europeans or Christians who should have behaved better then and still should now. But it is to get a clearer picture of what we as a species have been, rather than fictional representations of purely good and purely bad actors that have displaced the truth.

It is common today to charge historically Christian nations with violence or religious bigotry not only toward Native Americans but even toward Muslims. During the riots of 2020, one Islamic group called for renaming Saint Louis, Missouri, because the French king after whom the city is named, Louis IX (1214–1270), had fought against both Jews and Muslims and, in fact, had been captured and imprisoned by Muslims in Egypt during the Seventh Crusade. In modern pluralistic societies, where large numbers of people with very different beliefs must try to live together in some sort of civic orderliness, such religious tensions obviously need to be avoided. But it is not so easy to transpose postmodern American concerns into the Middles Ages, let alone the Age of Discovery.

Few Westerners know it, but in 1453—less than forty years before Columbus arrived in the Caribbean—the Ottoman Turks finally overthrew Constantinople, capital of the Eastern Roman Empire for over a thousand years, and continued with further advances. This process had a long history. Muslims had conquered much of the Middle East and all of North Africa and made repeated incursions into the Holy Land, Spain (for eight hundred years), Rome, Sicily (where they ruled for almost a century), and elsewhere. It is no surprise, then, that Louis IX fought Muslims, even as he was beyond all dispute one of the most saintly and charitable of men. In the context of his time, preventing Muslim advances preserved Christian civilization. Had he and others failed, European and American cultures might today resemble the Middle East, and the voyages of discovery might never have occurred.

The downfall of Constantinople in 1453 sent shockwaves throughout Europe and, in Spain, one reason why Ferdinand and Isabella, by fits and starts and finally in 1492, expelled Muslims was fear of Ottoman support for rebels. And it did not stop there. Muslim invaders pressed on into the Balkans and other Western territories, even reaching Vienna, where they were turned back only with some strokes of good fortune, primarily the last-minute arrival of Polish hussars, in 1683.

If revisionist views of European nations in the Middle Ages and the early Renaissance have sought to make them look like nothing so much as *Game of Thrones*, recent scholarship about pre-Columbian America makes much of the New World appear not so very different. Our picture of native peoples in the English-speaking world has been strongly shaped by images of the relatively thinly settled Indian lands that the English colonists encountered (especially after diseases from Europe felled large percentages of native communities). It was from them that we derived the notion of the "noble savage," physically fit, independent, living lightly on the land. That picture is not entirely wrong—for a rather small segment of indigenous populations. It depends, however, on focusing on small tribes (all of what is now New England held only about one hundred thousand natives in the early 1600s, about one-sixth the current population of Boston) and ignoring continual tribal warfare, with its scalpings, kidnappings, and torture of captives. Most of the native settlements along the New England shores, for example, were protected by ramparts from attacks by warriors of other tribes.

When it comes to the large city-states and even empires that have been uncovered in Meso- and South America in recent decades, the argument for a universal human nature (and not an entirely happy one) across differences of culture, place, and age gains significant support. People who have actually looked into, say, Aztec civilization know that Tenochtitlán—the core of today's Mexico City—appeared to the earliest Spanish explorers, some of whom had sailed to the most opulent Mediterranean cities, as far richer in buildings, population, foodstuffs, and various cultural achievements than any city in Europe, the Middle East, or North Africa. It was also the center of an empire—perhaps containing as many as five million people—built by conquest over neighboring peoples and dependent on human sacrifice to bloodthirsty gods who required human blood to maintain the equilibrium of the world.

The other great civilizations of the Americas—Olmecs, Toltecs, Maya, Incas—also produced impressive urban centers and political, economic, and social networks, so much so that, as archaeologists and others have uncovered the remains of those civilizations, estimates of the population of the Americas have soared wildly. Some of the increase is doubtless owing to the desire of some scholars to compensate—overcompensate, say other scholars—for the relatively small numbers once thought accurate. Estimates now range from 8 million to almost 120 million inhabitants. Obviously, discrepancies of more than an order of magnitude call into question the methodologies used to produce them. But that large urban centers existed with extensive networks and surrounding areas to feed and supply them is now beyond dispute.

It is also beyond dispute that, like other human population centers, these cities were not situated in an unsullied earthly paradise. They cultivated but also depleted natural resources. They fought typical wars of conquest with one another. They rose, flourished, declined, and disappeared, just like human habitations in other parts of the world. Most practiced slavery. They changed large features of the natural landscape—from the high altitude of Mexico City to the riverbanks of the Amazon. That a much more idealized version of native peoples has survived all these discoveries reflects a hunger in postmodern Western culture for something "other" and purer. But projecting your needs onto other peoples and ignoring their actual lives dehumanizes them in a sense. No people will long be held in esteem—once real history enters into the picture—if they are held up as an unreal idealization that has never existed since the Garden of Eden, owing to the sinfulness, limited vision, and weakness of our universal human nature.

That applies to current critics of the past as well. If you are going to pull down statues of Columbus because he and the culture out of which he came were imperfect, what ideals will you offer for the future? In a review of the first edition of this book (titled *1492 and All That: Political Manipulations of History*),[8] Oxford historian J. H. Elliot suggested that it was regrettable that a book like this even needed to be written.[9] But it did. And it still does—now partly rewritten and amplified to reflect some of the historical work that has been done in intervening years and to freshen arguments that may prevent us from making rash and destructive judgments.

A remarkable shift in how we view human history has become dominant since this book first appeared. For several centuries in the West, there has been a widespread belief in human progress, driven by science, technology, and pragmatic uses of reason. There remained some sense that great men—Columbus, Newton, and Jefferson among them—could alter the course of history. As the first chapter in this book outlines, Americans caught up in that progressive movement were happy to falsify the historical record in order to portray the Genoese explorer as a kind of precursor of later rebels who defied the received wisdom of religion and tradition to forge new paths for the human race. In that reading, Columbus was the forerunner of the Protestant Reformation, the Scientific Revolution, global capitalism, even the modern autonomous self.

8   *1492 and All That: Political Manipulations of History* (Washington, D.C.: Ethics & Public Policy Center, 1992).
9   J. H. Elliott, "The Rediscovery of America," *New York Review of Books*, June 24, 1993, https://www.nybooks.com/articles/1993/06/24/the-rediscovery-of-america/.

Columbus and the Crisis of the West

That reading was not true (Columbus was a thoroughly medieval Christian extrapolating from the geographical knowledge available for the most part since Greco-Roman times). But that misappropriation of Columbus did at least retain some sense of the daring and imagination that went into Columbus's voyages—and the global developments they unleashed. Much of that understanding, as is documented here, simply melted away in the anti-Western ideological triumphs of the past fifty or so years. Columbus has become, for many today, a blank slate on which to project the loves and hatreds of our time: Euro-centrist, racist, imperialist, "genocidal maniac," and so on.

But there is even worse. Not only has the old Western confidence in progressivism, unreliable and incomplete and deluding a vision though it was, collapsed into its mirror image, but a crushing materialism, joined incoherently with visions of a technologized human future, has replaced it. There's no better example of the process than the wild, worldwide success of a book such as Yuval Noah Harari's *Sapiens*,[10] which dismisses virtually all of previous history as a mere prelude to a posthuman future that seems to leave him and millions of readers untroubled, though untethered to anything recognizably congenial to *Homo sapiens*. In its own strange way, that detachment from everything in the past paradoxically represents a kind of culmination of the anti-Western, anti-historical purity that makes up the bulk of the story told in this book.

Part of the difficulty in properly assessing Columbus the man is that it took a complex and driven figure to carry out what, eventually, he did. So it is possible to say he was ambitious—because he was. And sought honors—which he did—and wealth too. And that there were religious motives mixed in with these others.

---

[10] Yuval Noah Harari, *Sapiens: A Brief History of Humankind* (New York: Harper Perennial, 2015).

Columbus, like many in his time, was a strong believer whose faith deepened as he grew older—not exactly an unknown phenomenon even today. But his religious side has looked, at least to the cynics, as either a hypocritical cover for worldly motives or a benighted medieval superstitiousness that he had clung to well into what was then the Renaissance. Yet the notion of preaching the gospel to all nations and using the riches of the East to recover Jerusalem from the Muslims, however strange an aspiration for modern eyes and ears, made perfect, even sublime, sense in his world.[11]

A modern reader need not be a believer to understand that the mentality of someone—and such an unusual someone—in a different age, half a millennium ago, should not be reduced to categories that come easily to mind for us. Indeed, anyone who wants to understand both the man and the things he achieved—and did not achieve—should expect to have to step outside of at least some habitual assumptions. If that does not happen, we will be proceeding under a schizophrenia that afflicts much of the Western world today: on the one hand, we take the principles of human dignity and liberty as self-evident—which they are not, anywhere outside the Christian-inspired civilization of the West.[12] And at the same time, we will repudiate the very source of the things we hold as most morally certain.

The author is quite aware that there are many people who do not care about such efforts, who want only to feel the thrill of sweeping moral condemnations of imperfect historical figures, figures who, like us, were deeply shaped by their own times, by contemporary insights and blindness—and occasional steps toward something

[11] See Carol Delaney, *Columbus and the Quest for Jerusalem: How Religion Drove the Voyages That Led to America* (New York: Free Press, 2011).
[12] See Tom Holland, *Dominion: How the Christian Revolution Remade the World* (New York: Basic Books, 2019).

Columbus and the Crisis of the West

greater than they could yet articulate. Yet even if a work like the
present one may not much affect our current civilizational crisis,
civilization depends on unrelenting efforts to pursue truth, however
unpopular, over uninformed emotion.

And besides: the history of both Native American peoples and
the Europeans who came to these shores is much more humanly
interesting and instructive than simple morality tales.

Introduction to the 1992 Edition

In the highest literary achievements of both Western and non-Western cultures, human history is often viewed through lenses combining national epic and personal tragedy. Texts as diverse as Virgil's *Aeneid* and the Hindu sacred poem *Bhagavad Gita* portray crucial events of the past — indeed, foundational historic battles, acknowledged to have produced much good in the present — as inextricably bound up with painful choices and morally worrisome violence. In the battle that will ensure the founding of Rome, Aeneas, after a moment spent agonizing over whether to spare Turnus, sees that the opposing warrior is wearing a belt captured from a slain comrade and kills him in the last lines of the epic. Before a crucial clash that will determine the future of India, Arjuna, in anguish over the need to do battle with beloved teachers, friends, and members of his own family, ultimately obeys the counsel of the god Krishna and goes to war. The glory of Rome and the splendor of India, as their own high cultures recognized, were rooted — as are all large-scale human endeavors — in human loss, contradictions, and moral doubt, for which Virgil invented the immortal phrase *lacrimae rerum*.

Among the peoples of the Americas, perhaps the Mexicans, whose high indigenous cultures already possessed their own epics and tragic songs, have best preserved this sense of the epic and tragic dimensions of sweeping historical change. The conquest of the Aztecs by the Spanish under Cortés did not simply replace one people and culture with another, as is often assumed. From the heroism, brutality, courage, and turmoil of that era—from the colossal confluence of Aztec and Spaniard—something new emerged: Mexicans. Appropriately, Mexico celebrates October 12 not as Columbus Day but as el Dia de la Raza, "the day of the race," the new people of mixed Native American and European heritage. In the United States, we are usually distrustful of grand epic visions and reluctant to accept human tragedy, both of which we would like to think belong to the bad, old, striving, and overreaching worlds left behind by our immigrant ancestors. We prefer to see American life as a perpetually fresh start—without, or at least beyond, history—that provides us with the opportunity to do or to become whatever we decide upon, ancient human limitations notwithstanding. The American story, in this view, is the story of a New World in several mutually reinforcing senses. Not only are we different from the Old World geographically; we hope we are different spiritually as well. We do not accept Europe's somewhat cynical expectations of government and society. As Luigi Barzini, a shrewd and sympathetic outside observer, noticed, the founding documents of the United States show that even perfection is not enough for us. We seek a "more perfect union ... immediately, to-day, tomorrow morning at the latest."[13] What other nation would have designated itself a novus ordo seclorum?

This drive for perfection and for deliverance from history has produced many of the most characteristically American achievements and is, for good and bad, a continuing American legacy. Yet as time has passed and American history has lengthened, the epic and the tragic, which sooner or later take their places as part

[13] Luigi Barzini, The Europeans (New York: Penguin Books, 1984), 11.

of human life, have emerged to trouble the New World story. As Gibbon rightly said, history *per se* is "a long tale of crimes and follies." Anticipating the quincentenary of Columbus's arrival in these lands, diverse voices have arisen to assert, on the one hand, the epic grandeur of the European migration and, on the other, the tragic consequences of that expansion for native peoples, for Africans imported as slaves, and for nature itself. Though other nations have their disputes about the meaning of October 12, 1992, in the United States that date swings sharply between outright celebration and outright condemnation.

In a culture that has long denied epic and tragedy, both praise and blame quickly become ultimate weapons. For the critics, who often give the impression of having just discovered some of the unfortunate, violent, but long-known facts of the American past, the presence of evil in the historical record totally discredits the myth of American exceptionalism and of the United States as a just society. These critics charge that Americans have hypocritically disavowed the unsavory parts of their past to protect a self-righteous, sanitized national story.

For many defenders, who frequently seem to regard any criticism of the United States as a prelude to total denunciation, admitting the tragic dimension of America's past threatens to obliterate the distinctive character of our history. Because so much of what tenuously binds together Americans of widely diverse backgrounds hinges on American ideals of liberty and justice for all, these defenders believe that serious criticism based on real American events may upset the entire national applecart. They point to the basic decency of modern-day America and suspect — not entirely wrongly — that many contemporary critics of the American past are really pursuing an agenda for the American present.

But radical critics and wholesale defenders of the American experiment, in fact, pay subconscious homage to an abiding New

Columbus and the Crisis of the West

World myth. As the historian David Noble has argued: "A central tradition in American historical writing has been the assumption that the United States, unlike the European nations, has a covenant that makes Americans a chosen people who have escaped from the terror of historical change to live in timeless harmony with nature."[14] The fundamental point of contention between the two warring parties is whether we possessed that "timeless harmony" in the past or can achieve it in the future. Popular attitudes often mirror this historical perspective. Americans tend to think of their country in terms of a basic human perfection, and bridle—either in criticism or defense—at any evidence that the United States is, or should be, just another nation in the history of the human race.

The present volume makes no claims to Olympian objectivity nor does it seek to conceal its own judgments. It does not even aspire to be comprehensive history. Probably no one alive knows enough to write the full story of European and native peoples either during or after the earliest period of contact—though many current commentators have had the hubris to attempt it. While this volume presumes that the United States is overwhelmingly a great good place now, it does not attempt to ignore or underplay the tragedy of its origins and development or its continuing problems. And entering, as it does, an already polemicized debate, it cannot help but reply to arguments that have come to dominate the public discussion.

Since the Civil War, we have become an indissolubly united nation, but our sense of the epic heroism and the tragic costs, for North and South, that secured that unity has grown progressively weaker as the benefits of American civilization have come to be taken for granted. The unanticipated success of Ken Burns's 1991

---

[14] David W. Noble, *The Eternal Adam and the New World Garden* (New York: Grosset & Dunlap, 1968), ix.

PBS television series *The Civil War* shows that Americans are capable of taking to heart the wrenching emotions produced by such conflicts. As we approach 1992, it would be useful to recover, in similar fashion, a just sense of both the glory and the agony that attended the arrival of Europeans on this continent. To anticipate one possible misconception: invoking the epic and tragic is not a way of using artificial literary categories to gain political and moral absolution for the past or the present. Rather, these concepts exist precisely because they reflect a deep and valid understanding of some permanent elements of human life. For example, the isolation of the Americas from the other continents for thousands of years prior to 1492 left native populations tragically helpless before diseases that arrived from abroad. Whether Europeans, Asians, or Africans had made the first trip linking these shores to the rest of the world, millions of deaths were poised to occur solely because of geographical accidents. Furthermore, though we must never lose sight of universal moral principles and judgments, we also need a solid sense of the ways in which those principles may clash with one another or become entangled in concrete circumstances. Tragedy, as we know from Greek drama, is not solely occupied with the triumph of evil over good, or one evil over another. Tragedy is probably sharpest when the situation dictates that a choice be made between incompatible goods, leading to the unavoidable loss of something humanly valuable. Even in epic achievements, human costs inevitably must be paid. Epic and tragedy do not conceal truth beneath artificiality but open windows onto a fuller reality.

Toward that same end, this book concentrates mainly on a range of moral questions about the European settlement of the Americas. In doing so, it necessarily also tries to get some facts straight that have become distorted by polemics. In the approach to 1992, many books have already been written to show the depravity of the Europeans and the purity of the native peoples. Some readers may think this book attempts the contrary. But instead of using Renaissance Europe or neolithic indigenous societies as a stick with which to beat the present, this brief study aims at examining what happened when widely divergent cultures — each with its share of humane individuals and cultural riches, as well as ruthless tyrants and cultural monstrosities — met and mingled.

Disentangling the various strands of this process is both complicated and subject to dispute at every point. Some disproportion also results from the fact that, with few exceptions, indigenous peoples left no written records. Not only did the victors write the history: for a long time, they were the only ones who *could* write the history. But the evidence we are fortunate enough to have seems to confirm that little of the cultural mixing in the Americas can be characterized in the strictly black-and-white terms usually applied to it by various factions. Discrete events were certainly at times horrifying evils; other events show human interaction of a gratifying sort not usually encountered in everyday life; still others show unprecedented situations demanding — but only rarely getting — heroic human solutions. The most important methodological issue here, however, is to see the original record as a reality in its own time and not to succumb, as far as is humanly possible, to the temptation to let contemporary issues crush fragile historical truths. There are dishonorable episodes that will always be a part of the American past. Our duty now is to make sure that in fleeing one type of dishonor, we do not rush headlong into another.

I am fully aware that this approach may satisfy no one but me. It is one of the major premises of this book, however, that there are various forms of imperialism. And none, perhaps, is so insidious as the imperialism that tries to defend some portion of the past at the cost of distorting it to satisfy the imperious, and seemingly noble, emotions of the present. Whatever their flaws or accomplishments, the Europeans and native peoples who first met and began the process in which we are now all living at least deserve to be understood in their own fullness. When we make them over into our own image and likeness, or redefine them in contemporary terms, we *use* other human beings, now dead, rather than working, as we should, to *understand* them.

Only when we have far more of the story straight, and are at ease in facing a nonidealized America with a concrete history, will it be appropriate to take stock of what has happened in the past — and to seek to draw some lessons from it for our collective and common future.

Note: The very terms "American," "indigenous," "Native American," "Indian," and "European," as well as many others, have been drawn into the intellectual and political turmoil over 1492. The use of these terms in this text is governed by the intention to give no deliberate offense to any person — or to the English language.

1

Myths and Anti-Myths

*The greatest event since the creation of the world
(excluding the incarnation and death of Him who
created it) is the discovery of the Indies.*

— Francisco López de Gómara, *Historia General* (1552)[15]

Of the many symbolic dates that have been suggested for the birth of the modern world, one of the strongest candidates is 1492. Depending on what we mean by "modern," of course, a case could also be made for the Renaissance, the Reformation, the Industrial or French Revolutions, the outbreak of the First World War, the confirmation of Einstein's theory of relativity, the dropping of the atom bomb on Japan, or several other events as being *the* turning point toward modernity. But events of that magnitude and kind — political, religious, military, scientific — have occurred around the globe during the tens of thousands of years of human history. If by "modern," however, we mean the human space in which we now find ourselves, one world in which the entire earth with all its peoples and cultures and technologies has become a single, if

---

[15] Francisco López de Gómara, *Primera Parte de la Historia General de las Indias*, vol. 22 (Madrid: Biblioteca de Autores Espanoles, 1852), 156.

Columbus and the Crisis of the West

tangled, social complex, and in which any event anywhere has importance for the whole species *Homo sapiens*, then 1492 stands unrivaled as the pivotal year for the birth of the modern world.

Such large-scale speculations are far from idle when we try to evaluate Columbus's voyages and their consequences. Since the very concept of the "world" as we know it depends on what happened in 1492, many more issues come into play in our assessments than the bare historical events. In a sense, the past five hundred years also come under scrutiny because various continuities and developments directly link 1492 with our own time. Most visibly, contact between the Old World and the New World radically changed flora and fauna, and therefore attitudes toward the environment—for both; affected population and mortality through war, disease, agriculture, and settlement patterns; and revolutionized European as well as Native American thought and culture. All these factors have had profound effects on the shape of the modern world.[16]

They also have introduced some uncertainties about how we should think about the past and conduct ourselves in the present. During the Columbus quincentenary in 1992, particularly since we were uncertain about so much else in American life, attitudes toward the previous five hundred years of history were already deeply divided. The past of not only America but of Western civilization and the entire world seemed divided between either a glorious, if

---

[16] Alfred W. Crosby, *The Columbian Exchange: Biological and Cultural Consequences of 1492* (Westport, Conn.: Greenwood Press, 1973); Henry F. Dobyns, *Their Number Become Thinned: Native American Population Dynamics in Eastern North America* (Knoxville: University of Tennessee Press, 1983); Edmundo O'Gorman, *The Invention of America: An Inquiry into the Historical Nature of the New World and the Meaning of Its History* (Bloomington: Indiana University Press, 1961). The theses of each of these volumes are discussed in following chapters of this book.

flawed, period of human achievement or a horror to be deplored. It was as if the world that began in 1492 could not decide whether it was a good or bad thing that it had come into being.

As the twenty-first century has developed, the negative side of the picture has all but eclipsed everything else in elite culture. Gone is the courageous and visionary Genoese explorer in a haze of alleged racism and imperialism. Emblematic of this whole shift in point of view was the announcement by the august *New York Times* in August 2019 of its 1619 Project. The announcement showed a coastline as seen from the Atlantic Ocean and asserted, "In August of 1619, a ship appeared on this horizon, near Point Comfort, a coastal port in the English colony of Virginia. It carried more than 20 enslaved Africans, who were sold to the colonists. No aspect of the country that would be formed here has been untouched by the years of slavery that followed. On the 400th anniversary of this fateful moment, it is finally time to tell our story truthfully."[17]

The *Times* editors claimed—and have been developing materials for use in schools based on the claims—that the whole American system was set up to establish and perpetuate slavery. It is undeniable, of course, that slavery is America's "original sin." But several distinguished historians responded to the *Times* project, pointing to the absurdity of the claim and the historical myopia it reflects. Five in particular—Victoria Bynum, James M. MacPherson, James Oakes, Sean Wilentz, and Gordon S. Wood—perhaps the greatest living scholars of American history, wrote a letter to the *Times*, saying, "We applaud all efforts to address the enduring centrality of slavery and racism to our history. Some of us have devoted our entire professional lives to those efforts." But they

---

[17] "The 1619 Project," *New York Times Magazine*, August 14, 2019, https://www.nytimes.com/interactive/2019/08/14/magazine/1619-america-slavery.html.

named a number of fundamental errors in the "framing" of the project as well as particulars, "matters of verifiable fact, which are the foundation of both honest scholarship and honest journalism," especially in interpretations of the Declaration of Independence, Lincoln, Frederick Douglass, and more. Most importantly:

> On the American Revolution, pivotal to any account of our history, the project asserts that the founders declared the colonies' independence of Britain "in order to ensure slavery would continue." This is not true. If supportable, the allegation would be astounding—yet every statement offered by the project to validate it is false.[18]

Despite these judgments by accomplished scholars, the *Times* and many American cultural institutions, to say nothing of public opinion, continue to propagate a vision of America as founded in, bred by, and still dominated by racism.

As this episode indicates, for the most part, professional historians have continued to do what they have done for decades; pointing out good and bad consequences of Europe's role in linking the Americas with the Old World and in creating the first true global networks. Scholarly knowledge about the several peoples involved in this monumental saga is more detailed and set in better perspective today than at any time in the past. But knowledge alone is not shaping current interpretations. A substantial group of historians and political actors have entered the public arena, seeking to use Columbus and various turning points in Western, American, and even global history as a springboard for advancing political agendas.

***

[18] Exchange of Letters, *New York Times*, January 4, 2020, https://www.nytimes.com/2019/12/20/magazine/we-respond-to-the-historians-who-critiqued-the-1619-project.html.

Earlier Political Distortions

This has happened before. In fact, it has been a persistent feature of the Columbus story since the very beginning of American history. Columbus's scholarly son Fernando wrote one of the earliest accounts of his father's exploits. Following Columbus's lead, Fernando portrays him as a lone genius opposed by dark enemies and scoffers. Sailing routes were the high-tech commercial secrets of the fifteenth century, and many of Columbus's texts deliberately conceal information that he does not wish to pass into the hands of others. Furthermore, Columbus himself was not above coloring the truth, to say nothing of lying, to protect and advance his claims on the Spanish monarchs. In an age when vast distances, slow communications, and new human complexities hampered government and oversight, it was perhaps understandable that he would also try—after the fact—to elaborate justifications for actions he had taken out of necessity and in the face of unprecedented circumstances.

Columbus, as will become clear in the next chapter, was an accomplished and bold sailor, perhaps the most adventurous in all history. He knew how to keep a crew reasonably in line on ship, but as a governor on *terra firma*, he was little better than disastrous in any but the most favorable circumstances. His third voyage ended with his being returned to Europe in chains and with the Spanish monarchs forbidding him to return to Hispaniola, the advanced base for exploration in the Americas, because of the ill feeling that had arisen toward him there among the *Spaniards*. When he was shipwrecked and marooned on Jamaica for over a year on his fourth and final voyage, he faced various temporary mutinies before being rescued. By the end of his life, Columbus would be entangled in acrimonious legal battles over his rights in the Indies. Some Spaniards thought he had misrepresented the ease with which wealth might be acquired in the New World; others accused him

Columbus and the Crisis of the West

of nepotism and highhandedness toward Europeans on the island of Hispaniola. It is no wonder, then, that in 1592, the one hundredth anniversary of his first voyage went largely uncelebrated. Columbus's real-life political disputes had to fade before he could emerge as a symbolic figure in the myth of America.

In 1692, his star still had not risen. But by 1792, his historical fortunes, owing to circumstances in the New World, were poised to explode. North America, growing in wealth and liberty, had just thrown off the yoke of George III. Reflecting the atmosphere of the time, King's College in New York, founded in 1754, renamed itself Columbia. Unhampered by much close knowledge of Columbus's life, several prominent Americans, including Ben Franklin, saw in the explorer a predecessor on the road to liberty, the initiator of an American spirit distinct from that of the old Europe. The new capital of the United States was therefore named the District of Columbia. Some zealous partisans of liberty had even wanted to name the new nation after Columbus.

And by 1892, the four hundredth anniversary of his first voyage to the New World, Columbus had, for most people in this country, been transformed into the precursor of a confident and progressive United States of America. Preparations for the official celebration, the Columbian Exhibition in Chicago, were so elaborate, in fact, that the program did not get into full swing until 1893. The opening proclaimed 1492 not merely a historical date but a turning point in the emancipation of mankind. Though Native American groups staged some protests and some scholarly criticism[19] of him as a sailor and as a man appeared even at that point—Columbus's

---

[19] For example, Justin Winsor's *Christopher Columbus, and How He Received and Imparted the Spirit of Discovery* (Boston: Houghton Mifflin, 1891); and Henry Vignaud's later *Études critiques sur la vie de Christophe Colomb avant ses découvertes* (Paris: H. Welter, 1905).

historical high tide—Columbus had largely become a myth serving several political and intellectual agendas and some popular uses.[20]

The motives behind this apotheosis were quite straightforward and understandable, if somewhat ill-founded. America was in an expansive mood, and Columbus was a useful symbol of enterprise and liberty—and not only for establishment WASPs. Italian-Americans, for example, looking for an opportunity to display their contributions to a then mostly unwelcoming American culture, erected a statue to Columbus in New York in what is still Columbus Circle.[21] A decade earlier, some American Catholics, mostly Irish, had founded the Knights of Columbus, both to strengthen ethnic identity and to hold up the navigator as a model for those who wanted to become better Catholics and better citizens. Despite the self-interest and elementary historical knowledge that went into them, these initiatives did have the virtue of pointing out the Mediterranean and Catholic contributions to an America that had lost sight of them.

The Vatican, too, found in the fourth centenary a historical opportunity. In the 1870s, a French count, Roselly de Lorgues, had proposed Columbus for sainthood, a cause later taken up by such distinguished French literary figures as Leon Bloy and Paul Claudel.[22] The First Vatican Council rejected that proposal "on moral

---

[20] For a brief overview of this history, see chapter 16, "His Place in History," in John Noble Wilford, *The Mysterious History of Columbus* (New York: Knopf, 1991).

[21] The Black Lives Matter protests of mid-2020 threatened even that venerable landmark, but while many statues of Columbus fell—Baltimore's was thrown into the harbor and had to be retrieved—Columbus Circle's did not. The city council, however, may complete what rioters could not.

[22] On these figures, see E. T. Dubois, "Leon Bloy, Paul Claudel, and the Revaluation of the Significance of Columbus," in *Currents of Thought in French Literature* (New York: Barnes & Noble, 1966), 131–144.

grounds," probably because of Columbus's long liaison with Beatriz de Arana, the mother of his illegitimate son, Fernando. (At the time, sensitivity to the admiral's alleged misdeeds against Native Americans in the New World was not very high.) In 1892, however, Pope Leo XIII did issue an encyclical praising Columbus: *Quarto abeunte saeculo*. While this document keeps Columbus separate from the saints, who have superhuman virtues, it does praise him for virtues of another kind: "For the exploit is in itself the highest and grandest which any age has ever seen accomplished by man; and he who achieved it, for the greatness of mind and heart, can be compared to but few in the history of humanity."[23] Although he allows that Columbus sought personal gain and glory, Leo believed, as did many people in the nineteenth century, that ambition was often a spur to achievement. Columbus's most monumental feat, however, was characterized as carried out under divine inspiration: he brought Christianity to "a mighty multitude, cloaked in miserable darkness, given over to evil rites, and the superstitious worship of vain gods." Columbus's opening up of new mission territory also compensated for some of the losses the Church in the early sixteenth century was about to suffer because of the Protestant Reformation.

All the popular late-nineteenth-century views of Columbus, even the Vatican's, stemmed directly from progressive ideologies, and produced, as well as drew strength from, remarkable misrepresentations of history. We have all heard it vaguely claimed, for instance, that Christopher Columbus proved to a disbelieving and dark, late-medieval Europe that the world was not flat. Jeffrey Burton Russell, a medieval historian, has assembled evidence exploding this and several other historical myths that have been attached to Columbus

---

[23] Leo XIII, *Quarto abeunte saeculo*, in *1878–1903*, vol. 2 of *The Papal Encyclicals*, ed. Claudia Carlen (Raleigh, N.C.: McGrath, 1981), 285–288.

since the nineteenth century.[24] Russell shows beyond dispute that any educated person in late-medieval Europe already knew, as did the ancient Greco-Roman world, that the earth was spherical.

Nineteenth-century historians simply invented a progressive-Columbus myth for several reasons. Some hated the Spanish Empire and Roman Catholicism. Others wanted to demonstrate the superiority of the modern world in general, and America in particular, to all earlier ages. Still others found it expedient to portray religion, particularly Christianity, as a reactionary force and an opponent of enlightenment.

The Flat Error

How was what Russell calls the "Flat Error" introduced? The answer to this question is instructive, especially if we wish to be on guard against distortions that our current proclivities may inject into new historical interpretations. Ironically, the process began as what appeared to be a much-needed scholarly revision of history.

Only two ancient Christian writers of any significance put forward a flat-earth theory: Lactantius (ca. 245–325), a Latin convert whose views antedated the sophisticated hermeneutics of Church Fathers such as Saint Augustine and Saint John Chrysostom and propounded a crude "biblical" cosmos; and Cosmas Indicopleustes, a Greek who, writing around 547–549, argued that the universe was a vaulted arch with the earth as its floor. Lactantius was posthumously condemned as a heretic, and Cosmas was — and is — so obscure that a student may easily complete a graduate degree in medieval studies without ever coming across his name. Of further importance in the present context is the fact that Cosmas was

---

[24] Jeffrey Burton Russell, *Inventing the Flat Earth: Columbus and Modern Historians* (New York: Praeger, 1991).

unknown to Western Europe until 1706 and could have had no influence in Columbus's time.

As anyone who has read *The Divine Comedy* will recall, Dante takes for granted a spherical earth and a Ptolemaic universe—in fact, makes them of major structural significance in his poem. All other serious medieval thinkers held the same belief. How, then, did their views get steamrolled into the Flat Error? (A *Wizard of Id* cartoon included among the illustrations in Russell's volume shows a mock-Solomonic king reconciling a dispute between the court's flat partisans and round partisans by proclaiming that the world is both flat and round: "I call it the Pizza Theory.") Russell points to two main schools of revisionist historians as the primary culprits: the progressives of the early nineteenth century and the Darwinians after 1870. Both groups had an interest in revising the record for contemporary purposes.

The Nineteenth-Century Columbus: Protestant and Progressive

Washington Irving, probably the best known of the progressives, concocted an image of Columbus as a modern man who had freed himself from the constraints of feudal and Catholic Europe to help create the democratic and Protestant New World. During a stay in Spain, Irving had read some of the original archival materials on Columbus, and he selected from them to make of that Catholic Genoese navigator the unlikely hero of American Protestantism and progressivism. Irving's *History of the Life and Voyages of Columbus*—a vivid, romanticized, dramatic, and often fictitious moral tale—was published in 1837.[25] Despite its shortcomings as truth,

[25] Irving's biography was first published in two volumes by Carey, Lea & Blanchard, Philadelphia, 1837. An accessible modern

the book set the tone of most studies and popular beliefs about the explorer for the rest of the century and, in some crucial ways, beyond.

Exploration in Columbus's time essentially called for state backing. Columbus's failure to gain support from the leading maritime explorers of his day, the Portuguese, and his subsequent difficulties in convincing Ferdinand and Isabella, king and queen of the newly united kingdom of Spain, are well known. His troubles stemmed in no small degree from the fact that learned opinion in his time held that the world was larger than Columbus thought and the landmasses smaller, which would mean a long open-water distance from Europe to Cathay (China). The Spanish monarchs even called together a few learned churchmen, some from the University of Salamanca, who were also skilled astronomers and geographers, to evaluate Columbus's project. It appears they recommended against it but out of knowledge, not superstition.[26]

In Washington Irving's "history," however, this judgment is shown to have all the trappings of the fanaticism and obscurantism once facilely ascribed to everything "medieval." And in the work of a host of later self-styled progressive writers, the Inquisition and "monastic bigotry" take on life as symbolic forces that must be overcome to create America. Irving transformed the persons consulted by the crown into a formal council of "learned" theologians who confronted Columbus with a passage from ... Lactantius! A

---

text has been edited by James W. Tuttleton (Boston: Twayne, 1987).

[26] Few facts survive about the council appointed to look into Columbus's enterprise that go back to anywhere near the date of the event; they cannot properly be used in anything like Washington Irving's interpretation. For a sober survey of the record, see Felipe Fernández-Armesto, *Columbus* (New York: Oxford University Press, 1991), especially 53–54.

textbook in 1880 paraphrases Irving's scene: "Is there anyone so foolish as to believe that there are people living on the other side of the earth with their heels upward and their heads hanging down?"[27]

Though, as was mentioned earlier, Lactantius had been declared heretical over a thousand years earlier, modern historical ignorance and arrogance made it an easy step to the kind of truth-versus-heresy morality play that has persisted even as late as this exchange in Joseph Chiari's 1979 play *Christopher Columbus*:

> COLUMBUS. The Earth is not flat, Father, it's round!
>
> THE PRIOR. Don't say that!
>
> COLUMBUS. It's the truth; it's not a mill pond strewn with islands, it's a sphere.
>
> THE PRIOR. Don't, don't say that; it's blasphemy.[28]

This misrepresentation flattered several American prejudices, but the parallel with other struggles between sweet reason and stubborn revelation did not go unnoticed elsewhere. In France and other continental nations, for example, Columbus, viewed as the bearer of universal enlightenment, was also to find a successful career.

Writing in the 1940s, Samuel Eliot Morison, a canny sailor and generally temperate historian of Columbus, describes Irving's scenes of Columbus in argument with the learned doctors as "pure moonshine" and continues:

> Washington Irving, scenting his opportunity for a picturesque and moving scene, took a fictitious account of this nonexistent university council published 130 years after

---

[27] Russell, *Inventing the Flat Earth*, 51. The original text is in John J. Anderson, *Popular History of the United States* (New York: Clark & Maynard, 1880), 19.

[28] Joseph Chiari, *Christopher Columbus* (New York: Gordian, 1979); quoted in Russell, *Inventing the Flat Earth*, 3.

the event, elaborated on it, and let his imagination go completely.... [This] has become one of the most popular Columbus myths; for we all love to hear of professors and experts being confounded by common sense.... The whole story is misleading and mischievous nonsense.... The sphericity of the globe was not in question. The issue was the width of the ocean; and therein the opposition was right.[29]

Other Political Uses

After 1870, the Flat Error was found to have a second use, this time among what might be called the anti-anti-Darwinists. Darwin's defenders were looking for any ammunition they could muster in their struggle with fundamentalist Christians. None of the major Church Fathers or medieval thinkers would have dreamt of relying solely on the Bible as a guide to scientific matters. Biblical hermeneutics were generally too sophisticated for that. But feeling threatened by some scientific advances, groups of modern Christians tried that desperate tactic. Their zealous oversimplifications gave Darwin's supporters—who were not very theologically sophisticated themselves—a powerful weapon with which to make all so-called biblical thought appear benighted.

Dug up by some scholar or other involved in these controversies, the long-forgotten and always negligible Cosmas Indicopleustes was translated into English for the first time in 1897 and was immediately portrayed not only as a fool himself but as the emblem of Christian foolishness. His name began to appear in histories and textbooks as if he had been the main cosmological theorist of the Middle Ages. The medieval Church had been a sponsor of

---

[29] Samuel Eliot Morison, *Admiral of the Ocean Sea*, vol. 1 (Boston: Little, Brown, 1942), 88–89.

science and learning, of course, with figures such as Roger Bacon and Albertus Magnus, modest though their scientific work was by modern standards. But this truth was lost as the dynamics of the Darwin controversy were projected back upon the earlier age.

And the transgressors were not only ignorant bigots. Andrew Dickson White, the founder of Cornell University, for example, became one of the principal late-nineteenth-century propagators of the Flat Error out of opposition to contemporary Christian obscurantists. Ignoring the medieval scholarship that was available even in his day, he accepted on faith the misstatements of several fellow polemicists. Russell comments: "White and his colleagues ended by doing what they accused the fathers of, namely, creating a body of false knowledge by consulting one another instead of the evidence."[30]

Though for at least the last fifty years, all this has been known to scholars as a simple comedy of errors, the myth persists. Not only does the Flat Error continue to appear in widely used primary, secondary, and college textbooks, but it even continues to have pernicious effects on some of the most influential modern histories. The distinguished historian and former Librarian of Congress Daniel Boorstin, in his lively and generally reliable volume *The Discoverers*, for example, has been taken in to a degree. In chapters entitled "The Prison of Christian Dogma" and "A Flat Earth Returns," Boorstin asserts that during the Middle Ages, Christians engaged in an "amnesiac effort to ignore the growing mass of knowledge [about a spherical earth] and retreat into a world of faith and caricature." As evidence, he cites the hapless and then-still-unknown Cosmas and, in the course of several pages, mixes that eccentric figure with more mainstream Christian thinkers, such as Augustine, to evoke

---

[30] Russell, *Inventing the Flat Earth*, 44.

a wholly imaginary "legion of Christian geographers" who believed that the earth was flat.[31]

Boorstin does not go on to make the further vulgar error that Columbus proved the world was round. Somewhat inconsistently, he admits that the experts had turned Columbus down "probably because they thought he had grossly underestimated the sea distance westward to the Indies."[32] Yet coming after the extensive misrepresentation of the state of geographical knowledge in Columbus's time, this brief concession has doubtless done little to prevent the survival of several nineteenth-century myths about Columbus in twentieth-century textbooks and popular lore. George and Ira Gershwin's song "They All Laughed" merely records the belief most people held in the earlier part of the twentieth century—and may still hold.

Twentieth-Century Myths

The tenacity of the progressive-Columbus myths that were gathering force in 1892 and beyond should alert us to the possibility that new, unconscious distortions—this time of a very different character—may have colored current versions of the story. For most public commentators now, Columbus is no longer viewed as a proto-progressive. On the contrary, for a spectrum of scholars and activists, this Christopher (which means "Christ bearer") has become the symbolic bearer not of Christ—except in the sinister sense of destroying native spirituality and culture—but of every evil that Western individualism, capitalism, industrialism, colonialism, and cultural "Eurocentrism" have visited on any part of the world in the last five hundred years. And the twenty-first century

---

[31] Daniel Boorstin, *The Discoverers* (New York: Vintage, 1985), 100–113.

[32] Ibid., 173.

has added to the evil litany by making Columbus appear the font and origin of American racism and "whiteness."

Every schoolchild used to be taught that Christopher Columbus, a Genoese navigator, discovered America in 1492. But for several years now, a chorus of voices (growing larger and louder as more and more contemporary evils are attributed to a man who lived five centuries ago) has assaulted every certainty, except the date, about the Columbus story. Some want to de-emphasize Columbus's significance preemptively by establishing that the Vikings, West Africans, or Asians were here first, though if they were, they left few signs and almost no written records. Others would like to convince us that Columbus or Colón or Colombo or whatever his name may have been was in fact—take your pick—Spanish or Portuguese, Greek or Jewish. Far from being a navigator, moreover, he had never commanded a ship "larger than a rowboat" before setting sail for the New World.[33] Still others, by far the most numerous and ideologically strident, wish to monopolize public attention with claims that Columbus's "discovery" of America is, in any case, nothing to celebrate. Indeed, for some, he and the Europeans who followed him are the scourge of humanity.

The very term "discovery" was ruled out of the official proceedings in the 1992 quincentenary by some of the principal participants. When Spain first began planning for the commemoration of its role in the New World, it tried to defuse hostile reactions from Native Americans and others who regard the very idea of the discovery of America as evidence of continuing cultural imperialism. Native populations, in this view, did not need to be "discovered." They knew who and where they were when the Spaniards arrived. Needing a more neutral term, therefore, Spain and its New

---

[33] Kirkpatrick Sale, *The Conquest of Paradise: Christopher Columbus and the Columbian Legacy* (New York: Knopf, 1990).

World collaborators (primarily Mexico) scoured the softer side of contemporary culture and hit upon *El Encuentro,* "The Encounter of Two Worlds."

The Smithsonian Institution in Washington, D.C., followed suit. Its major quincentenary exhibition, *Seeds of Change,* argues that even to speak of Old World and New World is to get the picture wrong. In the words of Herman J. Viola, director of the quincentenary programs at the Museum of Natural History, Columbus's voyage created "one new world from two old worlds."[34] This formula, too, seemed to skirt claims of precedence and superiority.

In itself, seeing 1492 as the meeting of two cultures—particularly the emergence of "one new world" from the process—has significant historical value. At the very least, it points to something in what William Carlos Williams once called "The American Grain" that is often overlooked: the continuing presence of native cultures in our world, particularly in certain parts of Latin America. But some native spokesmen refused to accept such compromises. For example, the South and Meso American Indian Information Center (SAIIC) in Berkeley, California, a self-described liaison between Indian peoples of the North and of the South, and between Indians and non-Indians, issued "A Call to Action!" in 1991 that included the following:

> We ask the Spanish government, the Vatican, and all Latin American and European governments who are promoting the Quincentennial Jubilee, how the steam-rolling of cultures for the enrichment of a European minority can be considered an "Encounter of Two Worlds." … The myths

---

[34] Quoted in the introductory film to the exhibition show at the Smithsonian Museum of Natural History, 1991.

about Columbus and the "encounter" are a completely false manipulation of history.[35]

Sympathetic persons were requested to send contributions to the SAIIC offices to help spread the word about the most evident consequences of Columbus's invasion:

> genocide, torture, political, ideological and cultural submission and death through diseases brought to the continent. Our land and our resources have been and continue to be plundered. Military, ideologic, economic and religious power are the instruments of domination in this conquest.

The Battle Lines

As this excerpt graphically shows, what began as a seemingly just attempt to make appreciation of the two cultures more equal in the Columbus commemoration quickly shifted into an acrimonious battle to make the non-European side a moralistic stick with which to beat European societies, including their political and cultural heirs in the Americas. Many of the more radical critics of those societies—environmentalists, feminists, African American organizations, multiculturalist advocates—vigorously entered the Columbus controversy. Scenting political opportunity, Cuba's Fidel Castro, one of the last communist dictators, declared himself an honorary Native American and denounced Columbus. (When Arthur M. Schlesinger Jr., slyly pointed out to him during a 1992 visit to Havana that "if it weren't for Columbus, you wouldn't be here," Castro conceded, "Well, Columbus brought good things as well as bad.")[36] Though

---

[35] SAIIC promotional mailing, 1991.
[36] Arthur M. Schlesinger Jr., "Four Days with Fidel: A Havana Diary," *New York Review of Books*, 26 March 1992, 26.

generalization about such a diverse group is difficult, it is probably fair to say that something like their common view was expressed by Russell Means, one of the leaders of the American Indian Movement: "Columbus makes Hitler look like a juvenile delinquent."[37] Means went on to say that asking Native Americans to celebrate on October 12 is like asking Jews to appreciate a "balanced view of the Holocaust" on Hitler Day. In the early decades of the twenty-first century, "genocidal maniac" was a term often used about the explorer with no apparent need to back up the claim.

Few major institutions are willing to defend themselves against this sort of moral and political onslaught. At the time of the quincentenary, most simply sought to avoid confrontation by side-stepping the Columbus issue entirely. In Washington, D.C., the exhibition at the Museum of Natural History, which documented the exchanges of food, plants, and animals after 1492, basically did not address Columbus at all. Neither did Washington's other main museum show that had been prompted by reflections on 1492. The National Gallery of Art displayed objects assembled from several cultures flourishing "Circa 1492," and the gallery's director, J. Carter Brown, stressed in the catalogue: "This show is not about a man called Christopher Columbus; his name does not even appear in the title."[38]

---

[37] Public statement on Friday, 24 November 1989, in protest outside the Florida Museum of Natural History's exhibit *First Encounters: Spanish Explorations in the Caribbean and the United States, 1492–1570*, quoted in Jan Elliott, *Exhibiting Ideology* (a review of *First Encounters*) (New York: Racial Justice Working Group, Prophetic Justice Unit of the National Council of Churches of Christ in the USA, 1990).

[38] J. Carter Brown, foreword to *Circa 1492: Art in the Age of Exploration*, ed. Jay A. Levenson (Washington, D.C.: National Gallery of Art, 1991), 9.

Columbus and the Crisis of the West

Instead of examining the record, good and bad, of the man whose efforts make 1992 a significant date, many institutions have, on the contrary, chimed in with support for the breathtaking range of the indictments against him.

Even the churches, which in some sense should be willing to defend their bringing of the good news to new peoples, cannot seem to find any value in the spread of Christianity to the Americas. The U.S. National Council of Churches (NCC), an umbrella Protestant organization that for years has advocated progressive causes, professed to see in the European arrival not a badly flawed social integration, at least partly redeemed by evangelization, but genocide *tout court*—several interlocking genocides and rapes, in fact, of the land, of peoples, and of raw materials. In the brief statement on the quincentenary that the NCC issued in 1990, genocide was mentioned several times per page, while evangelization, in a positive sense, was not mentioned at all.[39] For the NCC, evangelization was solely a pretext for exploitation; the quincentenary, then, should be an occasion not for rejoicing but for repentance.

In fact, only the U.S. Catholic bishops and their Latin American counterparts, along with a few prelates in Spain and Rome, were willing to praise the evangelization, though they admitted it was marred by profoundly un-Christian acts.[40] Yet many Catholics, too, have taken up the radical critique. Liberation theologians in Latin America seem to have replaced now a moribund Marxism with anti-1492 thought. One U.S. Catholic bishop, part Native American himself, even called on the Knights of Columbus to change

---

[39] National Council of Churches in the USA, *A Faithful Response to the 500th Anniversary of the Arrival of Christopher Columbus* (resolution adopted by the governing board, New York, 17 May 1990).

[40] National Conference of Catholic Bishops (U.S.), "Heritage and Hope: Evangelization in America" (pastoral letter), *Origins* 20 (6 December 1990): 415.

their name.[41] For many of the religious critics, genocide and rape of women, of the land, and of culture stand at the dark heart of all nonindigenous American societies and cultures, north and south.

The Indictment

Native American and African American self-assertion in 1992 and later was as understandable as Irish Catholic and Italian American self-assertion was in 1892. Both anniversaries allowed some forgotten truths to be told, whatever distortions may have simultaneously been introduced. But a much larger storm has also been brewing—what can only be described as a historical indictment of Columbus and European imperialism, as well as of European culture and all its works and pomps. These charges are aided by sympathy for some groups that were subjected to very real and almost unprecedented evils during the Age of Discovery. The activist militant group Columbus in Context, founded in New York in 1990, described the quincentenary as the best political opportunity for progressives "since the Vietnam War"[42] and issued a statement calling for the rejection of the mariner as a national hero: "He organized an extermination of native Americans. He was also mean, cruel and greedy in small matters as he was in vast ones." Hans Koning, a novelist and long-time opponent of Columbus who is the apparent author of this statement, argues that we must open our eyes to the past:

> We must end the phoney baloney about the white man bringing Christianity, and about Columbus the noble son of the humble weaver. Our false heroes and a false sense of the

---

41 Demetria Martinez, "Bishop Challenges Knights to Drop Columbus," *National Catholic Reporter*, 25 August 1991.

42 Quoted in Charles Krauthammer, "Hail Columbus, Dead White Male," *Time*, 27 May 1991, 74.

meaning of courage and manliness have too long burdened our national spirit.[43]

The radical critique clearly indicts the United States in general as much as it does Columbus.

Perhaps the most powerful formulation of this indictment to appear as 1992 approached, however, was Kirkpatrick Sale's revisionist biography *The Conquest of Paradise: Christopher Columbus and the Columbian Legacy* (see footnote 33). Significantly, Sale was not a professional historian but a political and environmental activist, a co-director of the E. F. Schumacher Society, and a founder of the New York Green Party. Sale's reading of Columbus's legacy had considerable impact on sympathetic teachers, journalists, and the general public because of both its stylistic and analytical brilliance and its widespread distribution as a main selection of the Book-of-the-Month Club.

Many newly emphasized truths about Columbus the man, his voyages, and his legacy are disturbing. Here was a daring sailor, a visionary who brought the Americas and Europe together, but also a man with many human flaws, the product, in part, of a culture in turmoil. His story is both epic and tragic in that his monumental achievement is intertwined with the high and low human qualities closely related in him. Kirkpatrick Sale believed, along with many others since Francisco López de Gómara first said it, that Columbus is "the most important figure in human history," but in a negative sense.[44] His account of 1492 and after is a relentless venting of bile. Sale is vivid, learned, obsessed, sneering, contemptuous, skeptical of anything that reflects well on Columbus or European culture, and ultimately credulous about every evil attributed or attributable

---

[43] Hans Koning, "Don't Celebrate 1492—Mourn It," *New York Times*, 14 August 1990.

[44] Alvin P. Sanoff, "The Myths of Columbus" (interview with Kirkpatrick Sale), *U.S. News & World Report*, 8 October 1990, 74.

to Columbus, by himself or others. In addition, he presents with renewed contemporary credulity the old myth of noble savages and ignoble Europeans.

Noble and Ignoble Savages

The opposition of noble savages to savage Western civilization is now a commonplace of our culture. First introduced by Montesquieu and later perfected by Rousseau about two and a half centuries ago, this theme has been transposed into several keys pitting East Indians, black Africans, Communist Chinese, revolutionary Cubans, Sandinista Nicaraguans, and Native Americans against evil Western counterparts. But Kirkpatrick Sale achieved a high-water mark in the purity of his noble savages and the utter blackness of his savage Western civilization.

If this seems an exaggeration, witness the following passage in which we are informed that not only did the noble savages at the time of Columbus's landing live in social harmony amid natural abundance of food and other needs; they lived, it appears, in a kind of prelapsarian garden where disease itself was virtually unknown:

> One reason that the Indian populations, in the Caribbean as elsewhere, were so vulnerable to diseases of any kind is that, to an extraordinary extent, the Americas were free of any serious pathogens. The presumed passage of the original populations across the Bering Strait tens of thousands of years before served to freeze to death most human disease carriers except a few intestinal ones, it is thought, and there were apparently none established on the continents previously, so in general the Indians enjoyed remarkably good health, free of both endemic and epidemic scourges. As

Columbus and the Crisis of the West

Henry Dobyns says in his examination of aboriginal North American populations, *Their Number Become Thinned*, "People simply did not very often die of illnesses" before the Europeans came.[45]

Importantly, the argument here is not that indigenous Americans were susceptible to European diseases because they had never before encountered them; rather, they were free of serious disease in general. They lived in a kind of medical paradise.

At times, Sale seems to suggest that, if only we were willing to fly over to eastern Siberia and make the trip alfresco again while the continent was being fumigated, we might return to this blissful state. There is little chance of our doing so, however, because, as Sale portrays us, we are all descendants of late-medieval European culture, which he characterizes as a culture of death. Some innocents may think of the early sixteenth century as the time of Reformation and Counter-Reformation, Renaissance progress, and a march toward a fuller humanism, but Sale will allow none of this. Where we may see complexity or ambiguity, Sale sees an evil monolith that has survived basically unchanged through the intervening centuries, "a Europe that in thought and deed was estranged from its natural environment and had for several thousand years [!] been engaged in depleting and destroying the land and waters it depended on, and justifying that with one or another creed or conviction."[46]

Though Sale lays much of the blame for Western ecocide on biblical impulses, he shows a kind of backhanded fairness here: he is willing to concede that Western civilization was deeply ill even before the advent of such antinatural spiritual movements.

[45] Sale, *Conquest of Paradise*, 160.
[46] Ibid., 74.

Classical scholars will be interested to learn that the Roman Empire fell because its exploitation of nature had led to "its own inability to feed itself."[47] For Sale, Europe's divorcing of itself from nature made it rootless and restless, sick and unstable, powerful but hollow. Late-medieval Europe, he argues (mostly by selective quotation from other historians), exhibited these characteristics in a uniquely strong form.

And he sees in Columbus the very incarnation of all these negative qualities. Sale's Columbus is not a daring seaman with a vision of something of which even the navigator himself was not fully conscious. Instead, this Columbus is a man without family or community ties, ready to sail anywhere because nothing constrained him or moved him to loyalty. His motives, insofar as identifiable motives drive such a deeply disturbed man, centered on early capitalist greed and early Renaissance ambition for power and status. Any doubts about this interpretation can be laid to rest by reading Columbus's *Journal* of the first voyage. There, according to Sale, the impulse toward exploitation of nature and the lust for gold dominate, and the meager description of the flora and fauna of the New World make it clear that Columbus has no idea of—let alone any interest in—what he is looking at.

Neither did the Europe of Columbus's time react to the discovery, in Sale's view, with the proper curiosity and wonder: "Certainly there was no intellectual explosion, nothing that 'caused Europe to realize that the perimeters of their world were changing' and 'to reevaluate their concept of the world' (as a recent study has put it)."[48] The Europeans, insofar as they looked up from their constant preoccupation with evil deeds and death, merely saw the new lands as wealth to be exploited. The right to colonization was assumed

[47] Ibid., 82.
[48] Ibid., 125.

Columbus and the Crisis of the West

by Christian intruders who missed "an opportunity for a dispirited and melancholy Europe to have learned something about fecundity and regeneration, about social comeliness and amity, about harmony with the natural world. The appropriate architecture for Colon to have envisioned along these shores might have been a forum, or an amphitheater, or an academy, perhaps an auditorium or a tabernacle; instead, a fortress."[49]

During his lifetime Columbus used to get gratuitous advice from people in "safe berths there in Spain." Writing from the relative security of the Empire State, Kirkpatrick Sale joins that line of long-distance critics. The lessons he drew from the Columbus story are perhaps the most telling aspect of his study:

> There is only one way to live in America, and there can be only one way, and that is as Americans — the original Americans — for that is what the earth of America demands. We have tried for five centuries to resist that simple truth. We resist it further only at the risk of the imperilment — worse, the likely destruction — of the earth.[50]

Sale ridicules Columbus, the medieval dreamer, for thinking he was near the earthly paradise when he discovered four rivers running together in a beautiful region of what is now Venezuela, a scene that reminded him of the description in the book of Genesis. Yet biblical myths are powerful. Sale titled his book *The Conquest of Paradise* and predicts something very like the Last Judgment if we do not repent of our Western ways. Native American ways mirrored a perfect life in the Garden of Eden and point the way toward the New Jerusalem. Claims of that magnitude are not uncommon in the new Columbus literature.

---

[49] Ibid., 113.
[50] Ibid., 369.

New Age and New World

As unlikely a candidate for pure angel or pure devil as Christopher Columbus may appear, his exploits have been drawn into the larger debate now going on about the nature of American culture. Just as, in 1892, confident, progressive Americans identified with a confident, progressive explorer, so in 1992, troubled, pessimistic Americans saw in Columbus an image of everything wrong with contemporary American life. A 1992 PBS television series on primitive peoples went so far as to accuse Columbus of exporting *consumerism* to the New World, though consumerism does not seem to have been exactly rampant in medieval Spain.[51] On the face of it, five hundred years of evil seems a lot to attribute to the influence of one man. Logically, if Columbus is to receive all the blame by virtue of a massive *post hoc, ergo propter hoc*, then he should also receive all the credit for whatever good has occurred in those five hundred years. Yet it is far more common to criticize him for the legacy of slavery, conquest, and imperialism, as well as for the cultural arrogance, male domination, militarism, and environmental insensitivities alleged to make up the core of modern American life.

The old heroic view of Columbus was a myth. But is the new view of this sailor from Genoa the needed corrective to former idealistic portraits? Is Columbus as brutish, and his legacy as unrelievedly evil, as the radical critics claim? Or is Harvard historian Stephan Thernstrom right when he says that Kirkpatrick Sale "tells the tale with about as much balance and judiciousness as we might expect in a history of the United States written in the Soviet Union in the darkest days of Stalin's rule."[52] Older biographers of Columbus such

---

[51] David Marbury-Lewis, *Millennium: Tribal Wisdom and the Modern World*, PBS, 11 May 1992.

[52] Stephan Thernstrom, "The Columbus Controversy," *American Educator* 16, no. 1 (Spring 1992): 31.

as Samuel Eliot Morison were not unaware of some bad precedents set by Columbus. Yet anything less than a sweeping denunciation of five hundred years of Western history—that is, anything less than lining up behind views like those of Sale—is now regarded by many people as a simple continuation of imperialism.

The following chapters examine several of the particulars in the indictment of Columbus. Hans Koning and Columbus in Context are partly right: we need to know the full truth about the American past, even when it cuts across present pieties of whatever stripe. Popular accounts of American history *have* been too uniformly rosy, obscuring the fact that the United States has been and is made up of a group of imperfect human beings with a mixed history, a foul rag-and-bone shop like all human societies. Knowing the full truth about our past—even the unsavory parts—need not weaken us. Rather, it should make us both more modest about our expectations and prouder of the true achievements that have taken place on these shores in the past five hundred years.

But we also need the truth to prevent a further imperialistic imposition on the very peoples the radical critics wish to defend. Some parts of Native American cultures were admirable and deserve preservation. Others decidedly were not, as shall be shown in some detail in the following pages. Using Native American culture as a pawn in contemporary political debates serves only to damage, once more, the true record of what they achieved—and did not achieve. It is no favor to Native Americans or African Americans today to redefine their heritage to suit, yet again, the needs of white culture, as if they were not poor fallible human beings with cultures composed of good and bad, as are we all.

Carrying out these two investigations requires serious work, not facile assumptions. Contemporary scholars frequently invoke the question of "the other"—a useful notion so long as we remember that it is always difficult to know the other, particularly when that other lived in a different culture several centuries ago. This sense of the difficulty in knowing the other, however, is rarely evident even in university environments. In early 1992, for example, the student senate at the University of Cincinnati voted to declare a "Columbus-myth-free Campus,"[53] giving voice to a sentiment probably well represented on many campuses in the 1990s. But that goal is far more demanding than the students supposed. It is highly doubtful that any of them—perhaps even any of the adults advising them—have much acquaintance with the myths, facts, lacunae, and legitimate difficulties in interpretation about Columbus. Nikole Hannah-Jones—the leader of the *New York Times*'s 1619 Project—was an undergraduate at the University of Notre Dame in 1995 and wrote that the European explorers were "barbaric devils" and that "I understand that because of some lacking, they needed to constantly prove their superiority." And she added, "The white race is the biggest murderer, rapist, pillager, and thief of the modern world," as well as a charge that would become common in institutions of higher learning: "Christopher Columbus and his like were no different than Hitler."[54] It's doubtful that she and the thousands of college students who have come to the same conclusions since did so on their own.

Two sound biographers of Columbus have observed that, along with its other educational failures, "the United States seems to have lost, rather than gained, knowledge about Columbus since 1892. Most people reach adulthood with only the most rudimentary

[53] John Leo, "P.C. Follies," *U.S. News & World Report*, 27 January 1992, 26.
[54] Jordan Davidson, "In Racist Screed, NYT's 1619 Project Founder Calls 'White Race' 'Barbaric Devils,' 'Bloodsuckers,' Columbus 'No Different Than Hitler,'" *Federalist*, June 25, 2020, https://thefederalist.com/2020/06/25/in-racist-screed-nyts-1619-project-founder-calls-white-race-barbaric-devils-bloodsuckers-no-different-than-hitler/.

knowledge about him, half remembered from a few lessons in elementary school."[55] And they had not yet seen the radicalization that would engulf American and European campuses. Arriving at truth, college students were once taught, takes intellectual effort; repeating ideas that happen to be in the air takes none. Without careful study, the impulse to cast aside other people's myths for what we think are obvious truths creates myths of its own; and myths may be consoling but, when taken for truth, may be dangerous.

A serious writer, the Oxford historian Felipe Fernández-Armesto, began his own 1991 biography of Columbus with this observation: "Considered from one point of view, Columbus was a crank."[56] He reached this conclusion—which at least was qualified in the sense that he admitted it was the view from only one angle—by approaching Columbus, like so many recent commentators, precisely from a psychological "point of view." In this reading, Columbus was a parvenu, always trying to make it big financially because he was a poor weaver's son and constantly seeking honors and titles for much the same reason. Unlike most other amateur psychologizers, Fernández-Armesto doesn't entirely dismiss the religious side of Columbus's psyche—the first term in the old "God, gold, and glory" summary of Columbus's motives—but sees in it something increasingly bizarre.

It's possible to find facts in the record to back up, at least in part, each of these generalizations, as well as many others. But they all come up against an initial and large problem. Global exploration was a serious business in the fifteenth century. So of course there were financial motives associated with every one of the voyages

---

[55] William D. Phillips Jr., and Carla Rahn Phillips, *The Worlds of Christopher Columbus* (New York: Cambridge University Press, 1992), 7.

[56] Fernández-Armesto, *Columbus*, vii.

undertaken to explore the African coast, reach the Indies, and cross the Atlantic, just as sailing around the Mediterranean was often a commercial enterprise. It also isn't surprising that Columbus sought titles, since the wealth that one trip might make could be lost in another. And religious goals—preaching the gospel to all nations and retaking the Holy Land from the Muslims—may seem a distant third, and perhaps even hypocritical, to a modern secular gaze.

But whatever mix of these elements may have existed in Columbus at any given moment, and however obsessive he may have seemed—and how could he have carried out such a grueling task otherwise?—rulers and financial investors in his day were just as shrewd about the people they backed as their counterparts are today.

There were plenty of other people in Spain clamoring for patronage and support for all sorts of purposes. At least some quite intelligent people must have believed that the "crank" had a fairly good case and that he himself was worth a calculated bet. The usual current evaluations of Columbus have emphasized his shortcomings and the personal crises he experienced during his later trials in the New World. But as we turn now to look more closely at the man himself, it's crucial to keep in mind that not only did he impress people in his day who were not easily impressed; he also carried out an amazing feat. We may not go quite as far as Francisco López de Gómara in the judgment with which we opened this chapter: "The greatest event since the creation of the world (excluding the incarnation and death of Him who created it) is the discovery of the Indies." We do, however, need to make room—even as we see all-too-human failures—for something it is only humanly right and just to call greatness.

2

El Almirante

*Let us hear what their comments are now—those who are so
ready with accusations and quick to find fault, saying from their
safe berths there in Spain, "Why didn't you do this or that when
you were over there." I'd like to see their sort on this adventure.*

—Columbus, *Lettera Rarissima*[57]

After centuries of controversies, the life of Columbus lies beneath
mountains of interpretation and misinterpretation. Sharp criticism
of *El Almirante* (the admiral), and sharp reaction to it, go back to
the very beginnings of his explorations, as the passage cited above,
written at a particularly threatening moment during Columbus's
fourth and final voyage to the New World, graphically shows. Then,
as now, it was easy for people who had never dared comparable feats
to suggest how the whole business might have been done better.
And in truth, Columbus's manifest errors and downright incapaci-
ties as a leader of men, anywhere but on the sea, played into the
hands of his critics and properly made him the target of protests. His

---

[57] C. Varela, ed., *Cristobal Colon, Textos y documentos completos*
(Madrid: Alianza, 1984), 323–324. A more literal but less clear
translation, along with the original Spanish text, may be found
in vol. 2 of Cecil Jane, ed., *The Four Voyages of Columbus*, reprint
(New York: Dover, 1988), 94–95.

Columbus and the Crisis of the West

failures in leadership often followed a familiar pattern: indulgence of one group or another (both native and European) followed by disorders, leading to atrocities against the Caribbean natives and harsh punishment, including executions, of Spaniards as well. Stubbornness, obsessiveness, and paranoia often dominated his psyche. Even many of his closest allies in the initial ventures clashed with him over one thing or another. In the wake of the titanic passions that his epochal voyages unleashed, it is no wonder that almost every individual and event connected with his story has been praised or damned by someone during the past five hundred years.

There has been a somewhat understandable bias in the historical characterizations of Columbus. The episodes in his life that attract the most attention are the moments of conflict or adversity. So, unrest among his men during the first voyage; or his troubles in keeping order—and his oscillation between unwise indulgence of both Spaniards and the indigenous followed by harsh punishments of both groups when things went awry—on Hispaniola during the second or third voyages; or the "voices" he heard when he was under stress or marooned: all these are scrutinized closely for what they reveal about the man. But as anyone might argue: judge me not when I'm in severe straits, facing situations almost impossible to manage, especially after I may have risked a great deal in hope of achieving great things. Any account of my life should also credit what I am like in more normal circumstances. And it's in those more normal circumstances that the "sweetness and benignity" described by Las Casas, and the "noble bearing," and even the "good intentions" need to be credited.

The long history of these varied interpretations should, at the very outset, lead to a certain caution. If it is true—as it doubtless is—that Columbus has at times been the object of uncritical hero worship and American national pride, the kind of figure who used to appear in grade-school textbooks, it is equally true that such times are

58

long since passed. There is real value in more critical, even skeptical, approaches to the historical records—so long as they do not become the sole or dominant way of reading what is a complex, rich, and multifaceted story, like all large-scale human things. If Columbus was in the past often turned into a plaster saint, the danger in the twenty-first century is more often an assumption that he must have embodied the most villainous traits of the Western civilization, which he helped to spread throughout the world. But even such extreme reckonings show, at the very least, his continued significance.

There is a reason why Vasco da Gama, for example, who succeeded in finding a water route to "the Indies" around the Cape of Good Hope in Africa, has never had the same kind of celebrity that attached itself to Columbus. Reaching the Indies was a bold and skillful effort—in its way requiring almost as much cleverness and sheer grit as the Atlantic crossing. But not quite. Sailing along an unknown and uncharted coast is not as easy as it may appear to the average landlubber. And doing so over long stretches takes rare courage and persistence. Still, it was not the same as passing long weeks out of sight of land. And there's also this: though reaching the Indies had an immediate financial benefit far greater than the voyages across the Atlantic, it still largely operated within the horizons of the previously known world. For all the claims of Native American defenders that indigenous populations didn't need to be "discovered"—that they knew where they were—the rest of the world did not know them. And they did not know the rest of the world. Columbus, both literally and figuratively, inaugurated our globalized world.

Elusive Facts

Attempts to account for the various and apparently contradictory things Columbus said and did have raised doubts about even the most basic facts of his personal history. In spite of all the scholarly ferment during the five hundredth anniversary of 1492 and after, however, many traditional teachings about Columbus's early life remain the most probable explanations for the data we have. Born in Genoa—like Venice, one of the most important Mediterranean trading powers of the time—he was a humble weaver's son who sailed early in his life to lands as distant as the Greek island of Chios and Ireland, perhaps even Iceland. He plied the Atlantic seaboard from England to Elmina, an important trading post far down the coast of Guinea in Africa. Eventually, most likely in the 1480s, he settled in Portugal, became a chart maker, and married a Portuguese wife of the lesser nobility. Sometime during these years, he conceived the idea of sailing west to the Indies and petitioned the Portuguese king for financial support and state sponsorship before turning to Spain.

But to careful scholars, much of this is plausible conjecture. In the introduction to the Columbus documents published by the Hakluyt Society in 1929 and 1932, Cecil Jane remarked that evidence available for determining the early practical experience and beliefs of Columbus is scanty and unsatisfactory: "In such circumstances, dogmatism on the question would be entirely misplaced. To assert that, before he had discovered the New World, Columbus held any given opinion would be to assert something wholly impossible of proof."[58] New evidence has surfaced since then that clears up certain problems beyond reasonable doubt. But Jane's warning should still be heeded. The primary material about Columbus leaves many issues unresolved, and perhaps unresolvable.

Anyone approaching this material for the first time should be especially cautious. Numerous theories have been proposed to fill in gaps and reconcile contradictions, including various solutions

[58] Jane, *Four Voyages*, xxviii–xxix.

to alleged mysteries about Columbus the man and his intentions. Denigrators of Columbus generally believe that the gaps exist because he was not considered very important at the time of his death. But this is to project scholarly frustrations back on a rather full record. Though Columbus's fortunes had certainly declined toward the end of his life and made the records of his final years less detailed than we might wish, the amount of biographical data concerning him is relatively large compared with that concerning his near contemporaries. John Cabot, for example, who "discovered" North America for the British, was also probably Genoese (Giovanni Caboto) and was born roughly the same time as Columbus. Yet no immediate written records of his voyages, or much about the man, have come down to us. Everything is second- or thirdhand, save a few documents placing him in Venice (if this is the same Cabot) and England.[59] Measured against the paucity of information about Cabot and other explorers of the Americas, Columbus's dossier is quite thick.

Through a Glass Darkly

But the wealth of material is deceptive. The several surviving letters, memoranda, wills, and annotations in books—all written by the admiral himself—do not yield an unambiguous portrait. Furthermore, two of the earliest secondary sources, Fernando Columbus's life of his father and Bartolomé de Las Casas's *History of the Indies*, are marked by partisan passions. Fernando clearly wishes to portray the admiral as a great, pious, and noble man hounded by

---

[59] A good short survey of the little that we possess about Cabot is presented in chapter 6, "John Cabot's Voyages," in Samuel Eliot Morison, *The European Discovery of America: The Northern Voyages* (New York: Oxford University Press, 1971).

fools and evildoers—as a grand figure whose claims on revenues from the New World for himself and his descendants should be honored by the Spanish monarchs in perpetuity. For Las Casas, a Dominican priest who became famous as the foremost defender of the Indians, Columbus evokes mixed emotions. He is a great hero whom Las Casas saw make his triumphal return to Seville on Palm Sunday 1493, after the first voyage, but also, inadvertently, a doer of certain evils.

Writing decades after 1492 with a fervor bordering on fanaticism, Las Casas intends to denounce mistreatment of the American natives and to convince the Spanish crown to stop it. While he holds Columbus, whom he knew personally, in high esteem, he also blames him for beginning that mistreatment, which he paints in lurid detail. Las Casas underplays or ignores more amicable relations between Spaniards and natives. His book *The Very Brief Relation*,[60] as many scholars have noted, gave Spain's sixteenth-century enemies—a large group of nations consisting of political competitors and emerging Protestant powers—the data with which to concoct the *leyenda negra* (black legend) of the Spanish Empire. Ironically, Spain's very openness to publishing and debating its actions in the New World made it appear far worse than countries such as England and the Netherlands, which also committed atrocities but without the negative publicity.

Las Casas is also our source—thirdhand—for one of the most crucial records: Columbus's *Log* of the first voyage. We know that scribes reproduced the original manuscript in two fair copies. One, presented to Queen Isabella, was eventually lost. The other was lost as well after Las Casas had made extensive extracts and paraphrases from it for his history. Scholars have reconstructed this *Log* from

---

[60] Bartolomé de Las Casas, *A Short Account of the Destruction of the Indies*, trans. Nigel Griffin (New York: Penguin Classics, 1999).

passages in Las Casas, but given the intervening hands and Las Casas's two powerful passions, love of Columbus and horror at the mistreatment of natives, we can only speculate on what distortions have been introduced into the text.

Even so, what we have is remarkable. One of the best historians of the period—and far from being a Columbus partisan—has written of the *Log* of the first voyage:

> On its own it is enough to establish Columbus as a man of extraordinary character and exceptional gifts. His reports to Ferdinand and Isabella are unique in the annals of the sea; no master ever compiled so detailed a log; no commander of the day ever wrote such copious reports; no navigator of that era—except perhaps Columbus's future rival Amerigo Vespucci—displayed such talent for observation, such sensitivity to the elements, such appreciation of nature. No sailor ever revealed so much of himself in a yarn. Columbus was a "poor foreigner" who never perfectly mastered written Spanish, as Las Casas complained; he was an autodidact who was never taught the art of writing. But he combined natural rhetoric with a responsive spirit, and he had a good tale to tell.[61]

After all the vituperation directed against Columbus for later problems, it is good to come upon a clear statement about other sides of a great explorer.

Fact and Imagination

The temptation to project modern categories back upon earlier historical periods is always strong. Reviewing these first late-fifteenth-century contacts now, with knowledge of what befell indigenous

---

[61] Fernández-Armesto, *Columbus*, 68–69.

peoples later, we are particularly inclined to read large-scale portents into small events. If Columbus mentions how easy it would be to subdue the natives, or expresses impatience with his failure to find the high and rich civilization of Asia, many historians readily fall into the error of seeing his attitudes as a combination of careless imperialism and greed, or even as a symbol of all that was to follow. We would do well to recall, however, that the Spanish record after Columbus is complex and not wholly bad, particularly in the religious defense of the newly discovered peoples and the gradual elaboration of native rights (see chapter 3).

In Columbus the man, several conflicting currents existed side by side. Las Casas is an important witness here because of both his passionate commitment to justice for Indians and his personal association with Columbus for several years. In a telling remark, Las Casas notes that while Christopher's brother, Bartolomé, was a resolute leader, he lacked the "sweetness and benignity" of the admiral.[62] Columbus's noble bearing and gentle manners are confirmed in many other sources. Nevertheless, Las Casas can be harsh in his criticism. Chapter 119 of *History of the Indies* concludes with the judgment that both brothers mistakenly began to occupy land and exact tribute owing to "the most culpable ignorance, which has no excuse, of natural and divine law."[63]

After five hundred years, it may seem impossible to reconcile the contradictory traits Las Casas mentions. He attempted an explanation of his own:

> Truly, I would not dare blame the admiral's intentions, for I knew him well and I know his intentions were good. But ... the road he paved and the things he did of his own free

---

[62] Morison, *Admiral of the Ocean Sea*, vol. 2, 164.

[63] Bartolomé de Las Casas, *Historia de las Indias*, vol. 1 (Mexico City: Fondo de cultura economica, 1951), 466 (author's translation).

will, as well as sometimes under constraint, stemmed from his ignorance of the law. There is much to ponder here and one can see the guiding principle of this whole Indian enterprise, namely, as is clear from the previous chapters, that the admiral and his Christians, as well as all those who followed after him in this land, worked on the assumption that the way to achieve their desires was first and foremost to instill fear in these people, to the extent of making the name Christian synonymous with terror. And to do this, they performed outstanding feats never before invented or dreamed of, as, God willing, I will show later. And this is contrary and inimical to the way that those who profess Christian benignity, gentleness and peace ought to negotiate the conversion of infidels.[64]

As this excerpt shows, Las Casas's style of writing and mode of reasoning do not always yield great clarity, and his assessment here begs several questions. Columbus's policies, and official Spanish policy generally, were much more given to gentleness and kindness in the beginning than Las Casas, who witnessed only later troubled times, allows to appear. Enslaving the native peoples — except in cases of just war and violation of natural law, as in the case of cannibals — was rejected by monarchs and people alike. Slavery was never much part of the admiral's interests anyway. The preponderance of the evidence indicates that he intended the island of Hispaniola, today's Dominican Republic and Haiti, to become something of a trading post like the ones Genoa had pioneered on the other side of the Atlantic. At least initially, he was not seeking to colonize, and when Spain sent twenty soldiers with him on the second voyage, he often clashed with them.[65] Later, as conditions

---

[64] Las Casas, *History of the Indies*, 53.
[65] Fernández-Armesto, *Columbus*, 102.

became more troubled, he seems to have envisaged a peaceful agricultural colony of some sort. But conflicts with natives and factional infighting among Spaniards drove the admiral, especially during the second and third voyages, to harsher measures, including enslavement of Indians captured in military actions when there seemed no other way to restore order. But this was not a policy intended to establish a regime of slavery. The preponderance of the evidence is that unruly Spaniards in conflict with unruly indigenous peoples forced his hand, and many of the same sources credit Columbus with at least ending the conflict.[66]

While Las Casas's condemnation is cast in terms of absolute justice and, as such, has permanent relevance to evaluating Columbus's role in the New World, we should also remember that Columbus was placed in unprecedented circumstances and should not be judged in the same way we would judge a modern trained anthropologist. Paolo Emilio Taviani, an admiring but not uncritical biographer of Columbus, demonstrates the difficulty attending every particular of the first contact:

> The European scale of values was different from that of the natives. "They give everything for a trifle"; obviously what was a trifle on the European scale was not so for the natives. For them "a potsherd or a broken glass cup" was worth "sixteen skeins of cotton." Columbus warned that would never do, because from unrestricted trade between the two mentalities, the two conceptions of value, grave injustices would result, and so he immediately prohibited the cotton trade, allowing no one to take any and reserving the acquisition entirely for the king of Spain. A just prohibition, not easy to impose on ninety men — what strength could it have when

[66] Ibid., 113.

nine hundred, nine thousand, or ninety thousand Europeans would arrive? Such were the first troubles in an encounter between two worlds that did not understand one another.[67]

If we wish to task Columbus for all the asymmetries that ensued, we should credit him as well for this initial attempt, later repeated by many Spanish governors and theologians, to find some just route through the thicket of massive cultural difference. He failed and tolerated far more wicked practices than unequal trade, but we should not let subsequent events blind us to his authentic concern for justice in the first contacts.

Some Brighter Moments

In spite of the cultural gulf, mutual affections and understanding did, at times, appear. After over two months of exploration in the Caribbean, Columbus's ship, the *Santa Maria*, went aground on Christmas 1492 in what is now Haiti. There Columbus encountered a people and a chief so helpful that his log entries for the following days view the entire episode as providential. He would never have chosen, as he admits, to come ashore or build the settlement of La Navidad (Christmas) there. He did not like the harbor. Yet he concluded that his relations with the Taínos and their chief Guacanagarí must be part of a divine plan in light of the friendship that sprang up between the two peoples.

Some Columbus scholars, perhaps a bit jaded from staring overlong at the historical lacunae and inconsistencies of the man, see in these log entries only an attempt to cover up the disastrous loss of the ship or a propaganda ploy to make the Spanish monarchs

---

[67] Paolo Emilio Taviani, *Columbus: The Great Adventure*, trans. Luciano F. Farina and Marc A. Beckwith (New York: Orion Books, 1991), 102.

think well of the discoveries. Robert H. Fuson, a modern translator of the log, is a marine historian rather than a Columbus specialist. He is sometimes rightly criticized for his rather naive historical interpretations.[68] But it is precisely because he is not predisposed to suspicion that he notices something overlooked by scholars occupied with weighing too many contradictory theories about the Haiti episode:

> Affection for the young chief in Haiti, and vice versa, is one
> of the most touching stories of love, trust, and understanding
> between men of different races and cultures to come out of
> this period in history. His [Columbus's] instructions to the
> men he left behind at La Navidad, for January 2, clearly
> illustrate his sincere fondness and respect for the Indians.[69]

The January 2 entry, as we shall see below, indicates that Columbus had some ulterior motives in placating the natives. But that does not negate his genuine good feeling toward them or his gratitude for their generosity. Even if we assume that Columbus is putting the best interpretation on events for Ferdinand and Isabella, some sort of fellow feeling undeniably had arisen, at least temporarily, across the vast cultural divide separating the Taínos and the Europeans. Despite the great evils that would come later, this altruism was not without its own legacies.

---

[68] On this point and for an exhaustive and exhausting analysis of the *Log*, see David Henige, *In Search of Columbus: The Sources for the First Voyage* (Tucson: University of Arizona Press, 1991). As Henige's dedication of this volume to Pierre Bayle and a legion of other details show, skepticism may become as confining a dogma as credulousness.

[69] Christopher Columbus, *The Log of Christopher Columbus*, trans. Robert H. Fuson (Camden, Maine: International Marine Publishing, 1992), 32. See also Oliver Dunn and James E. Kelley Jr.'s translation (Norman: University of Oklahoma Press, 1989).

An extreme but common form of the oversimple charges often leveled against the Europeans in general and Columbus in particular has come from the pen of the novelist Hans Koning. Writing to influence public sentiments about the quincentenary, Koning insisted that from 1492 to 1500,

> there is not one recorded moment of awe, of joy, of love, of a smile. There is only anger, cruelty, greed, terror, and death. That is the record. Nothing else, I hold, is relevant when we discuss our commemoration of its 500th anniversary.[70]

Riding the wave of revisionism about American history sweeping over education, which has only become virtually dominant in the more than quarter century since then, Koning made these claims under the title "Teach the Truth about Columbus."

The only problem with his assessment is that every particular in his catalog of what constitutes the truth is false. To take them in order: Columbus certainly records awe at his discoveries throughout his four voyages. His praise of the land's beauty was partly meant, of course, to convince the king and queen of the value of the properties Columbus had discovered for them. But some of it is simply awe; Columbus's enthusiasm for many of the new lands reaches a climax during his third voyage when he describes the sheer loveliness of the Venezuelan coast, which he believed to be the site of the original Garden of Eden, the earthly paradise.

Drawing on biblical and classical sources, he is reminded as he encounters the waters of the Orinoco River that "Holy Scripture testifies that Our Lord made the earthly paradise and in it placed the tree of life, and from it issues a fountain from which flow four

---

[70] Hans Koning, "Teach the Truth about Columbus," *Washington Post*, 3 September 1991.

of the chief rivers of the world."[71] He wavers a bit about whether the relevant texts confirm speculation that this could be the site of the earthly paradise, but he observes, "The very mild climate also supports this view, and if it does not come from there, from paradise, it seems to be a still greater marvel, for I do not believe that there is known in the world a river so great and so deep."[72] Indeed, the very name Venezuela (little Venice) was given to the region by the Spaniards because the Arawak Indians lived there in houses built on stilts in the lakes. Venice was and is, for many people, a little jewel of a city, and the name Venezuela was obviously intended as a compliment. If all this is not a record of something at least approaching awe, it is difficult to imagine what would be.

The relations between natives and Spaniards before 1500 are not, *pace* Koning, unrelieved darkness either. If anything, they are a frustrating reminder of a road not taken. Smiles there were—recorded smiles—at least on the native Taíno side: "They love their neighbors as themselves, and they have the softest and gentlest voices in the world and are always smiling" (*Log*, Tuesday, 25 December 1492). Columbus had reason to appreciate these people since they had just helped him salvage what was salvageable from the wreck of the *Santa Maria*. In the feast that natives and Spaniards held after the rescue, the cacique Guacanagarí placed a crown on Columbus's head. The admiral reciprocated by giving him a scarlet cloak and a pair of colored boots, "and I placed upon his finger a large silver ring. I had been told that he had seen a silver ring on one of my sailors and desired it very much. The King was joyful and overwhelmed." Guacanagarí grew so close to Columbus that he may have even asked if he and his brother might return with him to Castile, though language problems

[71] Jane, *Four Voyages*, vol. 2, 34.
[72] Ibid., 38.

may also conceal here Columbus's desire simply to take the chief back with him.[73]

When it came time to leave for Spain, Columbus placed thirty-nine men "under the command of three officers, all of whom are very friendly to King Guacanagarí," and furthermore ordered that "they should avoid *as they would death* annoying or tormenting the Indians, bearing in mind how much they owe these people." The emphasis added to this last quotation has a double purpose. Clearly, Columbus recognized the temptations his men would have; just as clearly was he determined, to the best of his ability, to anticipate and block those temptations. This is the entry of January 2 that Fuson reads as expressing sincere kindness and affection. That reading may be a little too simple, but it is difficult to believe that it is entirely mistaken.

What this incident and the founding of the settlement definitely are *not*, however, are instances of simple European arrogance and imperialism, or what John Noble Wilford, a modern biographer of Columbus, has called "a personal transition from discoverer to imperialist."[74] Even when full-scale war between some Indians and Spaniards broke out during Columbus's second voyage, Guacanagarí remained loyal to Columbus in spite of — or perhaps in opposition to — commands from another local chief, Caonabó, for a cacique alliance. No source denies this loyalty between the Taíno and the admiral, even under trying cultural tensions and warfare. Though we are right to abhor many far less happy subsequent events between the inhabitants of the two worlds, the record of the early interaction is richer and more diverse than most people, blinded by contemporary polemics, think.

---

[73] An early historian, Andres Bernaldez, recounts a similar request by another cacique on Jamaica during the second voyage. See Jane, *Four Voyages*, vol. 1, 164.

[74] Wilford, *Mysterious History*, 170.

The List of Charges

The principal moral questions about Columbus arise essentially from three of his actions:

1. He immediately kidnapped some Taínos during his first voyage for questioning and used them as interpreters. In that act, according to the critics, he showed not only his contempt for Indian life but his belief that Spanish language, culture, and religion were superior and rightly to be imposed on native peoples.

2. After the destruction of La Navidad and the turmoil that ensued during the second voyage, Columbus foolishly ordered exploratory missions without adequate safeguards to restrain outrageously violent men such as Mosen Pedro Margarit and Alonso de Ojeda. He then punished the natives who objected to Spaniards' living off the land or who resisted their commands. In addition to setting this evil precedent, he shipped home some natives to become slaves with a very poor excuse:

   > Since of all the islands those of the cannibals are much the largest and much more fully populated, it is thought here that to take some of the men and women and to send them home to Castile would not be anything but well, for they may one day be led to abandon that inhuman custom that they have of eating men, and there in Castile, learning the language, they will much more readily receive baptism and secure the welfare of their souls.[75]

3. Columbus instituted a system of gold tribute from the natives that was heavy—nearly impossible, in fact, given the

---

[75] Jane, *Four Voyages*, vol. 1., 88.

small quantity of gold on the island of Hispaniola—and that was harshly enforced.

Each of these charges is true, and no amount of admiration for Christopher Columbus can excuse what is simply wrong. And, of course, the situation grew even worse in some of the later voyages. The argument by Felipe Fernández-Armesto, one of the fairest Columbus historians, that "Columbus and his successors were guilty only of applying the best standards of their time" makes two shortsighted and ambivalent assumptions.[76] First, it assumes that such behavior represents the best contemporary standards. As we shall see in the next chapter, when we examine the religious influences during the exploration and some of the philosophical developments the discoveries stimulated, it did not. Many in Europe knew the bad behavior was wrong and said so. Second, the argument assumes that individuals should not be criticized for acting like the majority of their contemporaries because they are bound by culture and history. The latter argument draws strength from current philosophical schools that hold there are no privileged or absolute positions outside of historically conditioned views. But if we think we should condemn Aztec human sacrifice as wrong—not simply a different cultural form, but wrong—then we must admit there are universal principles that also allow us to criticize improper European use of force, enslavement, and exploitation.

Yet just as we try to understand the reasons behind Aztec human sacrifice or Carib cannibalism, and both tribes' imperialism toward other native peoples, we should also try to see what led to Columbus's behavior. Columbus, as Las Casas testified above, was not by nature a violent man like Ojeda or Cortés. The first sign of harshness by him, in fact, seems to have been his acquiescence,

[76] Felipe Fernández-Armesto, "In Defense of Columbus: The Trouble with Eden," *Economist*, 21 December 1991–3 January 1992, 74.

during the second voyage, in a death sentence against some Indians on Hispaniola who had been caught stealing. Significantly, the pleading of another Indian moved him to remit the sentence in that case (the wavering, too, is characteristic of his uncertainty in handling questions of governance). Though he apparently regarded the Indians as inferior and always approached them with much the same assumption of superiority that Spaniards approached the Guanches of the Canary Islands and the native tribes they encountered on the Atlantic Coast of Africa, he seemed at least partly — and when circumstances allowed — aware that good treatment was both morally called for and favorable to Spanish interests.

A fairer reading of the record reveals some mitigating factors, though these by no means add up to an exoneration:

1. Though Columbus did kidnap some Indians, two interpreters among them, he set one of them free immediately upon returning to Hispaniola during the second voyage.[77] The other seems to have disappeared from history. He hoped that the Indian set at liberty would tell others of Spain's wonders and of Columbus's good intentions. This was self-serving, crude, and manipulative on his part, but it shows some perspicacity and basic goodwill.

2. Slavery was always a bone of contention between Columbus and the Spanish monarchs: the monarchs vehemently opposed this way of "civilizing" their subjects in the Indies. Columbus was not clear in his own mind about the issue. As late as the third voyage, the last in which he would be permitted to visit the growing colony on Hispaniola, Columbus ordered that slaves could be taken only during a just war. His thinking was muddled, as was the thinking of the world for at least another half

[77] Morison, *Admiral of the Ocean Sea*, vol. 2, 90.

century until several crucial questions about Indian rights and just claims were sorted out (again, see chapter 3).

3. The imposition of gold tribute for Spanish services stemmed from the belief that much gold existed on Hispaniola. And Indian failures to meet what seemed to the Spaniards modest levies were mistakenly attributed to laziness. Indians loved the tiny hawk's bells that the Spaniards brought as trinkets; asking them to fill a bell with gold every two months seemed a reasonable request. Since all governments tax in some fashion, Spain was doing only what caciques and Carib conquerors had been doing for time immemorial. The Spanish system did not "introduce" a new evil to an idyllic people without politics, but it proved peculiarly burdensome because it was imposed from the outside and in ignorance of the realities on Hispaniola.

Furthermore, contrary to many wild modern charges, the Spaniards never intended to commit "genocide." In even the most cynical reading, a ready supply of native workers served Spanish self-interest. European and African diseases, however, soon laid waste whole tribes.

Fernández-Armesto argues that Columbus's recourse to violence on Hispaniola resulted mostly from his basic inability to rule well, from "misjudgment rather than wickedness."[78] Gonzalo Fernández de Oviedo, who became the official Spanish historian of the New World, said that to govern the Hispaniola colony correctly, a person would have to be "angelic, indeed superhuman."[79] Columbus was far from either; in fact, he was far from possessing even normal political acumen. During his second and third voyages, he clearly

[78] Fernández-Armesto, *Columbus*, 112.
[79] Quoted in Morison, *Admiral of the Ocean Sea*, vol. 2, 304.

tried to avoid facing political difficulties on Hispaniola by exploring further afield — exploration being what he was good at, and he knew it.[80] The problem was not merely lack of political skill. As a foreigner in Spain, he felt that he could trust only family members and close personal friends. (In fact, recent research has revealed that the Columbus family belonged to an anti-Spanish faction in Genoa, a political embarrassment that may help account for some of Columbus's reticence about his early life.)[81] The resentments arising from difficult conditions, moreover, served to reinforce his tendencies toward paranoia. His rule of both Indians and Spanish oscillated between being too indecisive and too harsh.

We should also understand, however, the kinds of Indians and colonists he had to govern. Columbus had trouble enough with the natives and complained:

> At home they judge me as a governor sent to Sicily or to a city or two under settled government and where the laws can be fully maintained, without fear of all being lost.... I ought to be judged as a captain who went from Spain to the Indies to conquer a people, warlike and numerous, and with customs and beliefs very different from ours.[82]

Even the Taínos were probably far less gentle than Columbus earlier reported and "not so innocent as Las Casas tried to show."[83] The Caribs, their fierce, cannibalistic enemies, seem to have been as terrified of the supposedly pacific Taínos as vice versa. And recent archaeological investigations suggest that the Taínos, contrary to

80 Fernández-Armesto, *Columbus*, 122.
81 Phillips and Phillips, *Worlds of Christopher Columbus*, 90.
82 Jane, *Four Voyages*, vol. 2, 66.
83 See chapter 7, "The Ball Game," in Eugenio Fernández Méndez, *Art and Mythology of the Taíno Indians of the Greater West Indies* (San Juan: Ediciones "El Cerni," 1972), 62.

Columbus's impression of them as being without religion, had a complex system of belief and ritual akin to those in Central America and Mexico. They appear to have played a ritual ball game reenacting the cosmic struggle between light and darkness and ending with the religious sacrifice of one or more human victims. An early Spanish conquistador estimated that twenty thousand people were sacrificed yearly on Hispaniola alone, though that figure may be wildly exaggerated.[84] In any event, native tribes were profoundly *other* to the unsophisticated sailors and explorers in Columbus's day—and remain profoundly other even to us today.

The Spaniards with whom Columbus had to deal were not much better. After the second voyage, he asked the monarchs to think carefully about whom they were sending on the voyages and to choose "such persons that there be no suspicion of them and that they consider the purpose for which they have been sent rather than their personal interests."[85] Not only were some of the colonists unusually violent, but many Spanish gentlemen who had come expecting easy wealth resented Columbus, the need to work, and the unhealthy conditions on the island. In dealing with these settlers, as Las Casas observed, "The Admiral had to use violence, threats, and constraint to have the work done at all."[86]

Nicolás de Ovando, an experienced and talented leader appointed later by Spain to rule Hispaniola, also had difficulties in establishing order, but he succeeded in a relatively short time. Columbus did not possess Ovando's gifts. Given all the adverse circumstances, it is not surprising that Columbus himself ended up in chains at the end of the third voyage. Complaints about his governance prompted Ferdinand and Isabella to send Francisco

---

[84] Ibid., 61–69.
[85] Jane, *Four Voyages*, vol. 1, 94.
[86] Wilford, *Mysterious History*, 173.

de Bobadilla to help administer the colony. When Bobadilla disembarked, he found five Spaniards hanging from the gallows; they had been executed for crimes by Columbus's orders. Seven more Spaniards were scheduled for the same punishment. In the widespread turmoil, Bobadilla decided to arrest the admiral, put him in chains, and ship him back to Spain in 1500. Columbus was forbidden afterward to visit Hispaniola. Officials there were so determined to keep him from exerting any further influence on the island that they would not let him come ashore even during a bad storm while he lay at anchor outside the harbor on the fourth voyage.

Modern Eclipse

In our time, a basic skepticism toward heroes, a general guilt over colonialism, and a profound alienation from contemporary culture have led some writers to overemphasize the less savory side of the Columbus story. Sometimes, as in Koning, that perspective eclipses everything else. The desire to correct an idealized image of Columbus tempts us into new falsehoods and blind spots. For that very reason, the record has to be examined carefully. A useful thought experiment is to try to imagine what a historian, looking back at 1992 on the occasion of the sexcentenary in 2092, might regard as errors induced by twenty-first-century biases.

One strong current tendency, for example, is to belittle even the courage and vision, and the indisputable achievement, of Columbus in making the first Atlantic crossing. In the modern world, long trips are far less daunting and stir people's imaginations far less than at any previous time in human history. We step onto comfortable airliners and arrive within hours at any destination on the globe. Only a few decades ago, most people were astonished that a lone man—Charles Lindbergh—could fly the tiny *Spirit of St. Louis* from New York to Paris. Even ships take only six days to cross the Atlantic today, and they are usually equipped with amenities, safety features, and communications equipment that make them almost as comfortable as a modern city—and given the nature of the modern city, probably less risky to life and limb. Our low opinion of the physical bravery required to make the first Atlantic crossing reflects more our own material advantages than the reality of the deed.

The first European Atlantic crossing (at least the first that we are sure took place) began on September 8, 1492, from the Canary Islands, then already on the margins of the known world, on three modest, seventy-foot boats; land was not sighted again until roughly forty days later, on October 12, somewhere in the Caribbean.[87] Significantly, Spain sent no soldiers with Columbus; this initial foray was a voyage of exploration, not conquest. After months of exploration, the return trip began on January 16, 1493, and came to a harrowing end when three days of unusually fierce storms separated the two remaining ships. Columbus limped into the Azores on February 17 and then took a couple of weeks more to reach Lisbon on March 4. The entire journey had taken almost six months.

But the rigors of that ordeal paled in comparison to those suffered by Columbus and more than one hundred explorers while they were marooned on Jamaica during the fourth voyage. The

---

[87] The exact site of landfall continues to be hotly disputed and will likely remain so, barring some conclusive archaeological discovery. San Salvador, formerly Watlings Island under British rule, is the most popular candidate, with Samana Cay in the next place. Other sites have been suggested because they show convincing geographical features. Robert Fuson gives a handy list of the candidates, their major sponsors, and the dates they have been proposed in the introduction to his translation of *The Log of Christopher Columbus*. The inconclusiveness of this dispute mirrors the indeterminable nature of many questions relating to the voyages.

governors on the quickly growing colony of Hispaniola spent a year sorting out political questions before bothering to send a rescue ship. Threatening natives, unfamiliar food, and the Indies' pleasant but quite different climate made every maneuver difficult. It shows a profound lack of imagination and sympathy to say, as many have, that it was no great feat and someone would have done it sooner or later anyway. Many explorers, even years after 1492, would not return to tell their stories.

Experience, Courage, Knowledge

Columbus's achievement lay not only in his daring but also in his determination to take a risk on the basis of growing knowledge. Columbus was primarily a practical sailor, but a sailor who read and thought under the influence of a vision. Observation of the winds in the Atlantic convinced him that he might catch westbound winds from the Canaries and eastbound returning winds farther north. In this he was brilliantly right. His study of the Florentine cartographer and mathematician Paolo Toscanelli's work and his careful perusal of various other geographical and travel books made the trip seem possible. Columbus seriously erred here, however. As we saw in chapter 1, he grossly underestimated the distance west across the Atlantic from Europe to Japan (an error he shared with his contemporary, the cartographer Martin Behaim, who constructed one of the first modern globes).[88] But he was lucky in that today's Cuba is located almost exactly where he thought Japan should be.

Still, as the records from his voyages show, he was not only a keen navigator but also a sharp observer who, though operating with only rudimentary technologies, made some amazing discoveries

[88] Phillips and Phillips, *Worlds of Christopher Columbus*, 79.

in addition to the lands he found. Felipe Fernández-Armesto sums it up thus:

> Despite nearly five hundred years of assiduous detraction, his prior role in the discovery of America remains the strongest part of Columbus' credential as an explorer. But we should recall some of the supporting evidence too: his decoding of the Atlantic wind system; his discovery of magnetic variation in the Western hemisphere; his contributions to the mapping of the Atlantic and the New World; his epic crossing of the Caribbean; his demonstration of the continental nature of parts of South and Central America; his *apercu* about the imperfect sphericity of the globe [the earth bulges in the Atlantic near Brazil]; his uncanny intuitive skill in navigation. Any of these would qualify an explorer for enduring fame; together they constitute an unequalled record of achievement.[89]

Probably no one until that first New World voyage had deliberately, and successfully, spent so much time sailing out of sight of land as had Columbus. The Portuguese who started working their way down the West African coast in the fifteenth century and the Chinese who began exploring the Indian Ocean at about the same time both engaged in some brave seamanship. But the Portuguese also prudently followed the shoreline and kept a sharp eye for homebound winds. The Chinese, despite the multiculturalist wish to accord Admiral Zheng He and a non-Western country a place in the age of exploration, visited only previously known ports.[90]

Several other daring expeditions were attempted earlier, notably by two Portuguese sailors, Fernão Dulmo and João Estreito, who

---

[89] Fernández-Armesto, *Columbus*, 191.
[90] F. W. Mote, "China in the Age of Columbus," in Levenson, *Circa 1492*, 337–350.

in 1487 sailed west, never to be heard from again.[91] Reports of others sailing out of England and elsewhere were common in the late fifteenth century, but no one left a definite record of discovery and return. Most disappeared without even leaving their names to history. Clearly, such efforts show that an exploratory mood was growing in the European Atlantic, but they should not be read through the distorting lens of hindsight. The disappearances cannot help but have introduced further doubts and fears among those considering similar undertakings.

Columbus's marked and persistent certainty that he could reach the Indies has led to some speculation, based on rumors dating back to his own lifetime, that Columbus had rescued a shipwrecked Portuguese sailor who told him about land in the west. The story appears to be false, and both his son and other sympathetic early commentators attribute it to the ill will of detractors. But even if it were true, the fact that no ship, so far as the principal countries of Europe knew, had ever returned from across the Atlantic would hardly have increased anyone's confidence to make the attempt.

God's Messenger

In the preface to the *Libro de las profecías* (*Book of Prophecies*) he compiled near the end of his life, Columbus relates and perhaps exaggerates to Ferdinand and Isabella how he became convinced that the voyage was not merely possible but his own special vocation:

> During this time, I have searched out and studied all kinds of texts: geographies, histories, chronologies, philosophies, and other subjects. With a hand that could be felt, the Lord opened my mind to the fact that it would be possible to sail

[91] Wilford, *Mysterious History*, 7.

from here to the Indies, and he opened my will to desire to accomplish this project. This was the fire that burned within me when I came to visit Your Highnesses.[92]

Adding that God wished there to be a *milagro ebidentisimo* (very conspicuous miracle) in this enterprise, Columbus acknowledges and repeats that, though he had read and studied much on his own, he is an uneducated man; "for the execution of the journey to the Indies, I was not aided by intelligence, by mathematics, or by maps. It was simply the fulfillment of what Isaiah had prophesied."[93]

When Columbus mentions "a hand that could be felt," he is not speaking metaphorically. At several critical points in his life, he seems to have even heard a "voice" speaking prophetically to him.[94] Early and late in life, Columbus appears to have believed he had a calling from God to make his trip. It was not the first time in history that a man felt inspired by God to do one thing but, in the event, achieved another. Though commentators have long noticed Columbus's religiousness, it has not received proper treatment, and certainly has been misunderstood, until very recently. Most historians have accepted the religion as sincere, but perhaps a psychological defense mechanism, particularly when it manifests itself in the face of danger from storms. But Columbus's extensive writing on the subject is, in our singularly secular age, widely regarded as misguided at best, pathological at worst, and therefore not to be credited with much importance. Yet it is an absolutely crucial element in understanding everything for which he is remembered.

---

[92] "Introductory Letter," in Christopher Columbus, *Libro de las profecías*, trans. and ed. Delno C. West and August Kling (Gainesville: University of Florida Press, 1991), 105.

[93] Ibid., 111.

[94] Fernández-Armesto, *Columbus*, passim.

Columbus and the Crisis of the West

His *Libro de las profecías*, which he assembled with the help of Gaspar de Gorricio, a monk from the Carthusian monastery at Las Cuevas, is a mass of scriptural and other texts that Columbus believed predicted his voyage to the New World. Akin to the mystical speculations of Pascal and the enormous commentary of Isaac Newton on Old Testament prophecies, this work is an embarrassment to many of Columbus's admirers[95] and a target for his detractors.[96] Practical men, men of a scientific bent are not supposed to indulge in these spiritual lucubrations. Along with late letters and other materials, the *Profecías* has usually been dismissed as evidence of a broken man whose mind has plunged back into mysticism in the worst sense of the word—understandable only as a compensatory reaction to the unpleasant realities of Columbus's closing years. The book was not even translated from the original Latin into a modern language until 1984.[97]

Though Washington Irving and many other major biographers knew of this text, it was long not accorded its proper value, perhaps owing to the myth of Columbus the progressive. In fact, the modern English translator and commentator on it, Delno C. West, found that the copy at Princeton's Firestone Library, which he first examined in the 1980s, still had the pages uncut.[98] West says of the importance of the text:

> The apparent inconsistencies in his story and action are not so much weaknesses and lapses as his own attempts at

---

[95] Samuel Eliot Morison, for example, gives the *Libro de las profecías* only three passing references in the two large volumes of *Admiral of the Ocean Sea*.

[96] See Sale, *Conquest of Paradise*, 188–191.

[97] Cristobal Colon, *Libro de las profecías*, trans. and ed. F. Morales Pedron (Madrid: Collecion Tabula Americae, 1984).

[98] Introduction to Columbus, *Libro de las profecías*, 4.

accommodation to political realities in a world in which his particular kind of motivation was rare and difficult to engage. He was a man of visions, dreams, hope. All of these goals were unintelligible to many of his contemporaries and to nearly all of his biographers and readers in the succeeding five hundred years. But the goals were perfectly clear in the light of his biblical sources and world events as seen through the eyes of prophecy.[99]

Though West's statement is a little too sweeping and perhaps sails a little too close to a conventional Columbus as Catholic saint, his work has uncovered essential and largely overlooked dimensions of the admiral and his relentless push toward the Indies.

Religious Enthusiasms

Columbus's growing obsession with religion shows, amid sincere and solid devotion, unhealthy features. It has been suggested that physical or mental illness accounts for some of the more bizarre beliefs he came to hold. Modern pathologists have even diagnosed Columbus, probably correctly, as suffering from Reiter's syndrome, a severe rheumatoid arthritis.[100] But Reiter's syndrome, though it debilitates the sufferer periodically, does not produce mental instability. The fundamental question is: Did Columbus's vision change late in his life? Or was he only emphasizing something in his thought and action that had always been present? West has discovered that among the notes in Columbus's handwriting at the back of his copy of the *Historia rerum ubique gestarum*, a popular

---

[99] Ibid., 74–75.

[100] Several recent biographers accept this diagnosis on the basis of G. Weissmann, *They All Laughed at Christopher Columbus: Tales of Medicine and the Art of Discovery* (New York: Times Books, 1987).

medieval book about foreign lands by Aeneas Sylvius Piccolomini (later Pope Pius II) is "an earlier, smaller version of the *Libro de las profecías*."[101] The entries bear the date 1481, over ten years before the first voyage to the Americas. Columbus was only thirty at the time. Whatever developments his beliefs underwent, it seems indisputable that something resembling a prophetic, even apocalyptic, vision guided Columbus from his early manhood on.

These early religious concerns show that his later professions were not merely a cover for Spanish imperialism and personal ambition, even though they were clearly mixed in with both of those things. Scholarly opinion has come to recognize how deeply Columbus was influenced by medieval Franciscan traditions of the end time, particularly by those of the prophet Joachim of Fiore (1135–1202). Several New Testament texts posited that the world would not end before the gospel had been preached to all nations. Columbus firmly believed that he was preparing the way for finally accomplishing this task. He knew from reading Marco Polo, for example, that out of curiosity about Christianity, Kublai Khan had asked the pope to send missionaries to Cathay. Political and military turmoil had prevented the two priests assigned from completing their journey. Columbus's pressing forward and certainty about the nearness of Cathay resulted from his belief that he had been called on to finish that business.

Golden Means to Sacred Ends

These discoveries enrich our understanding of Columbus's relentless pursuit of gold. Like many of the Spanish who came to the New World, he sought profit, in the most tangible sense of the word, for himself and his descendants. Yet few accusations of raw personal

[101] Columbus, *Libro de las profecías*, 86.

greed surface in the many accounts we have of Columbus, some by his mortal enemies. Nor do his habits, despite the privileges he tried to secure, much reflect a man savoring the prospect of massive personal wealth. The Franciscans, the Catholic religious order most dedicated to the vow of poverty, were always hospitable and helpful to him in his petitions to important Spanish figures. Several recent students of Columbus's millennial vision have noted that when he traveled through Spain, he stopped at monasteries rather than the homes of caballeros or grandees.[102] During his later years, Columbus's typical dress in Spain was indistinguishable from that of lay members of the Observantine Franciscans, an austere group within the Franciscans. No conclusive evidence exists that Columbus was a lay Franciscan, but these are just some of the indications that he was. The gold he sought, though partly intended for himself and his heirs, was mainly to be used for far different purposes and became bound up with what one historian has called a "spiritual quest."[103]

Though Columbus contrives to keep Ferdinand and Isabella interested in his "enterprise of the Indies" by emphasizing the beauty and wealth of the New World and the general friendliness of its inhabitants, he also frequently encourages them to use the wealth he has uncovered to mount a last crusade to retake the Holy Land. The long struggle to expel the Moors from Spain, which ended only in January 1492, kept the crusading spirit alive there longer than elsewhere in Europe. Furthermore, the Turkish conquest of

---

[102] Leonard I. Sweet, "Christopher Columbus and the Millennial Vision of the New World," *Catholic Historical Review* 72, no. 3 (July 1986): 381. See also Marcel Bataillon, "The Idea of the Discovery of America among the Spaniards of the Sixteenth Century," in *Spain in the Fifteenth Century: 1369–1516*, ed. Roger Highfield (New York: Harper & Row, 1972), 453.

[103] Sweet, "Millennial Vision," 378.

Columbus and the Crisis of the West

Byzantium in 1453 had made all of Europe feel threatened. But Columbus had far greater aims in mind: that the Spanish king would complete the New Testament prophecies and usher in the end time.

Ferdinand himself seems not to have found the idea preposterous. In light of the Islamic threat, he took special pride in seeing himself as a crusading liberator and even coveted the title "King of Jerusalem." He submitted proposals for the conquest of Jerusalem to his Cortes—his groups of royal advisers. In this he may have been taking advantage of a mistaken belief, which Columbus accepted as true, that Joachim of Fiore had predicted the retaking of the Holy Land by a king of Spain. None of Joachim's writings, however, suggest Spain as the instrument of the final struggle. Various skeptical parties, including Machiavelli (who in *The Prince* praises Ferdinand as an exemplary and effective two-faced ruler), have argued that Ferdinand was not serious about these proposals.[104] According to this view, Ferdinand, confident that the Cortes would reject the idea, proposed the crusade to win credit for his good intentions.

The medieval preoccupation with crusades to retake the Holy Land may not be very intelligible to most modern readers. Indeed, crusades are often invoked along with "the Spanish Inquisition," as instances of Christian prejudice and bloodthirstiness. But this shows a blind spot in our intellectual vision. We find it hard to believe that religious reasons in themselves can be motivating people when materialist explanations—desire for power or wealth—are near to hand, as they almost always are. Yet Iran in the 1970s and 1980s acted against its own worldly interests in what it saw as adherence to religious principle. In 1494, just two years after Columbus's New

---

[104] Felipe Fernández-Armesto, *Ferdinand and Isabella* (New York: Taplinger, 1975), 132–133.

World landfall, the Dominican monk Girolamo Savonarola came to power in Florence — then in the full flower of the Renaissance. Religious zeal led to bonfires of the beautiful vanities that we associate today with the very name of Florence.

Religious impulses have strong worldly consequences. Few people have any difficulty understanding, for example, why modern Jews desired and vigorously defend the state of Israel. Jews, like Christians, believe in a God who is simultaneously transcendent and the Lord of history. In that perspective, the special places where, and persons to whom, He has shown Himself are not merely negligible vehicles but part and parcel of a Creator God. In fact, all the religions of the Book, including Islam, share the perception (which exists in different form among some nonbiblical peoples as well) of sacred sites. The desire to possess, and to worship at, these sites is as natural as the Jewish desire for the biblically promised homeland.

Holy wars to capture such sites may seem improper to persons who believe religion should lead to pacifism or at least promote peace, but most of us can understand why peoples from various cultures show a special attachment and willingness to go to war to gain ancestral and sacred lands. That's true for Native Americans, Middle Eastern Muslims, Russians, and Chinese as well as for medieval and Renaissance Christians. The Old Testament certainly seems to support that kind of war under certain conditions; the ancient Hebrews had to defeat the Canaanites. Similarly, the founders of the modern Jewish state had to take Palestine by force. This enterprise, however, should be distinguished from the use of force in proselytizing, a practice that seems to have been countenanced without qualms only by Islam among the three faiths of the Book and even among Muslims only intermittently.

The Crusades have gotten a bad reputation because of the human corruption that accompanied such an allegedly holy cause.

Columbus and the Crisis of the West

As T.S. Eliot has portrayed the situation in his "Choruses from 'The Rock'":

> Some went from love of glory,
> Some went who were restless and curious,
> Some were rapacious and lustful.
> Many left their bodies to the kites of Syria
> Or sea-strewn along the routes;
> Many left their souls in Syria,
> Living on, sunken in moral corruption;
> Many came back well broken,
> Diseased and beggared, finding
> A stranger at the door in possession:
> Came home cracked by the sun of the East
> And the seven deadly sins of Syria.

But Eliot concludes:

> Not avarice, lechery, treachery,
> Envy, sloth, gluttony, jealousy, pride:
> It was not these that made the Crusades,
> But these that unmade them.[105]

We are unused to this idea and rightly resist easy resort to religious violence in modern pluralistic societies, but the medieval view of a crusade is not simply irrational or corrupt, or a cynical cover for materialistic interests.

At any rate, Columbus was willing to put his treasure where his heart lay. In 1498, before his third voyage, he made a will that was later altered in various ways. But one point remained firm until his death: he directed the executors of his estate to set up a fund—not

---

[105] T.S. Eliot, *Collected Poems, 1909–1935* (New York: Harcourt, Brace & World, 1962), 110.

large, but not negligible either—in Genoa's Bank of Saint George to help pay for the liberation of Jerusalem.[106]

Medieval and Not

While these religious passions clearly link him to medieval categories of thought, Columbus was willing to risk his life to show that some medieval lore was incomplete, false, or misconstrued. Columbus may have been medieval in a variety of ways, but there were some important respects in which he was not. Though he was committed to converting the world, for example, he was not rigidly intolerant. Even late in life he wrote, "I believe that the Holy Spirit works among Christians, Jews, and Moslems, and among all men of every faith, not merely among the learned, but also among the uneducated."[107] Some of the "sweetness and benignity" of character mentioned by Las Casas perhaps shows through here.

Nor does he greatly manifest the characteristic medieval superstition about imaginary terrors or boundaries beyond the known world. The experiences of a sailor, and also of a certain type of religious mind, prevent him from accepting tall stories without corroboration. Some parties have accused him of credulity, or at least fanciful misunderstanding, in accepting the Taínos's stories that the Caribs were cannibals.[108] Though he is eventually convinced of their view, he resists that interpretation for quite a while. In several places in his *Log*, he says things such as this:

> The Indians with me continued to show great fear because of the course I was taking and kept insisting that the people of Bohio had only one eye and the face of a dog, and they

[106] Sweet, "Millennial Vision," 381,

[107] Columbus, *Libro de las profecías*, 107.

[108] See Sale, *Conquest of Paradise*, among others.

fear being eaten. I do not believe any of this. I feel that the Indians they fear belong to the domain of the Great Khan.[109]

Whatever misunderstandings may be occurring in such early exchanges because of the language barrier (Columbus himself notes this difficulty, by the way), it is clear that Columbus does not arrive at his belief that the fierce Caribs were cannibals merely because he had read of *anthropophagoi* in ancient and medieval texts. And it appears his belief was correct. A modern biography adds: "To deny that cannibalism existed, one needs to assume that a wide range of European commentators simply made up the stories, an interpretation that defies reason, logic, and the available evidence."[110] Only in the log entry of January 13, 1493, after more than three months in the Caribbean listening to the fears of natives, does Columbus report Indian tales of cannibalism without some skepticism.[111]

Columbus's willingness to disregard certain medieval notions has led many people to see him as poised between the Middle Ages and the Renaissance. To them, his search for wealth, station, and knowledge manifest the very characteristics that define the Renaissance shift to emphasizing the life of man in this world. Lending weight to this side of the scale is the fact that Columbus also had an artistic side. Las Casas says of his abilities as an artist, "So fine was his hand that he might have earned his living by that skill alone."[112] His ultimate goal in compiling the book of prophecies was eventually to present the monarchs with an apocalyptic poem, of which we have some preliminary portions. Though by

---

[109] Columbus, *The Log*, 115, 117, 132, 138, and 154 for Columbus's initial doubts. Quotation in text on 132.

[110] Phillips and Phillips, *Worlds*, 295n22.

[111] Columbus, *The Log*, 172.

[112] Las Casas, *Historia de las Indias*, vol. 1, 30–31 (author's translation).

no means proof of a poetic talent of the first rank, the verses of this sailor-turned-explorer-turned-millenarian thinker add another dimension to an already complex man.[113]

Misrepresentations and Misunderstandings

Many historians and ideologues, however, overplay Columbus's Renaissance side for various reasons, usually having to do with modern agendas. His "medievalism" notwithstanding, he is made to stand as a symbol of incipient European capitalists and even imperialists, with all the ignoble characteristics often associated with those figures.[114] This charge reflects a misrepresentation of and condescension toward both the Middle Ages and the Renaissance not easily compatible with the facts. The Middle Ages were not sedentary or self-satisfied or uninterested in profitable commerce, by any means, merely limited by the knowledge and technology available until the fifteenth century. Medieval Venice and Genoa were the twin centers of Mediterranean naval commerce that paved the way for later commercial activities around the world. In *The Medieval Expansion of Europe*, J. R. S. Phillips shows that the push into the New World was a growth in the scale of exploration but is better understood as a continuation of, rather than a new departure from, impulses already present in Europe for centuries.[115] Columbus

---

[113] Columbus, *Libro de las profecías*, 258–259.

[114] One scholar (Taviani, *Columbus*, 263), however, placing yet another symbolic load on Columbus, has argued that he embodies "the creative genius of Italy shaping the beginning of the modern age." Columbus's pivotal position on the way toward the modern world perhaps makes such terminological tugs-of-war inevitable.

[115] J. R. S. Phillips, *Medieval Expansion of Europe* (New York: Oxford University Press, 1988), 255.

personally, moreover, exhibits a Franciscan delight in nature and the goodness of creation very much at odds with the facile contemporary picture of him as the precursor of rapacious, environmentally damaging capitalism. For Columbus, the New World was a kind of medieval *locus amoenus* (pleasant place) in which human, animal, vegetable, and inanimate nature show a primitive harmony. That he, like his contemporaries, did not anticipate the harmful effects of human use on the environment—effects that have become clear only in the last century or so—merely reflects the relatively small scale of human enterprises in his time.

Even some of the best recent writers on Columbus cannot quite give up certain mental habits and prejudices in their views of history—an incapacity that, paradoxically, mirrors the limitations they attribute to Columbus. John Noble Wilford, in his generally lucid but badly titled *The Mysterious History of Columbus*, often succumbs to the clichéd opposition between medieval and Renaissance. Wilford's training as a science writer perhaps betrays him here. He contrasts the allegedly dogmatic Columbus who never relented in his belief that he was somewhere in the "Indies," for example, with the Florentine humanist Amerigo Vespucci after whom America is named. Vespucci was from a noble family, and his vivid accounts of exploration were the primary vehicles through which the term "New World" came to be applied to the newly discovered lands. Wilford regards Vespucci as more of a Renaissance humanist than the Genoese admiral was—an "open-minded observer" who helps conceptualize the new situation.

This opposition of two contemporaneous figures reflects one of the subtler forms of bias that continues in Columbus studies. Tzvetan Todorov, a literary theorist who has concocted an elaborate and dubious history of European intellectual imperialism in the New World, has asserted that Columbus was medieval in everything not touching navigation.[116] In other matters, he submitted to and argued from authority. Vespucci, in the spirit of the Renaissance, was in this regard an empiricist. But, contrary to what Todorov may think, the Renaissance itself was not primarily empirical.

The rediscovery of antiquity shifted the appeals to authority to other texts in addition to Scripture (and the few Greek and Roman writers known to the Middle Ages). Such empiricism as began to develop was guided by ancient authors. Vespucci's empiricism is comparable to Machiavelli's, which is to say that both retreated from Scriptural categories to classical ones. Columbus and Vespucci both use the word "continent" for what is now South America. Columbus probably continued to believe that it was part of Asia; Vespucci's beliefs are also uncertain, though at times he seems to have made the breakthrough to the new conceptualization.

The Mexican historian Edmundo O'Gorman has carefully traced the growing mental change caused by the new lands in his ingenious *The Invention of America*. He shows with clarity that neither Columbus nor Vespucci unequivocally understood that they were exploring "America." That realization—and the host of implications it brought in its wake—came, perhaps, with Martin Waldseemüller's 1507 *Cosmographiae Introductio*, in which Amerigo Vespucci's name is first applied to "America."

What is at work here is a search for the roots of modern empiricism in the earliest European experience of the Americas, empiricism being one of the strongest currents in modern philosophy. But it is not very plausible that either Columbus or Vespucci fits the need. Vespucci is primarily a litterateur who writes well of the new sights; as such, he has no grand theory of geography. His accounts are marked by a closed-mindedness of their own, for example, in

---

[116] Tzvetan Todorov, *The Conquest of America: The Question of the Other*, trans. Richard Howard (New York: Harper & Row, 1985), 84.

his belief that the nakedness, promiscuity, and lack of political organization among native groups were evidence that they "live according to nature." This is as false—and European—a dogma as Columbus's medieval belief that all the continents were one divided landmass. The realization of the type of newness the Americas represented appears to have been the work of several minds rather than any one.

One of the oddest new approaches to Columbus makes use of esoteric postmodern literary theory to show how European language itself became a tool of conquest in the New World. In his critically acclaimed study *Marvelous Possessions*, Stephen Greenblatt argues that medieval astonishment at strange peoples and sights, which evoked puzzled respect for "the other," was transformed in the late fifteenth century into something wholly different. "Renaissance wonder" became "an agent of appropriation," reflecting a new desire for ownership and colonialism.[117] Greenblatt admits that what he calls "the language of Christian imperialism" did not *necessarily* promote appropriation, since religious figures such as Las Casas and Francisco de Vitoria made anti-imperial religious arguments (see chapter 3). But, he contends, in the European Christianity of the time, religious and worldly desires were readily "convertible."[118] For Greenblatt, Columbus was rarely a cynic, a skeptic, or a hypocrite. Rather, the admiral was a product of an increasingly pathological European culture that united religious aims and greed.[119]

Greenblatt's book is ingenious and careful in its reading of early-contact history. But for all its innovations and discoveries, *Marvelous Possessions* basically reproduces the old view that the

---

[117] Stephen Greenblatt, *Marvelous Possessions: The Wonder of the New World* (Chicago: University of Chicago Press, 1991), 24.

[118] Ibid., 71.

[119] Ibid., 58, 70.

Renaissance brought a rapacious spirit to bear on the physical world. It chides Europeans, moreover, for first reacting to different cultures the way people everywhere do—with misunderstanding and the use of familiar concepts to categorize the "other." Except for its fine literary examination of a wealth of cultural and historical material, this analysis offers little that is new.

Bad in Any Case

Perhaps the traditional opposition between the medieval and Renaissance Columbuses is fading in the postcolonial and postmodernist world. In Kirkpatrick Sale, Columbus is uniquely and doubly condemned for being medieval *and* for being of the Renaissance. His medieval side reflects superstitions, and his Renaissance side shows the destructive force of naked instrumental and mathematical reason, which Sale largely identifies with Renaissance Europe. Nevertheless, Sale also feels free to castigate Columbus for his lack of interest in numbers, that is, for not giving us the exact mathematical coordinates of the island where he made first landfall. Poor Columbus is merely the product of various opposing evil traditions that define Europe and Europeans—of which we are all the heirs, save, of course, the Kirkpatrick Sales who transcend cultural determinism.

All these attempts at neat categorizations assume that we can define a man, as well as a historical period, with far sharper boundaries than is ever the case. The mixture of human weakness and human greatness in even a key figure is never easy to calculate. The novelist Anthony Burgess created a Mozart who says, "My desire and my hope is to gain honor, fame, and money."[120] That sentence

---

[120] Anthony Burgess, *On Mozart: A Paean for Wolfgang* (New York: Ticknor & Fields, 1991).

plausibly formulates a great deal of truth about Mozart's life. Yet few music lovers would deduce from this that Mozart's work is therefore solely the product of ambition and cupidity or would try to explain the man and his music by sociological analysis of the late eighteenth century. Columbus similarly spoke of "God, gold, and glory," and many of the Europeans who followed him were driven by multiple motives, not all of which were, by any means, merely self-serving—witness the saintly missionaries, if no one else.

Kirkpatrick Sale, as usual, well formulates the ultimate issue behind much of the public controversy over 1992:

> In the final analysis, it is not so important whether Columbus was a good man. What matters is that he brought over a culture centered on its own superiority. The failings of the man were and remain the failures of the culture.[121]

This is a strained argument and, as we shall soon see, historical determinism of this kind makes it impossible to account for the many Europeans who thought differently—and the nature of Western civilization more broadly, which is really the target. It certainly does matter, if only for the sake of historical justice, that we try to discern the mix of good and evil in Columbus *per se*. Furthermore, no one can simply be identified with a whole culture. Every individual both draws on and opposes elements in his surroundings. If the preceding pages show anything, they show that Columbus, like the rest of us, was not simply good or bad. As a great human spirit, both his virtues and his faults appear larger and more vivid than they do in most people. And his historical influence reflects the dimensions of what he was. The argument about the European sense of superiority, however, can be engaged

---

[121] Sanoff, "Myths of Columbus."

quite well without dragging in Columbus, as if he were a mere conduit for European culture.

One reason that freedom arose in the West is the traditional Western separation of the City of Man from the City of God—the working out of Jesus' saying about rendering unto Caesar the things that are Caesar's, and to God the things that are God's. As we shall see in the next chapter, many of the early missionaries and theologians showed, in the very face of state power and financial interests, that Christian principles pointed toward other paths than those most often taken by settlers in the New World. Columbus and Las Casas were sometimes at odds over specifics but were not fundamentally opposed on these matters. Las Casas is the greater figure for his moral passion and courage, but Columbus, in spite of his faults, deserves no little admiration. Emblematic, perhaps, of their relationship was Simón Bolívar's view in 1819, that a newly liberated area of South America be named Colombia and its capital Las Casas: "Thus will we prove to the world that we not only have the right to be free, but we will demonstrate that we know how to honor the friends and benefactors of mankind."[122]

---

[122] Simón Bolívar, *Selected Writings*, ed. Harold A. Bierck Jr., vol. 1 (New York: Colonial Press, 1951), 119, quoted in Lewis Hanke, *Aristotle and the American Indians: A Study in Race Prejudice in the Modern World* (Bloomington: Indiana University Press, 1975), 114.

3

Vox Clamantis in Deserto?

*Spanish civilization crushed the Indian; English
civilization scorned and neglected him; French
civilization embraced and cherished him.*

—Francis Parkman, *The Jesuits in North America*[123]

One of the most persistent and least examined strands in the anti-
Columbus myth is the charge that, in the decades following 1492,
missionaries and other religious groups did little but sprinkle holy
water on a brutally destructive imperialistic conquest of native
cultures. For the most part, this mistaken impression stems from
simple, long-standing ignorance. Religious figures as diverse as Friar
Bernardino de Sahagún in Mexico, Roger Williams in Rhode Island,
and the Jesuit Jean de Brébeuf in New France were among the
very first Europeans to learn native languages and, in the process,
to begin inventing the modern disciplines of anthropology and
ethnology. They also preserved a good deal of what we know about
several precontact native cultures. Naturally, Christian evangelization of Indians raises many contemporary ethical questions—but

[123] Francis Parkman, *The Jesuits in North America*, in vol. 1 of Francis
Parkman: *France and England in North American* (New York: Library
of America, 1983), 432.

not only on the European side. While in a modern understanding, Christians had obligations to respect native cultural and individual rights, most of us would also agree that human sacrifice, ritual cannibalism, slavery, and torture were native practices that cried to heaven for change. On balance, European religious institutions, far from being mere tools of colonialism, were often among the strongest defenders of native life and culture in the New World, even as they changed them in sometimes better ways.

To say this, however, we must remind ourselves again of both the tragic and epic dimensions in this story. Once contact was established, native cultures were destined to be changed forever, as were European peoples. Just as the isolation of the Americas from the rest of the world made millions of deaths from disease inevitable — whether the first non-Native American arrived from Asia, Africa, or Europe — so native religion and culture would have changed whether they first confronted Buddhism or Islam, Judaism or Christianity. Though some revisionists have tried to equate Western religion itself with epidemic disease, the parallel is simply wrong. Despite the complicity of some religious individuals in violence against indigenous peoples, Christianity in general was not a moral or spiritual pathogen. The proof of this is that few Native American religious systems could be revived in their entirety today without generating great controversy, even among Native Americans themselves. The heroic attempts by missionaries to bring more humane practices to very different and hostile peoples can no longer be seen in the pious images of the past. Yet there was an element of epic grandeur, mixed with baser elements, in that story.

Contemporary critics frequently assume that a general religious imperialism occurred analogous to the military imperialism — an assumption that neither the historical record nor many morally relevant facts warrant. Francis Parkman's view, quoted above, oversimplifies and even misrepresents the early history to a great degree.

But it does suggest the need to examine at least three very different large-scale approaches to Native Americans, as well as diverse currents within each of the three, to arrive at an accurate picture. And, at least for Christians, it helps to keep in mind that the faith itself makes clear that all are sinners, including missionaries and those who claim to be pursuing justice, something observable in all cultures. And that spiritual truth has the practical benefit of preventing us from demanding perfection either from past figures or from ourselves.

The Religious Black Legend

Anglo-Saxon and Protestant bias against Spanish and French Catholics long colored criticism of the earliest missionary activity in the New World. For centuries, various Protestant enemies of Spain used information about Spanish atrocities in the New World—much of it provided by the Dominican friar and defender of the Indians Bartolomé de Las Casas and debated in remarkably open fashion by Spanish secular and religious leaders—to create the "black legend," a kind of catch-all for anti-Spanish propaganda. Lurid illustrations by artists such as Theodor de Bry mixed with anti-Catholic slurs to create an image that, to this day, inspires prejudices about Spanish America. (Pro-Spanish advocates created a corresponding "white legend," listing all the benefits European culture and Christianity brought to the New World and excusing or ignoring errors and atrocities on that basis.)[124] New France received slightly better treatment, but grudgingly. Parkman, that energetic but decidedly Yankee historian, feels free to tell his readers in an

---

[124] For both legends, see Charles Gibson, *The Black Legend: Anti-Spanish Attitudes in the Old World and the New* (New York: Knopf, 1971).

otherwise straightforward and fair report on the Jesuit missions to the Huron and other northeastern woodland tribes, "As for the religion which the Jesuits taught them, however Protestants may carp at it, it was the only form of Christianity likely to take root in their crude and barbarous nature."[125]

A double bias — against both allegedly benighted Catholics and allegedly benighted natives — appears clearly here. G. K. Chesterton once observed that much English history of the first Spanish explorations in the New World reflects "the desire of the white man to despise the Red Indian and the flatly contradictory desire of the Englishman to despise the Spaniard for despising the Red Indian."[126] Despite such biases, however, this older criticism did at least pay attention to facts, to the actual deeds and misdeeds of the first Europeans in the Americas.

A new, contemporary form of the black legend manifests no such virtue. Its proponents know few facts and, though profoundly influenced by the earlier prejudices, now condemn all European religious figures in the New World, Catholic and Protestant, Spanish and not. Most prominent native spokesmen and their supporters give the impression that Christianity and genocide are indistinguishable from one another and that all true Native Americans reject both. Oddly, though hundreds of thousands of Native Americans in the United States and tens of millions in Latin America seem happy to be Christians and to support their churches, even some prominent church leaders have accepted this view.[127]

---

[125] Parkman, *The Jesuits in North America*, 623.

[126] G. K. Chesterton, *Illustrated London News*, 23 April 1927, in vol. 34 of *Collected Works* (San Francisco: Ignatius Press, 1986).

[127] Some Catholic bishops in Latin America have argued that Protestant groups have been especially active in perpetuating stereotypes about early Catholic missions in the New World. In 1991, Cardinal Nicolás de Jesús López Rodríguez, president of the Latin American

As mentioned in chapter 1, during the quincentenary, prob-ably the most violently moralistic comment on the early role that Christianity played in the New World came from the U.S. National Council of Churches (NCC). After an introductory page studded with several charges of genocide, rape, and "ecocide," the NCC's official resolution—*A Faithful Response to the 500th Anniversary of the Arrival of Christopher Columbus*—called for repentance, not celebration, and described the role of religion in the New World as follows:

> The Church, with few exceptions, accompanied and legiti-mized this conquest and exploitation. Theological justifica-tions for destroying native religious beliefs while forcing conversion to European forms of Christianity demanded a submission from the newly converted that facilitated their total conquest and exploitation.[128]

The almost ritualistic repetition of "conquest and exploitation" in a mere two sentences, and the equivocation about European forms of Christianity (what other forms were there at the time?) are indicative of several contemporary biases within this argument and many similar critiques of the missionaries who came soon after Columbus.

Bishops' Conference, remarked on the lack of rancor indigenous peoples manifest toward the Church in all opinion surveys that have been conducted. He also designated "growing reform Protes-tantism as being one of the principal interested parties to oppose itself to the presence of the Catholic Church in the Americas." Quoted in *Liaisons Latino Americaines*, no. 86 (Paris, Novembre 1991). While both the cardinal's contentions may be somewhat exaggerated, these matters rarely appear in contemporary discus-sions of 1492 and after.

[128] National Council of Churches, *A Faithful Response.*

Columbus and the Crisis of the West

Facile Condemnations

Vast overreaching and a predictability born of lack of any real knowledge mar all such accounts. Stafford Poole, a close student of the early European religious activities in Latin America, writing late in the twentieth century, questioned, for example, whether "genocide" actually occurred:

> As elaborated in this century, the term applies to a calculated, deliberate extermination of an entire identifiable people for racial or other reasons. Despite the dreadful consequences of the European invasion of Latin America, there never was any planned or calculated desire to destroy the people as such.... There are other terms to describe what happened in the Western Hemisphere, but genocide is not one of them. It is a good propaganda term in an age where slogans and shouting have replaced reflection and learning, but to use it in this context is to cheapen both the word itself and the appalling experiences of Jews and Armenians, to mention but two of the major victims of this century.[129]

Among the various early European settlements, only the English at Jamestown—and only some of them—ever seem to have contemplated extermination of Indians.[130] Certainly, no church group is recorded to have accepted such a course.

Furthermore, while missionaries may have accompanied conquerors, very few simply legitimized their actions. Junípero Serra, for example, a Franciscan and one of the founders of California,

---

[129] Stafford Poole, "Iberian Catholicism Comes to the Americas," in *Christianity Comes to the Americas*, ed. Stafford Poole, Charles H. Lippy, and Robert Choquette (New York: Giniger Books, 1992), 125–126.

[130] Gary B. Nash, *Red, White, and Black: The Peoples of Early America* (Englewood Cliffs, N.J.: Prentice-Hall, 1974), 62–63.

walked the entire distance between San Diego and Mexico City to seek—and get—formal legal protections for the native peoples who were being abused by Spanish soldiers.[131] Unscrupulous and greedy churchmen may have sought their own advantage, but the nature of the religious vocation is such that those kinds of Christians are a minority at any time. Quite a few religious leaders, especially in Spanish territories, clearly thought political dominance was a prerequisite to efficient evangelization, but that position did not entail blanket acceptance of everything Spaniards wanted to do. From the very beginning, religious scruple vied with worldly interests. The instances of *religious* imperialism in the most serious sense of forced conversion and gross mistreatment for heresy are not nearly as common—or unopposed—as is usually assumed.

Sailing on Columbus's second voyage, the first official representative of Christianity arrived in the New World in 1493. The priest Bernal Buyl was both apostolic vicar and a personal representative of Ferdinand and Isabella, who liked to style themselves *los reyes católicos* (the Catholic monarchs). When Columbus discovered that all the men he had left at La Navidad on the island of Hispaniola had been killed in his absence, Buyl advocated a hard line against the Indians. But Columbus chose, despite some troubling evidence, to believe the explanations of his old friend Guacanagarí that other tribes were responsible and to ignore Buyl. After a year of various conflicts with Columbus and other Spaniards in the New World, Buyl resigned and returned to Spain. His story, however, shows one pattern: religious rigor (Buyl) opposed to a mixed secular and religious leniency (Columbus). But other patterns—by no means exceptions to some harsh rule—also developed.

---

[131] See Kevin Starr, *Continental Ambitions: Roman Catholics in North America: The Colonial Experience* (San Francisco: Ignatius Press, 2016), 213–225.

Columbus and the Crisis of the West

Serious religious debates began immediately over ethical conduct in the New World. Slavery, for example, was early opposed. J. H. Elliott, one of the premier historians of imperial Spain, points out that as early as 1500, theologians and others protested when Native Americans arrived on Spanish docks to be sold as slaves. This led Queen Isabella, who had already freed several Indians Columbus had sent back, formally to outlaw the practice. Not even a decade had elapsed since first contact with the New World.[132] The legislation permitted well-defined exceptions that had already been established for other places outside the Americas—warriors could be taken captive in just combat when Spaniards were attacked or when tribes practiced cannibalism, human sacrifice, or other crimes against natural law. Unfortunately, these exceptions provided crude and unscrupulous people with numerous loopholes to do whatever they wished.

Anti-Spanish Bias

The NCC document, however, makes no mention of these reactions or of the passionate and sophisticated defense of the natives and of native culture developed very early on by Spaniards, particularly in the Church—an omission that has not gone unnoticed by Hispanics.[133] As the American historian James Muldoon has commented:

> Hispanic critics of the NCC resolution have a point. The resolution was directed only at Columbus's voyages and, by implication, at the establishment of Spanish domination

---

[132] J. H. Elliott, *Imperial Spain, 1469-1710* (New York: Penguin Books, 1963), 70. Elliott is also a very useful guide to other facts needed to assess moral issues raised by New World contacts.

[133] See in particular Mario Paredes, "A Hispanic Reaction to the NCC," Northeast Hispanic Catholic Center, New York, 25 July 1991, reprinted in *Origins* 20 (16 August 1990): 173–174.

over much of the Americas. The English, French, Dutch, and even the Portuguese seem to have escaped this sweeping condemnation.[134]

In fact, the NCC seems blissfully unaware of the interesting and sometimes inspiring history of early Spanish religious activity in the New World, and the document—reflecting the organization's basic ideological thrust—does little more than repeat fashionable clichés about the "complicity" of missionaries in the oppression of native peoples then and now. It cites, vaguely, only two sources for these assertions, both largely uninformed and highly ideological: *Black Elk Speaks* and Howard Zinn's *A People's History of the United States*.

This lack of curiosity about Christian history by a professedly Christian organization is telling and a grave moral failing. Had the authors of the statement gone outside their two meager counter-cultural sources, they might have discovered unfamiliar cultural and religious riches within their own traditions. They would have found a wealth of reflection on the nature of the native peoples and their cultures that would have helped them understand how Western cultures, precisely because of their encounters with Native Americans, gradually came to a more inclusive recognition of universal humanity. But the NCC appears to have been more interested in issuing a universal indictment of the West on the basis of prejudice against Hispanic culture—and the West more broadly.

Myopic Progressives

Defenders of the NCC statement and critiques like it contend that they are opening up Eurocentric history to alternative views. In

---

[134] James Muldoon, "The Columbus Quincentennial: Should Christians Celebrate It?" *America*, 27 October 1990, 300.

Columbus and the Crisis of the West

fact, they present the most historically myopic visions imaginable. Not only are they ignorant of Native American cultures, but their ignorance of Europe makes it impossible for them even to know what would, or would not, constitute a sinister Eurocentric view. A crucial issue in any history of the Americas is the origin of the concepts of universal human rights and respect for alien cultures that underlie contemporary critiques. We now take these principles for granted. But such concepts existed nowhere in the world prior to certain developments in Europe, inspired by Christianity, least of all among non-Western cultures and New World tribes, who had their own versions of cultural superiority. Only because of some serious thinking in Western nations were the seemingly strange new peoples held to be rational — and therefore fully human — and international law developed to reflect that humanity. These were two new achievements even if practice in the New World followed theory very slowly and imperfectly.

To its credit, Spain began grappling with these moral and philosophical questions almost immediately, though some confusion and disorder naturally attended the initial Spanish contact with the New World. The brutality and greed that arrived with the less savory characters brought by later voyages compounded an already difficult cultural problem. Columbus himself, as we saw in the previous chapter, did not know what to do about these developments other than to try to restrain the worst excesses and to beg the monarchs to consider carefully whom they were sending to the Americas.

When he returned to Hispaniola on his third voyage in 1498 — which ended in his being sent back to Spain in chains after his harshness to both indigenous people and Spaniards — he immediately saw what evils had emerged in the scant six years since he had first crossed the Atlantic. It was his original intention that the island would be a trading post with peaceful settlers. He wrote, instead, to the king and queen upon his arrival:

Our people here are such that there is neither good man nor bad who hasn't three Indians to serve him and dogs to hunt for him and, though it were perhaps better not to mention it, women so pretty that one must wonder at it. With the last of these practices I am extremely discontented, for it seems to me a disservice to God but I can do nothing about it, nor the habit of eating meat on Saturday [*sic*, Friday] and other wicked practices that are not for good Christians. For these reasons it would be of great advantage to have some devout friars here, rather to reform the faith in us Christians than to give it to the Indians. And I shall never be able to administer just punishments, unless fifty or sixty men are sent here from Castile with each fleet, and I send there the same number from among the last and the insubordinate, as I do with this present fleet—such would be the greatest and best punishment and least burdensome to the conscience that I can think of.[135]

Columbus was accused of many things during this third voyage—allegedly large numbers of indigenous killed, casual acceptance of slavery and rape, and much more. Historians find the support for some of these charges credible, the most extreme either weak or exaggerated. But in the letter quoted above, we see clearly his sincerity and desire to reform a situation—even the Christianity of the Spaniards—that he could not control. Indeed, his indulgence toward the people he sent back to Spain created an anti-Columbus faction at court. And his confusion and occasional overreactions to circumstances on the island led to his being sent back himself and, later, to his prohibition from returning.

Many of the missionaries also did not know at first what to make of this unprecedented situation. But in 1511, less than two decades

---

[135] Quoted in Fernández-Armesto, *Columbus*, 133–134.

after Columbus's first voyage and only five years after his death, Antonio de Montesinos, a Dominican priest speaking on behalf of himself and two colleagues, denounced mistreatment of Indians in a homily given to outraged settlers on the island of Hispaniola. Montesinos pulled no punches. Invoking the biblical verse "I am the voice of one crying in the wilderness," he continued:

> This voice says that you are in mortal sin and live and die in it because of the cruelty and tyranny that you use against these innocent peoples. Tell me, by what right or justice do you hold these Indians in such cruel and horrible slavery? By what authority do you wage such detestable wars on these peoples, who lived mildly and peacefully in their own lands, in which you have destroyed countless numbers of them with unheard of murder and ruin.... Are these Indians not men? Do they not have rational souls? Are you not obliged to love them as you love yourselves?... In your present state you can no more be saved than the Moors or Turks, who do not have and do not want the faith of Christ.[136]

Montesinos's listeners in the pews, like many other settlers who would be chastised in the future by church and civil authorities, were predictably furious. He needed a protective escort to leave the church.

But in his fiery denunciation, the priest was following and proclaiming the decree issued years earlier in 1503 by Ferdinand and Isabella granting liberty to the Indians. The Mexican historian Rafael Altamira has said of that decree:

> What a memorable day for the entire world, because it signals the first recognition of the respect due to the dignity

---

[136] Quoted in Poole, "Iberian Catholicism," 79.

and liberty of all men no matter how primitive and un-
civilized they may be — a principle that had never been
proclaimed before in any legislation, let alone practiced in
any country.[137]

The proclamation was mostly disregarded in the Caribbean, probably because of the corrupt conditions that Columbus's letter had
spelled out, but Altamira rightly argues that the appropriate response to such an early expression of good principles in such difficult circumstances should be gratitude and surprise rather than
condemnation for the limited effect those principles had in practice. Because we now assume that human rights are obvious and
universal, we don't much look into their origins, for which we owe
a debt to these first Spanish impulses.

Not only did the king and queen approve of Indian liberty, but
two years earlier, in 1501, they had instructed Governor Nicolás
de Ovando about the Indians' religious life as well:

Because we desire that the Indians be converted to our holy
Catholic faith and that their souls be saved, for this is the
greatest good that we can wish for, and because for this they
must be informed of the matters of our faith, you are to take
great care in ensuring that the clergy so inform them and
admonish them with much love, and without using force,
so that they may be converted as rapidly as possible.[138]

Reading these statements now, we cannot help but recognize that,
however admirable, they were not enough to stop some horrible

---

[137] Quoted in Lewis Hanke, *All Mankind Is One: A Study of the Disputation between Bartolomé de Las Casas and Juan Ginés de Sepúlveda
in 1550 on the Intellectual and Religious Capacity of the American
Indians* (DeKalb: Northern Illinois University Press, 1974), 7.
[138] Ibid., 8.

atrocities. Some critics dismiss the religious aims as a mere ra-
tionalization justifying imperial interests. Yet the record is clear
that Seville took what practical steps it could to enforce its views
of proper treatment of natives. Most contemporary critics of the
Christian evangelization, however, are simply unaware that such
sentiments existed at all.

In fact, a fair study of the first half of the sixteenth century
reveals a steady and growing ethical concern among the Spanish
about how to understand and deal with the peoples of the New
World, who were so different from the Jews, Muslims, Africans,
and Asians with whom Europeans were already familiar. Surprisingly humane legislation was regularly passed, if just as regularly
ignored. Debates arose over factual and moral questions. Some
colonists believed that the Indians were only beasts, incapable
of governing themselves; others thought them fully rational and
capable of self-governance.

Naturally, some self-interest and personal rivalry played a role
in these disputes. The first viceroy of New Spain, the shrewd and
competent Antonio de Mendoza (who ordered the compilation
of native history and customs now known as the *Codex Mendoza*),
advised his successor to circumvent all special interests with a
simple practical rule:

> Treat the Indians like any other people and do not make
> special rules and regulations for them. There are few persons
> in these parts who are not motivated in their opinions of the
> Indians, by some interest, whether temporal or spiritual, or
> by some passion or ambition, good or bad.[139]

---

[139] A long excerpt from Mendoza's *Relacion de mando* (report to his
replacement) may be found in Woodrow W. Borah, *Justice by Insurance: The General Indian Court of Colonial Mexico and the Legal
Aides of the Half-Real* (Berkeley: University of California Press,

Mendoza practiced what he preached. He gathered a team of both native and Spanish artisans at the Franciscan college in Tlatelolco who produced a beautifully illustrated *Codex*.[140] That early wisdom bore the seeds of impartial treatment for all, regardless of origin—a uniquely American tenet necessitated by the rich mixture of various peoples on these shores.

The Sacred and the Profane

In the decades after Columbus, little by little, Spanish authorities did promote such principles, often at religious prodding and at great risk. The first viceroy of Peru, Blasco Núñez Vela, was killed by his own people when he attempted to implement the New Laws of 1542, which mandated protections for the indigenous population. In the early decades of the sixteenth century, laws had been passed prohibiting the Spanish from even using abusive names for the natives. Though all this legislation demonstrated a basic goodwill, it also shows that resistance by colonists, the vast distances involved, and lags in communication lasting months made keeping good order in the New World an almost impossible task.

But the laws and those charged with enforcing them were not always ineffective. When word of abuses reached the Spanish court, both secular and religious leaders were sometimes punished or recalled. The emperor Charles V himself ordered one Francisco de Chaves to pay for the construction of an Indian school in recompense for mistreating Indians. And a far more notorious

---

1983), 66–67. For Mendoza's kind but realistic assessment of the Indians, see A. S. Aiton, *Antonio de Mendoza: First Viceroy of New Spain* (New York: Russell & Russell, 1927), 94.

[140] The Mexican government has digitized a copy of the *Codex* and made it available online: https://codicemendoza.inah.gob.mx/index.php?lang=spanish.

case involved the bishop of Yucatán, the Franciscan friar Diego de Landa. Landa was perhaps the most gifted linguist to study the Mayas in the early decades of European rule. He not only mastered the language but also recorded Mayan customs and history, becoming one of the most important anthropological sources for native culture at the time of first contact. Furthermore, his phonetic transcriptions of the words represented by Mayan glyphs—the only true writing in the New World—have been crucial to the recent successes in deciphering them. His missionary work, however, was overzealous. Landa tortured Indians he suspected of heresy and burned hundreds of Mayan books, which were lost forever. In 1564, following the outcry his actions evoked, he was recalled to Spain to stand trial.

Sadly, Landa and other missionaries failed at times to heed their own church leaders. Decades earlier, in 1537, Pope Paul III had stated authoritatively in the encyclical *Sublimis Deus* what was to be argued again and again for the rest of the century:

> Indians and all other people who may later be discovered by the Christians are by no means to be deprived of their liberty or the possession of their property, even though they be outside the faith of Jesus Christ; and they may and should, freely and legitimately, enjoy their liberty and the possession of their property; nor should they be in any way enslaved; should the contrary happen it shall be null and of no effect.... By virtue of our apostolic authority we declare ... that the said Indians and other peoples should be converted to the faith of Jesus Christ by preaching the word of God and by the example of good and holy living.[141]

Despite abuses and occasional forced conversions, the words gentleness and affability were frequently invoked in various parts of the

[141] Hanke, *All Mankind Is One*, 16.

New World to encourage missionaries to adopt the most effective and Christ-like approaches to the natives.[142]

The Defender of the Indians

The most significant New World religious figure in the first century after Columbus was the Dominican friar Bartolomé de Las Casas. Las Casas was only nine years old in 1493 when he saw Columbus make his triumphant return to Seville from his first voyage to the New World. The noble bearing of the admiral impressed him, and the memory of that event remained with him for the rest of his life. That life was intimately bound up with the history of the Americas, particularly with protecting indigenous peoples, a labor that earned Las Casas the title *defensor de los Indios* (defender of the Indians).

Las Casas was slow to arrive at this vocation, but when it came upon him, it came with a vengeance. No trace of moral uneasiness about Indian welfare seems to have troubled his early years. His father and several uncles made the second voyage with Columbus, and in 1501 Bartolomé and his father accompanied the newly appointed governor Nicolás de Ovando to Hispaniola. But having already begun his studies for the priesthood before he left for the New World, Las Casas made his way back to be ordained in Rome sometime around 1507. The next year, he received an *encomienda*—a grant of land and Indians to work it—in Cuba and returned there to a prosperous life as a priest. Though, in theory, the recipients of *encomiendas* were required to watch over the physical

---

[142] Among many other instances, Parkman cites, for example, the martyr Jean de Brébeuf's letter to the general of the Jesuits: "Ce qu'il faut demander, avant tout, des ouvriers destinés à cette mission, c'est une douceur et une patience à toute épreuve." *The Jesuits in North America*, 494.

and spiritual welfare of the Indians, in practice they often treated them as little more than slaves.[143]

It was only a few years later that Las Casas suddenly found himself overwhelmed by a desire to defend the Indians. He had been acquainted with indigenous peoples since his father brought him home a slave (freed by the decree of Isabella in 1500) and had seen their mistreatment both on his early trips and in his capacity as a chaplain in Cuba. But the first time he seems to have thought seriously about the situation was after a Dominican priest refused him absolution during confession because he was holding Indians as an *encomendero*. In later years, Las Casas would infuriate Spanish colonists with his *Confesionario*, a guide directing confessors to deny absolution to those who owned and abused native people.

The Dominican Order played a crucial role in the development of better relations with the Indians in the New World. Founded in the early thirteenth century as a movement to teach and preach the truths of the Catholic faith, the Dominicans always recognized the need for "assiduous study." This requirement put them in the forefront of Christian philosophical and theological thought. Two of the most prominent Dominicans, Albertus Magnus and Thomas Aquinas, made wide-ranging contributions to intellectual life in the High Middle Ages. And in the new era inaugurated by Columbus, the Dominicans continued to develop their particular fields of interest: they pondered deeply questions of justice, rights, and law in the newly discovered lands.

---

[143] The origins of the *encomienda* system, which was a source of much abuse, are debated. Some have attributed it to Columbus himself. Felipe Fernández-Armesto, a virtual living encyclopedia of the period, believes it began not as a deliberate policy by any individual or Spain, but as a natural development as Spaniards and natives interacted. See *Columbus*, 142–143.

By contrast, most Franciscans and diocesan priests more readily accepted the necessity of Spanish military and political domination as a prerequisite to missionary activity. Generalizations about these issues, of course, leave out notable exceptions and nuances. Some Franciscans, too, thought and acted honorably in their own ways. And the Dominicans had serious differences of opinion. Las Casas himself became a Dominican in the 1520s, largely through the influence of Domingo de Betanzos. But he would later violently disagree with Betanzos's doubts, even questioning his motives, over whether at least some Indians were sufficiently rational for self-government.

Nevertheless, the most important *thinking* about right action in the New World and follow-up in political circles came almost entirely from Dominican figures. It is no accident that a Dominican brought the moral problems of the *encomienda* to Las Casas's attention in the confessional. When first confronted, Las Casas meditated on his confessor's objections, but not until 1514, while he was preparing a sermon, did he come upon a text that brought him up short: "The sacrifice of an offering unjustly acquired is a mockery; the gifts of impious men are unacceptable" (Eccles. 34:18). He announced from the pulpit the following Sunday that he was giving up his *encomienda*. From that moment on, he became a tireless—bordering on obsessive—advocate of Indian rights.

Las Casas joined his fellow Dominican Antonio de Montesinos, mentioned earlier, in lobbying on behalf of Indians at the Spanish court. And their work met with some immediate success. Las Casas not only asked for and got some opportunities to try different approaches in the New World, he also influenced legal and theological debates in the Old. In 1530 he wrote a treatise, *De unico vocationis modo* (The only way of summoning), now lost, that argued persuasion was the only biblically correct method of preaching the gospel.[144] With Bishops Zumárraga and Julián Garcés, he was able to send papers to Rome in 1536 that helped shape the pope's defense of the newly discovered peoples in the encyclical *Sublimis Deus*. His work was also instrumental, along with theological developments at the University of Salamanca, in framing the Spanish New Laws of 1542. But in 1550, he engaged in his most important battle: a theological dispute at the monastery of San Gregorio in the Spanish city of Valladolid.

The Importance of Valladolid

In that year, the Spanish crown appointed a theological commission to come to some decision about the issues that had already long been debated about the natives in the New World. As Lewis Hanke, perhaps the most learned American analyst of the role religion played in the Spanish expansion, has pointed out, "For the first time, and probably for the last, a colonizing nation organized a formal inquiry into the justice of the methods used to extend its empire."[145]

Throughout the first half of the sixteenth century, religious figures had argued over the proper conduct of church and state in the New World. To inhabitants of modern democracies, human beings are human beings and have rights, and only wicked arrogance accounts for any questioning of their humanness. But until relatively recently, no culture in the world—particularly none outside the European sphere of influence—widely accepted that understanding and put it into practice. Ironically, the much-maligned Spanish

---

[144] Though, for a long time, only a few chapters of this work were known to have survived, a reconstructed text has been produced in the series *The Classics of Western Spirituality* (New York: Paulist Press, 1992).

[145] Hanke, *All Mankind Is One*, xi.

began the elaboration of these universal principles through theological reflection on indigenous peoples.

Charles V ordered the theological commission to hear the arguments at Valladolid and reach a conclusion. He also suspended any further military activity until the ethical questions were settled. During the previous decades, some disputes had grown up within the religious orders themselves about whether natives were rational and could govern themselves. At Valladolid, Juan Ginés de Sepúlveda, a learned humanist and the most eminent living commentator on Aristotle's *Politics*, made the case that Indians were what Aristotle called "slaves by nature," i.e., people insufficiently rational to govern themselves. They could be subjugated by Spaniards—but only for their own good and in the interest of rational government.

Our immediate reaction to this is—quite properly—revulsion. In the sixteenth century, Sepúlveda did not find much intellectual agreement either. His *Second Democrates*, in which he first made these arguments, circulated in manuscript through the universities, where it was condemned almost universally.[146] Then as now, even among those who took Aristotle as the serious moral thinker that he is, there was great uncertainty about what he meant by "slaves by nature"; who, if anybody, belonged in that category; and what were the grounds for deciding? Yet for all his intellectual arrogance and ignorance of the New World (Sepúlveda had never made the Atlantic crossing), he had hold of a serious point that he argued crudely.

When we think of Indians today, we think of a weak, essentially benign group of peoples, badly treated for centuries, and this view colors our historical judgment. But the peoples and cultures of the New World before the spread of European influence differed widely from one another and did not always display characteristics that

---

[146] Poole, "Iberian Catholicism," 87.

anyone would wish to defend today. Despite the special pleading by defenders of Native Americans,[147] cannibalism existed without a doubt among the Aztecs, Guaraní, Iroquois, Caribs, and several other tribes. Pedro Fernandes Sardinha the unfortunately named (Sardine) first bishop of what is now Bahia, Brazil, for example, was eaten by the Caeté, a local tribe.[148] Human sacrifice was practiced by the high cultures and several groups not so developed. Indigenous slavery and torture were widespread from the Southern Cone to the Pacific Northwest all the way into today's Canada. The cultural differences between Europe and the Americas were accented by the bloodshed and cruelty on both sides and made mutual understanding difficult. But if, say, the Aztec Empire had been left alone and were still intact today, most of us would argue that humanity and reason cried out for intervention in that culture. The same was true, however, of most other indigenous groups, toward whom today almost everyone feels basic human sympathy.

Given circumstances like these, we should not be too quick to dismiss every argument in favor of Spaniards taking up the responsibility to govern natives as a sign of mere cynical opportunism. However wrong the anti-self-government position of Domingo de Betanzos, for example, he made a serious attempt to discern truth and responsibility.[149] Betanzos had not only led Las Casas into the Dominican Order, he had supported his early lobbying efforts on behalf of the Indians at the Spanish court. But with time and greater experience of the New World, Betanzos became less convinced of the wisdom of allowing every group of Indians to govern themselves as they had before the Spaniards arrived.

---

[147] E.g., W. Arens, *The Man-Eating Myth: Anthropology and Anthropophagy* (New York: Oxford University Press, 1979).

[148] Leslie Bethell, ed., *The Cambridge History of Latin America*, vol. 1 (New York: Cambridge University Press, 1984), 272.

[149] Poole, "Iberian Catholicism," 87.

Las Casas is the one figure that even the most radical critics credit with a truly humane approach to indigenous peoples, but by no means did he stand alone. As has been discussed earlier, several religious and secular authorities also believed Indians warranted the same treatment as other men. But it was Las Casas who lobbied tirelessly for decades and made a massive theological defense of the Indians at Valladolid. Although the judges did not submit a final verdict on the Las Casas–Sepúlveda debate, the evidence of Indian rationality and the corresponding Spanish duties had been thoroughly and publicly presented for all fair-minded people to examine. Las Casas cited examples of native government, art, architecture, sailing skill, and various other accomplishments, pointing out that these could not be regarded as the products of "irrational" brutes that were "slaves by nature."

In fact, it is a delicate ethical question whether in his zeal to protect Native Americans Las Casas did not go too far. In 1963, around the four hundredth anniversary of his death, at least one serious historian argued on the basis of modern psychological theory that Las Casas was a clinical paranoiac.[150] Certainly, there was no compromise in him; he decried his opponents as evil, never merely mistaken in their judgments. His passion was apparent in his obvious inflation of numbers and other exaggerations. While Sepúlveda briefly summarized his arguments for the theological experts at Valladolid, Las Casas went on obsessively—for days—with a torrent of testimony far beyond the capacity of his listeners to absorb. One of Las Casas's most extreme positions was that human sacrifice among certain native civilizations should not be taken as evidence of willful evil requiring harsh measures. For him this ritual practice reflected an ill-informed piety among natives who

---

[150] See Ramón Menéndez Pidal, *El Padre Las Casas: Su doble personalidad* (Madrid: Espasa Calpe, 1963).

had no way of knowing better. Unlike Jews, Muslims, and Asians, he contended, natives in the Americas had been isolated from the rest of the world and had never had a chance to be guided by the revelation of the Old or New Testaments. Even Las Casas's ally, the Dominican theologian and legal theorist Francisco de Vitoria (another pivotal figure in the developing ethical reflections on issues raised by the Americas), disagreed with him on this point. Vitoria concluded that natural law simply demanded the protection of innocents.

Some critics have accused Las Casas of a certain coldness of feeling (*frialdad sensitiva*) in pursuing the defense of Native Americans so unswervingly. But others have seen in his approach a truly remarkable early attempt to understand native religion from the inside. The Mexican historian Teresa Silva Tena has suggested that Las Casas produced perhaps the most interesting sentence written by a Spaniard in the sixteenth century when he claimed that the human sacrifices to be found among indigenous religious practices, "even if cruel, were meticulous, delicate, and exquisite," and that they testified to fervent religious observances among the peoples who practiced them (*aunque eran crueles, pero eran menudas, sotiles y exquisitas*).[151]

The debate at Valladolid did not give the Spanish government the clear theological and moral conclusions it desired. In a sense, however, this did not really much matter. Las Casas's testimony bore fruit. His central views, shared by many Dominicans in the New World and in Spain, slowly reshaped Spanish activity. The worst abuses of native peoples became less severe and more infrequent—and more often accompanied by moral opposition.

---

[151] Silva Tena also remarks that the phrase would have been envied by Octave Mirbeau and the Marquis de Sade, in "El Sacrificio Humano En La *Apologética Historia*," *Historia Mexicana* 16 (1967): 349.

Vox Clamantis in Deserto?

New World Achievements

Meanwhile, in the Americas, the missionaries had not been either idle or simply legitimizing conquest. Quite often, in fact, they tried to set up Christian enclaves outside secular jurisdiction—a continuation of the old medieval rivalries between church and state. Schools existed where Indians learned Latin and writing, while Spaniards learned native languages and wrote down Indian history and cultural lore. Had the best missionary schools been allowed to go their own way, an even better cultural mix, benefiting both the Old World and the New, would have had a fair chance of emerging. Some early fruits of such integration were the Nahuatl-Latin herbal of Juan Badiano and Martín de la Cruz, and the Franciscan Bernardino de Sahagún's rich compilations of information about native culture. In fact, in later debates, native achievements in these schools and the accumulated cultural record were used as evidence of the Indians' rationality and, therefore, humanity. One product of missionary schooling, the learned native Antonio Valeriano, later became *gobernador* of Tenochtitlán (Mexico City).

In complex ways, a religious melding of cultures occurred also —some within decades of the first encounters. The cult of the *Virgen de Guadalupe* spread quickly after 1531 when, according to tradition, the Blessed Virgin Mary appeared to an Indian named Juan Diego on Tepeyac, a hill north of the current Mexico City. That apparition became a religious and ethnic rallying point for the mestizo peoples of the New World—among other devotees—that persists until today (the basilica erected near the site is one of the most visited places of religious pilgrimage in the world).[152] For the Indians, the Virgin came to replace one of their goddesses. Mary's

---

[152] Cf. D. A. Brading, *Mexican Phoenix: Our Lady of Guadalupe: Image and Tradition across Five Centuries* (New York: Cambridge University Press 2001).

image on Juan Diego's cloak shows a woman with delicate Indian features standing above symbols associated with the pagan past. In Mexico and much of the rest of Latin America, this appearance radically changed secular and religious history. Christianity was no longer simply arriving from without; it had also become a creative energy arising from within native culture.

Unfortunately, the potential revolution in relations this religious development offered was partly lost because of the European monopoly on clerical leadership. The historian Robert Ricard has argued, plausibly, that "if the colegio at Tlatelolco [a seminary for native born students in Mexico] had trained only one bishop for the country, the whole history of the Mexican church would have been far different."[153]

Vitoria and the Beginnings of Modern International Law

Defenders of the Indians had to achieve two objectives in the years leading up to the debate at Valladolid. First, they had to prove that the Indians were rational and deserving of respect. Second, and no less important, they had to make sure that the law respected their dignity as rational beings. The Dominican friar and theologian Francisco de Vitoria performed the second task and is now generally recognized, along with Francisco Suárez and Hugo Grotius, as one of the founders of modern international law.

Revulsion at Pizarro's conduct in the conquest of Peru first stimulated Vitoria's thinking about Spanish actions in the New World, but he was soon carried by the very force of his thought to examine a whole gamut of issues relating to the widely differing

[153] Hanke, *All Mankind Is One*, 27.

and previously unknown peoples. Though Vitoria's contributions in this field are enormous, few know the extent and nature of the principles he elaborated. In *The Conquest of Paradise*, for example, Kirkpatrick Sale quotes Vitoria only once: "The imperfect creature falls to the use of the perfect." Sale means to suggest, wrongly, that Vitoria—and a long European philosophical tradition—sanctioned imperialism and ecological exploitation.[154] Vitoria did write this sentence, but anyone familiar with Scholastic philosophy will recognize immediately that this familiar formula from Aristotle is hardly a justification for brutal imperialist politics. In fact, Vitoria's work led in a far different direction.

Basing his arguments on the best legal and moral authorities in the Scholastic tradition, particularly Aquinas, Vitoria proceeded to develop principles of international law that became crucial to the universal recognition of the rights of all human beings. In the very heat of conquest and colonization, Vitoria contended that the Europeans had no right *at all* to take land already under cultivation and inhabited by natives. Vitoria was a distinguished theologian and a Dominican priest, but even a man with his reputation could not have been entirely safe from potential reprisals. His stand took courage, and the Spanish crown, to its credit, often asked him to sit on deliberative councils about the Indies.

Vitoria's formulations in various writings give an idea of precisely how simplistic and ill-informed is the impression created by Sale's single quotation and many more like it:

- Every Indian is a man and thus capable of attaining salvation or damnation.
- The Indians may not be deprived of their goods or power on account of their social backwardness, nor on account of their cultural inferiority or political disorganization.

---

[154] Sale, *Conquest of Paradise*, 134.

- Every man has the right to truth, to education, and to all that forms part of his cultural and spiritual development and advancement.
- By natural law, every man has the right to his own life and to physical and mental integrity.
- The Indians have the right not to be baptized and not to be forced to convert to Christianity against their will.[155]

So much for the simple domination of perfect over imperfect beings.

Believing that native peoples had full human rights, Vitoria did allow, however, that Europeans could occupy land not already claimed by Indians, provided they did no harm to nearby natives. This restriction may seem of little significance in light of what happened to native territories, but it is worth keeping in mind that this was a bold assertion. The Treaty of Tordesillas (1494), proclaimed by no lesser a figure than the pope, had preemptively assigned different portions of the new lands to the Spanish and Portuguese without concern for who might already inhabit them. Vitoria sought not only to restrain the crown and the colonists but also to alter a decision by the highest religious authority in the Christian world on the basis of Christian principles. He went even further; Vitoria argued that the pope should never have made

---

[155] The material on Vitoria is surprisingly small for such a pivotal figure, reflecting some historical myopia. A substantial portion of his work with commentary has been edited by Anthony Padgen and Jeremy Lawrence in *Vitoria, Political Writings* (New York: Cambridge University Press, 1991). The passages cited here are taken from selections from Vitoria's work jointly published by the University of Salamanca and the Catholic University of America in Spanish and English for the quincentenary as *The Rights and Obligations of Indians and Spaniards in the New World*, ed. Luciano Pereña Vicente (Salamanca and Washington, D.C.: University of Salamanca and Catholic University of America, 1991).

such a treaty because, just as the emperor had no absolute right to rule everywhere, the pope had no universal temporal jurisdiction. Some further principles of Vitoria's are worth quoting:

- The Indian rulers, whether natural or elected, enjoy the same fundamental rights as a Christian or European prince.

- According to natural law, a non-Christian cacique or king does not lose his dominion or jurisdiction due to his infidelity or idolatrous practices, and even Christian subjects are obligated to obey him.

- The Indian peoples may defend themselves with arms and may rebel against foreigners who unjustly seize their territories or who govern the republic to their own advantage or to the advantage of their own people.

- The Spaniards may justly defend themselves against belligerent Indians so long as they stay within the limits of legitimate defense; but they may not use victory as an excuse for seizing the Indians' towns or for enslaving their inhabitants; a properly defensive war does not justify conquest when the Indians believe, on account of ignorance, that they are justly defending their property.

- However, recourse to war and to said security measures may never serve as a pretext for slaughtering, or sacking or occupying the towns of the Indians, who are by nature fearful and humble, and who have more than sufficient reason for distrusting the Spanish conquistadors, whose ways are strange to them and who are armed and more powerful than themselves.[156]

Anyone familiar with just-war theory will recognize that Vitoria is here applying its principles of self-defense, just cause, discrimination, proportionality, and last resort to Spaniards and Indians

---

[156] Vitoria, *Rights and Obligations*, 17–19.

equally. His awareness of the many difficult and delicate questions that had to be faced—to say nothing of the self-serving interpretations of principles to which the Spaniards were prone—makes this strong attempt at equality all the more striking. Writing in the 1530s with several decades of New World history available to him, Vitoria admitted few reasons, and those mostly in theory, for Spaniards' taking over the governorship of natives. Prominent among those reasons were the protection of innocents from human sacrifice and cannibalism, and native blocking of peaceful evangelization.

Alarm bells go off for many modern scholars who read such exceptions, but they went off for Vitoria too. He argues in many passages that these exceptions are probably only theoretically possible, not likely in actual fact. Furthermore, he warns that unscrupulous men are apt to use these good principles for evil ends, and that the monarch should therefore be very careful about authorizing any military action.

In applying universal human concerns to specific political situations, Vitoria recommends the classical virtue of prudence. He puts himself in a long line of distinguished Scholastic thinkers when he writes, "For the common good and in order to achieve greater harmony and peace among people, the ruler may licitly tolerate laws and customs that go against natural law."[157] While Spain has an obligation to reform inhuman practices gradually, "Spain's right to remain in the Indies with the intention of overseeing and governing the natives is acceptable only because of the need for change there and only on the condition that their reform and protection be carried out to the benefit and development of indigenous peoples."[158]

[157] Ibid., 23, 29.
[158] Ibid., 23.

Perhaps the most striking strain in Vitoria's thinking was his insistence that difference of religion alone could not justify resort to war. (In rare cases, blocking peaceful evangelization might justify war, since it violated natural liberties.) Not only does Vitoria place the weight of his own reputation behind this principle; he also cites Thomas Aquinas and other Doctors of the Church and adds, "I know of no one of the opposite way of thinking."[159]

Vitoria treated these subjects primarily in two small collections of lectures that have been published under the titles *De Indis* and *De Iure Belli.* James Brown Scott, the most distinguished English-language expositor of Vitoria, has said, "In the lecture of Vitoria on the Indians, and in his smaller tractate on War, we have before our very eyes, and at hand, a summary of the modern law of nations."[160] Vitoria himself said modestly but truly of the lectures, "The whole of this controversy and discussion was started on account of the aborigines of the New World, commonly called Indians, who came forty years ago into the power of the Spaniards, not having been previously known to our world."[161]

Vitoria's positions develop the best of the prior Western international-law tradition in the face of a new challenge. Many of the passages above show the beginnings of principles we take for granted in international forums today. Vitoria is far closer to being an advocate of what is good in the Universal Declaration on Human Rights than he is to being Kirkpatrick Sale's fictitious theorist of cultural and environmental domination. Even more important for the history of the Americas is that Vitoria and his school at the ancient and prestigious University of Salamanca sent disciples

---

[159] Ibid., 31.
[160] James Brown Scott, *The Spanish Origin of International Law* (Washington, D.C.: Georgetown University Press, 1928), 21.
[161] Ibid., 22.

throughout the New World.[162] As Doctor Samuel Johnson, a Tory critic of European arrogance and imperialism, was to say centuries later, "I love the University of Salamanca; for when the Spaniards were in doubt as to the lawfulness of their conquering America, the University of Salamanca gave it as their opinion that it was unlawful."[163]

Black Robes

Much further afield from the immediate impact of 1492 is the story of the Jesuit missions in New France during the seventeenth century. Several serious studies have adequately described the mixture of idealism and heroics, error and failure, that characterized the Jesuit missionaries. (The popular film *The Mission* lovingly—if somewhat idealistically—portrays an oasis of peacefulness and intercultural development guided by the Spanish Jesuits in eighteenth-century Paraguay, a model not entirely missing in other places, such as the series of California missions founded by the Spanish Franciscan Junípero Serra.) They have had their rabid partisans and severe critics. Yet the Jesuit record is essential to understanding both the diverse ways in which European Christianity interacted with Native American culture and the later religious consequences of Columbus's voyage to the New World.

Early New France was not so much a colony as a trading post for furs and other items: a valuable economic arrangement to Europeans and Indians alike. As a result, conflicts over land claims and occupation did not play as great a role there as they did in the early history of British and Spanish America. Missionaries, too, were

---

[162] Poole, "Iberian Catholicism," 84.
[163] James Boswell, *Life of Johnson*, ed. George Birbeck Hill, revised by L. F. Powell, vol. 1 (Oxford: Oxford University Press, 1934), 455.

affected by this situation. Instead of being able to follow European settlements or military exploits, the French Jesuits had to go out and live among Indian tribes essentially unprotected. This took no little courage because, as they doubtless knew, in Spanish America, missionaries unprotected by arms, no matter how peaceful in their approach to Indians, had almost always been murdered.

Rather than forcing "European forms of Christianity" upon native tribes, as some charge all missionaries did, the Jesuits in New France, like their counterparts in China, sought to present Christianity in native terms and forms. They found in the rituals and beliefs of the main Eastern Woodland groups — Algonquian, Huron, and Iroquois — some parallels with Catholic sacraments and dogmas amid other, less congenial matter. Unlike Protestants, who saw in nature only unredeemed and fallen humanity, the Catholic system taught that grace builds on nature. The "black robes," as the Indians called the Jesuits, tried to take advantage of these natural affinities.

The Jesuit *Relations*, yearly reports back to the head of the society in France, are a goldmine of early-contact material.[164] In spite of the misunderstandings they contain and prejudices they perpetuate (they were widely read in seventeenth-century France), we have no more comprehensive source of information about native culture and religion in the Northeast region. Though the crudeness of some interpretations might make a modern anthropologist wince, a fair observer would have to say that the Jesuits truly tried to understand, according to their lights, the peoples they lived among. (Another popular film, *Black Robe*, based on a novel by

---

[164] Reuben Gold Thwaite edited these in *The Jesuit Relations and Allied Documents*, 73 vols. (Cleveland: Burrows Brothers, 1896–1901). A good selection from this massive record is Edna Kenton, ed., *The Jesuit Relations and Allied Documents* (New York: A. Boni and C. Boni, 1925).

Columbus and the Crisis of the West

Brian Moore, graphically shows both the cultural gaps the "black robes" strove to overcome and the gruesome tortures they were willing to endure—and did—to evangelize.)

Several of their discoveries remain of great interest. Some tribes had legends resembling the story of the Fall, even including a woman who tempted her husband with the fruit of a tree. Tales of a great flood and of a primeval man killing his brother also echoed the Bible. The Hurons and the Iroquois seemed to have had a more-developed concept of the afterlife than the Algonquians in the region. Whatever their anthropological soundness, these detailed findings show what attention and care went into the first contacts.

And that sensitivity persisted and continues to have repercussions. As late as 1724, Joseph Lafitau, another Jesuit who lived among Indians for several years, was making careful studies of native culture and claiming that his discoveries had proved doubly enlightening. While his knowledge of the ancient Greek classics, particularly of the religious rites in Homer, had given him insights into Indian rituals, his familiarity with "the customs of the Savages afforded ... illumination the more easily to understand and explain several matters to be found in ancient authors." Lafitau's observations are still of value today and have influenced the classical scholarship of the distinguished modern cultural historian Pierre Vidal-Naquet.[165]

The Jesuits' work also required a great deal of bravery. Paul Le Jeune, one of the earliest missionaries, remarked in 1632 on the "shocking cruelty to captives" among the warring tribes.[166] Seventeenth-century France, like the rest of Europe at the time,

---

[165] This material was presented by Bernard Knox in his 1992 Jefferson Lecture, "The Oldest Dead White European Males," reprinted in *New Republic*, 25 May 1992, 27–36.

[166] Parkman, *The Jesuits in North America*, 670–671.

was not exactly unfamiliar with torture and executions, but the Frenchmen found native treatment of prisoners excessive even by those standards. Isaac Jogues, who himself was later tortured and killed, recorded one instance of what he thought was human sacrifice, a debatable but not wholly implausible construal of what went on at times among the Iroquois.

To get a concrete sense of the world in which the Jesuits operated and the practices they sought to change, it is instructive to recall what happened to Jean de Brébeuf. Brébeuf was a talented linguist who learned several Indian languages. Like many of the Jesuits, he constantly had to defend himself from Indian charges of sorcery. (Even writing and reading were so alien to native ways of thought that they evoked fear.) Naturally, many Indians believed that sorcery was the cause of the disastrous epidemics brought by the French, which ravaged tribes, upending their ordinary way of life.

Brébeuf was working among the Hurons, tending the sick and trying to teach Christianity, when he was captured along with his colleague Gabriel Lalemant by the Iroquois. They tortured him to death, in steps: (1) Boiling water was poured over his head three times in imitation of baptism. (2) Hatchets were heated in a fire, strung together, and placed around his neck. (3) A belt of resin and burning pitch was attached around his waist. (4) His lips and tongue were cut off. (5) Pieces of his flesh were cut off, roasted, and eaten in front of him. (6) His heart was dug out and eaten. (7) His blood was drunk. Whatever shortcomings the Jesuits may have had, it is difficult not to admire, as the torturers themselves did, the courage they brought to a seemingly hopeless enterprise.

It is worth pausing a moment here on the question of cannibalism. A prominent scholar of Native American culture, Alvin M. Josephy, has argued in the introduction to a collection of essays by different hands, *America in 1492: The World of the Indian Peoples before the Arrival of Columbus*, that Columbus foolishly believed the

Columbus and the Crisis of the West

Taíno tales of Carib cannibalism because of medieval superstition. (As mentioned in the previous chapter, we know from reliable sources that Columbus actually resisted these tales, precisely because he thought them fictitious, until his experiences convinced him otherwise.) But other contributors to the volume show that the practice was widespread even among the Caribs,[167] and Josephy himself admits as much by making the astonishing assertion that the Indian practice of eating the flesh of brave captives paralleled in religious meaning the Christian sacrament of the Eucharist. In this view, the participants in both rituals desire to attain power and unite with a strong being. While such an aim may, in a very general way, be common to both, the fundamental confusion about significant differences as well is a case of special pleading.

Christians never ate actual human flesh, nor does their sacrament involve the torture and death of another human being. They believe that God himself chose to suffer and submit to death. Although distant echoes of human sacrifice and cannibalism (pointed in a far different direction) may still exist in Christian sacraments, it is a disservice to both real native beliefs and Christian teaching to conflate them. Brébeuf saying Mass and his Iroquois torturers do not have the same moral status—at least to us today. No one thinks that eating consecrated bread and drinking consecrated wine in church on a Sunday morning is a crime against universal human rights. Torture and cannibalism are such crimes. However much we may try to understand the meaning of these acts from the standpoint of someone within a native culture, we would not take

---

[167] See Louis C. Faron, "A Continent on the Move," in *America in 1492: The World of the Indian Peoples before the Arrival of Columbus*, ed. Alvin M. Josephy Jr. (New York: Knopf, 1992), 177–214. Although Josephy clearly intended to weigh in on the indigenous side in the 1992 debate, his aims are not always supported by the contributors to this volume.

a casual attitude toward them if they were still regularly occurring. In fact, we would agree on suppressing them, whatever the damage to native culture.

The Jesuit missions bore little fruit. The Hurons were converted and subsequently wiped out by a combination of disease and tribal warfare. Several Jesuits died horribly trying to present Christianity to native peoples in terms they could understand. Of course, other Christians were neither so delicate nor so heroic. But when we speak glibly of forced conversions and imposing European Christianity on native peoples, it is only fair to honor a group—one of several—that did neither and at least attempted a culturally sensitive approach, while showing an astonishing willingness to pay any price to make its efforts succeed.

Puritans and Nature

The ways in which the British brought Christianity to the New World are more complex. Unlike the Catholic Church, British Protestantism had no missionary orders and was riven by post-Reformation factions. The Puritans of Plymouth Colony looked upon themselves as a new saving remnant, reminiscent of the ancient Israelites who had gone out of Egypt into the wilderness. The colonists of Massachusetts Bay still felt themselves tied to the Church of England, a link that played no small role in Roger Williams's dissent and departure for Rhode Island. Quakers were burned as heretics in Massachusetts and eventually founded a colony of their own in Pennsylvania. Catholics led a precarious existence in Maryland. Virginia settlers wavered between Anglicanism and Puritanism. Under the circumstances, it is not surprising that there was little organized effort to convert Indians.

Tricks and force may have later been used to make Indians Christians, but such practices did not characterize the earliest English settlements. Puritan ideology made it difficult to arrive at a definite conception of who the Indians were. Were they a lost tribe of Israel, or were they merely unregenerate heathens like the Canaanites in the Old Testament? At least those few Puritans who occupied themselves with the Indians took the Indians as they found them. John Eliot, for example, showed true commitment to proper evangelization in learning indigenous languages (he translated the Bible into an Algonquian dialect) and in trying to convert natives through patient instruction. Understandably, Indians often fled Puritan religious talk, but that only shows they were free to do so.

The debate in English circles was not primarily, as among the early Spanish, about whether natives had rational souls. That issue, perhaps owing to the precedents set by the Spanish theologians, seems to have been settled in Puritan minds in the natives' favor. Daniel Gookin, an early Puritan missionary, probably expressed a typical sentiment, however, when he said that, except for their rational souls, Indians were "like unto the wild ass's colt, and not many degrees above beasts in matter of fact."[168] To Puritans, the Indians seemed the very image of men without true religion and civilization.

Nevertheless, to their credit, at least some of the English sought to remedy this situation. Though John Eliot's labors were poorly supported by a community that had more pressing concerns, he did manage to arrange some instruction for promising young Indians, even university training at Harvard. Among the documents establishing that university, there is an allowance for "all other necessary provisions that may conduce to the education of the English and Indian youth of this country in knowledge: and holiness."[169]

---

[168] Quoted in Catherine L. Albanese, *Nature Religion in America: From the Algonkian Indians to the New Age* (Chicago: University of Chicago Press, 1990), 35.

[169] William Kellaway, *The New England Company, 1649–1776: Missionary Society to the American Indian* (London: Longmans, 1961), 109.

Though this inclusion of Native Americans was more a matter of theory than of practice, one Indian did take a B.A. at Harvard before 1700. (A few decades later, Dartmouth College would be explicitly founded to teach natives Christian theology, among other subjects.)

Other early British settlements adopted differing attitudes toward Indians. Roger Williams, like Eliot, learned native tongues and even wrote a guidebook, *A Key into the Language of America* (1643). Williams tried to keep on good terms with Indians, a desire largely upset by King Philip's Rebellion in the 1670s. In general, however, Parkman is probably correct that the English mostly "scorned and neglected" Indians. If some of their basically respectful religious initiatives had generated more financial and social support, subsequent U.S. history might have been far different.

An Appraisal

When all is said and done, Vitoria, Las Casas, the Jesuits, the English missionaries, and other Christian groups did not have the full effect they might have had on behavior and evangelization in the New World. In part, this failure reflected the usual tragedy of human history — vices gaining the upper hand and ethical principles lagging far behind. But in part, too, it reflected the sheer difficulty Spain, France, and England had in understanding and governing the New World over such vast and watery distances. Hasty and overzealous religious did not help the situation, moreover, with their superficial baptisms and insensitive impositions. And a moral lacuna remained for even the best representatives of Christianity: African blacks were sold into slavery in various parts of the New World without very much of the moral indignation raised by the mistreatment of Native Americans until centuries later — when slavery started to be abolished, largely owing to British Methodists.

Columbus and the Crisis of the West

But the contact with native peoples planted a seed among religious thinkers, which was later to bear fruit in European culture as a whole. The Peruvian novelist Mario Vargas Llosa has argued:

> Father Las Casas was the most active, although not the only one, of those nonconformists who rebelled against the abuses inflicted upon the Indians. They fought against their fellow men and against the policies of their own country in the name of the moral principle that to them was higher than any principle of nation or state. This self-determination could not have been possible among the Incas or any of the other pre-Hispanic cultures. In these cultures, as in the other great civilizations of history foreign to the West, the individual could not morally question the social organism of which he was a part, because he existed only as an integral atom of that organism and because for him the dictates of the state could not be separated from morality. The first culture to interrogate and question itself, the first to break up the masses into individual beings who with time gradually gained the right to think and act for themselves, was to become, thanks to that unknown exercise, freedom, the most powerful civilization in our world.[170]

That civilization, Western civilization, owes no little debt of gratitude—though it rarely shows it—to the first Christian missionaries who grappled with problems, many still not fully resolved, in the New World.

---

[170] Mario Vargas Llosa, "Questions of Conquest," *Harper's*, December 1990, 51.

4

Colonialism, Indigenous Peoples, and the European Legacy

Whatever the particular crimes of Europe, that continent is also the source — the unique source — of those liberating ideas of individual liberty, political democracy, the rule of law, human rights, and cultural freedom that constitute our most precious legacy and to which most of the world today aspires.

—Arthur M. Schlesinger Jr.[171]

The nature of many elements involved in the study of 1492 — European colonialism, the alleged exploitation of natural resources, confrontation with premodern civilizations, and their sequels — made it perhaps inevitable that Columbus would be drawn into contemporary debates over culture, "identity" (including its potent ally "systemic racism"), environmentalism, and the wholesale rejection in several quarters of what is assumed to be "Western" civilization. As anyone familiar with contemporary disputes about school and college curricula knows, these movements attempt to give a dominant place in education and therefore in society as a

---

[171] Arthur M. Schlesinger Jr., *The Disuniting of America: Reflections on a Multicultural Society* (New York: W. W. Norton, 1992), 127.

whole to allegedly marginalized groups. African American, Native American, feminist, homosexual, and environmental perspectives should replace the dominant paradigm, which is reviled as "white supremacy," which is to say Eurocentric, male, heterosexual, and exploitative. The study and privileging of dead white European males must give way to a focus on other cultures and their distinguished members. In this perspective, Columbus—almost entirely shorn of any historical facts—symbolizes everything that cries out for repudiation. In fact, standing as he does at the very gateway to the Europeanization of the Americas, Columbus has come to represent for some people the most wicked dead white European male of them all.

The professors and students who in the 1980s chanted "Hey hey, ho ho, Western culture's got to go" at Berkeley and elsewhere, were not talking about a wider but a narrower world. Who in his right mind advocates throwing out a whole culture? And it might fairly be said that the more recent focus on "identity" conceived of as membership in favored groups—usually on the basis of race, class, or gender—with a grievance against "society" has shown itself to be even more radical, seeking virtually to destroy the Western heritage with little knowledge of what it is, what might replace it, and what the consequences and costs would be. People who take that framing for granted find it hard to believe that—for most members of the human race, throughout history, even today—family, community (or nation), and religion have been the most important markers of their "identities." Indeed, under the new dispensation, family, nation, and religion look like biases, even "hate" to some people who seek their sense of themselves in postmodern categories. Columbus and the Europe that came with him have, properly speaking, little to do with this contemporary struggle within Western societies. But they have been drawn into it anyway.

Were Indians Environmentalists, Feminists, Multiculturalists?

The usual indictment form the anti-Western argument takes is, first, to identify some feature of contemporary American society as a gross evil—e.g., racism, sexism, inequality—and then to claim that it did not exist in the Americas or would not have existed here if Columbus and his European followers had not brought it. For example, an allegedly staggering, industrialized United States is invited to look to Native Americans as models of good ecological behavior. But the evidence for such assertions—both of the failure of modern American society (which offers prosperity, health, and wide freedoms to people of varied origins in basically clean and pleasant environments) and the remedies in native cultures—is, at most, slender.

Though it is difficult and hazardous to generalize about such diverse peoples, Native American tribes probably did not even possess the idea of nature as a whole, a concept that appeared in the West with the pre-Socratic philosopher Heraclitus. Furthermore, Native American religions did not present sharp distinctions between the spiritual and physical worlds. And it would be projecting Western categories upon their thinking to regard this undifferentiated, non-Western way of looking at reality as implying that, for indigenous peoples, all of nature was somehow sacred. Åke Hultkrantz, a student of Native American religion, has remarked that some contemporary Indian pronouncements make it

> sound as if the whole universe, particularly the natural environment, is sacred. This is not so; if it were, Indians would not point out certain stones, mountains, and lakes as sacred. Conservationists have mistakenly assumed that Indians are ecologists because they supposedly care for all

of nature. In fact, there are many proofs of the devastation
of nature by Indians.[172]

What Westerners regard as Indian respect for nature focused on
some particular animal, plant, or place that might manifest the spirits
of what was thought needful for human life. Making use of that thing
might drive away or offend a spirit that had to be appeased, and thus
the item was respected in order to avoid wounded prerogatives and
dire consequences. Indeed, fear of the spirits and of the physical world,
which played a large role in native life, has very little, if anything, in
common with our contemporary concern for the balance of nature.

Anyone who studies North American Indian cultures seriously
will find interesting and complex peoples and, in many respects, an
intriguing natural charm. But a thorough student will also come to
realize that the Indians could not afford to indulge Romantic fantasies
about what we call "nature"; they knew only too well that their environment could be as cruel as it was kind. They tried, as best as they
were able with the knowledge and tools at hand, to bend things to
their use. Critics often denounce "white" culture as utilitarian—and
since the Scientific Revolution, there has been an excessive focus
on technological reason to the neglect of older and deeper strains in
the West that need to be recovered. But Indian cultures were (and
are) utilitarian as well. Among many Indians, Hultkrantz has found,

we seek in vain for a pure aesthetic beholding of nature.
An educated Senecan Indian well initiated into the traditions and values of his people once told me of the widely
divergent reactions of Indians and whites when they move
to new regions. The white man, he said, is impressed by
the appearance of the landscape and meditates over its

[172] Åke Hultkrantz, *Native Religions of North America* (San Francisco: Harper & Row, 1987), 24.

beauty, whereas the Indian first of all asks, where are my medicines?[173]

Western sentiment about nature over the last few centuries arose in large part from relative security and strength vis-à-vis natural powers. Confidence enables us to enjoy nature and appreciate its order because it is no longer such a harsh and, at times, overwhelming adversary. Despite the problems caused by Western technology, no one would want to give up the advances the West made in medicine, food, housing, and even communications for a romantic primitivism.

And at least some Indians take a much less Romantic view of nature than do modern environmentalists. Hultkrantz speculates that the contemplation of nature common among European peoples since the Romantics was a mode of thought unknown to the precontact Indian:

> Just as little as they performed art for art's sake—it was always a part of their technological, social, and symbolic activities—did they pursue a contemplation of nature to satisfy their aesthetic "needs." Their cultures simply did not provide for such needs.

Paradoxically, the sometimes-frightening power of Western technology has induced some Westerners and even some Indians to adopt extreme, near-quietist stances toward nature. In a famous and often-quoted interview in the late 1890s, for example, a Sahaptin Indian of Washington State was reported to have reacted with the following declamation to the suggestion by whites that the tribe cultivate the land:

> You ask me to plow the ground! Shall I take a knife and tear my mother's bosom? Then when I die she will not take me to her bosom to rest.

---

[173] Ibid., 125.

> You ask me to dig for stone! Shall I dig under her skin
> for her bones? Then when I die I cannot enter her body to
> be born again.
> You ask me to cut grass and make hay and sell it, and
> be rich like white men! But how dare I cut off my mother's
> hair?[174]

Some environmentalists have taken statements like this as proof of
a profound and universal Indian reluctance to disturb nature. But
anyone familiar with the various native tribes of North America
knows that agriculture, mining, and harvesting went on for centuries among them. The Sahaptin's statement, if indeed he made such
a declaration, was a late reaction to "white" practices more than
an accurate representation of native belief. This kind of credulity
is quite common among those who, without looking too closely at
indigenous groups, wish to find their own modern concerns reflected
in native traditions. The utopian desire for undisturbed land tempts
some "whites" to think that even using minerals somehow violates
the sacred order of nature — which they assume does not admit of
rational human needs.

Balances and Imbalances

In fact, even alleged Indian ideas of human harmony with nature
do not necessarily offer comfort to a modern ecologist. When Indians wanted to cut trees, for example, they felt obligated to give
the spirit to whom the trees belonged something in return, lest the
spirit grow angry and remove all trees. In many tribes, the spirit was
offered tobacco, and then the trees were cut. We usually conflate
this religious practice with the modern wish to preserve, enjoy,

---

[174] Ibid., 129.

and respect nature, but such an image may be very wide of the mark. In purely physical terms, these religious practices could lead to great damage. "In theory the Iroquois were conservationists," William Fenton has said, but in practice they "often contributed to the decline of species." They broke off entire tops of trees to harvest cherries and, even before the white man's arrival, probably overhunted deer and beaver.[175] Significantly, because of the way they exhausted resources, small native bands such as the Iroquois usually had to move their villages about twice per generation.[176]

While it might be somewhat edifying for our desacralized and industrialized culture if modern environmentalists followed Indian customs and prayed before acting, it would not disguise the evidence that, even in the thinly settled region of the North American Woodland cultures, Indians often exhausted the resources of a certain area and then moved on. The difference between them and, say, a modern paper company was that they were so few—and land so plentiful—that their actions threatened few major or long-term consequences. Today, in fact, paper companies will take steps to replant a forest, if for no other reason than economic self-interest. But such conscious care could not exist without a certain understanding of the physical world that was only partly present to Native American peoples.

That understanding was not apparent among larger, more developed native civilizations either. The troubles in their own relationship to nature had more far-reaching, visible consequences than did those of their woodland counterparts. For a long time, archaeologists believed that the Mayas—a developed, urban people—were

---

[175] William N. Fenton, "Northern Iroquoian Culture Patterns," in vol. 15 of *Handbook of North American Indians*, ed. Bruce G. Trigger (Washington, D.C.: Smithsonian Institution Press, 1978), 298.
[176] Ibid., 302.

gentle, scholarly astronomers. It was only with the gradual success in deciphering Mayan glyphs, the one true writing system among Native Americans, that they learned otherwise. The great Mayan city-states in Mesoamerica abruptly collapsed about six hundred years before Columbus arrived in the Americas, their people returning to a much lower level of material culture. No one is sure exactly why this happened, but exploitation of and stresses on the environment seem to have been factors. The evidence suggests that the Mayas regressed owing to their exhaustion of the tropical forests, as well as to endemic warfare among their city-states, epidemics, and political turmoil.[177] Whatever harmony with nature that may have existed among the Mayas appears to have been, as in other cultures with which we are familiar, hit and miss and profoundly subject to the human propensities toward evil and error.

Likewise, roughly about the time Columbus arrived in the Caribbean, the great Cahokian Mound Builder culture of southern Illinois—which may have had some cultural connections with the larger civilizations south of the Rio Grande—simply dispersed itself, probably *mutatis mutandis* for similar reasons. It is not unreasonable to speculate that weakness made the more primitive Native American tribes somewhat ecologically benign, and the more advanced Native American civilizations showed pathologies as bad as, or worse than, those in other developed civilizations. While the plagues, wars, and famines of medieval Europe may suggest a civilization in turmoil, for instance, none of these natural and man-made disasters led to a decline in European society comparable to the disappearance of the Mayas or the Mound Builders.

---

[177] For a sympathetic but reliable guide, see Linda Schele and David Freidel, *A Forest of Kings: The Untold Story of the Ancient Maya* (New York: William Morrow, 1990). And the more recent Michael D. Coe and Stephen D. Houston, *The Maya*, 9th ed. (New York: Thames & Hudson, 2015).

Varieties of Harmony

The Native American pathologies could be very bad indeed, and not only for environmental reasons. Many modern Westerners who blithely invoke the image of indigenous peoples living in harmony with nature—and with one another—often regard Christianity and Judaism as having inherited from the Bible a uniquely evil injunction to "subdue and dominate" the earth. This way of reading Genesis is clearly tendentious, but a powerful misinterpretation, since in the biblical perspective human beings are called upon to be stewards of creation. As decent a man as Albert Camus, who, though not a Christian, was generally fair to Christianity, argued in *The Rebel*, "For the Christian, as for the Marxist, nature must be subdued. The Greeks are of the opinion that it is better to obey it. The love of the ancients for the cosmos was completely unknown to the first Christians."[178] This is mistaken in several ways. The early Church Fathers wrote whole treatises on Creation and spoke of nature as "the second book of revelation."[179] Human beings were tasked in Genesis with being stewards of God's world. The modern misconceptions stem from a confusion: identifying (incorrectly) modern industrialism and a nature shorn of purpose since the Enlightenment and the Scientific Revolution with the deep Judeo-Christian roots of Western culture. Other cultures, many assume, had religious principles that demonstrated reciprocal and harmonious relationships with the physical world.

But reciprocity and harmony are equivocal terms. In different cultures, they may not necessarily result in what we would recognize

---

[178] Albert Camus, *The Rebel*, trans. Anthony Bower (New York: Vintage Books, 1956), 190.

[179] See Robert Royal, *The Virgin and the Dynamo: The Use and Abuse of Religion in Environmental Debates* (Grand Rapids: William B. Eerdmans, 1999).

as the good, the true, or the beautiful. For Algonquians, Iroquois, and other groups, kidnapping one another was part of a system designed to maintain a reciprocal balance among tribes. Widows of warriors had the right to demand the capture of men from other tribes to replace those lost, and this, in turn, induced the other tribe to seek its own replacements. The result was a never-ending series of feuds and mutual abductions. The people who put forward Native Americans as models of reciprocity may not exactly have such intertribal arrangements in mind.

Perhaps the most terrifying example of what the bare search for a natural harmony, absent other considerations, can mean occurred among the Aztecs. Like other Mesoamerican high cultures (Olmecs, Toltecs, Mayas—and even the Incas in South America, who mostly sacrificed children), the Aztecs thought that without blood offerings, the balance of nature would be upset and monstrous beings would emerge from the darkness to tear the cosmos apart. Jacques Soustelle, an admiring but honest historian of Aztec ritual, describes the special sacrifices required to keep the heavens revolving:

> The astronomer priest made a sign: a prisoner was stretched out on the stone. With a dull sound the flint knife opened his chest and, in the gaping wound they spun the firestick, the *tlequauitl*. The miracle took place and the flame sprang up, born from this shattered breast; and amid shouts of joy messengers lit their torches at it and ran to carry the sacred fire to the four corners of the central valley. And so the world had escaped its end once more. But how heavy and blood-drenched a task it was for the priests and the warriors and the emperors, century after century to repel the unceasing onslaughts of the void.[180]

---

[180] Jacques Soustelle, *Daily Life of the Aztecs on the Eve of the Spanish Conquest*, trans. Patrick O'Brien (Palo Alto: Stanford University Press, 1970), 101–102.

This, too, is harmony with nature, but a harmony that depends, as all such philosophical concepts do, on your beliefs about nature and the gods. Even the most ardent anti-Western activist may pause in the face of such natural harmony and decide that there may be limits to modern multiculturalism and native wisdom after all.

Pre-Columbian Paradise?

In recent decades, a large body of archaeological material has appeared that is gradually replacing uninformed and idealistic portrayals of ancient Native Americans as innocents living in harmony with nature. That idealism is most graphically represented in the peaceful and colorful murals of the Mexican artist Diego Rivera, which enjoyed a renewed appreciation as the five hundreth anniversary of Columbus's first voyage approached. Rivera's paintings show exactly the contours of the paradise many people would like to believe existed in pre-Columbian America: vistas of fertile plains spreading between breathtaking mountains; gaily dressed Indian peasants bending over neatly arranged plots of corn; community life steeped in the rhythm of the seasons, religious festivals, and songs. In short, an America before machines and automobiles, cities and suburbs, alleged alienation and cultural vacuity. While nostalgia for earlier, supposedly simpler times is a perennial theme of literature and art, rarely is the wish further from the reality than it is in Rivera's work. The murals may be pleasing art, but they are bad history.

The Nobel Prize–winning Mexican poet Octavio Paz has written some of the most lucid and accessible essays on pre-Columbian civilization in Mexico. These graceful commentaries combine both archaeological and historical research with genuine affection for Mexico's dual heritage. Paz, in short, seems to have no partisan axe to grind. The Mexican town he grew up in contained the usual seventeenth-century Spanish Baroque convents and nineteenth-century buildings, but these stirred his imagination far less than the small Indian pyramid he and friends discovered while on a picnic one day. Mexico's Spanish and Indian heritage are deeply present in Paz's poetry, particularly in his *Piedra de sol*, a long poem based on the Mayan calendar.[181]

Paz has described the Mesoamerican Indian culture as a world of city-states perpetually at war with one another under the leadership of kings who proclaimed themselves divine. Anti-Western ideologues may write glibly of a European culture of death, but some high Indian cultures, such as the Aztecs and the Mayas, were far more openly cults of blood and death than anything in the Old World. If the biblical religions are anti-natural, what of this:

> The religious foundation common to all the Mesoameri-can peoples is a basic myth: the gods sacrificed themselves to create the world; the mission of the human being is to preserve the universal life, including his own, feeding the gods with the divine substance: blood. This myth explains the central place of sacrifice in Mesoamerican civilization. Thus, war is not only a political and economic dimension of the city-state but a religious dimension.[182]

Paz's appraisal is consistent with that of one of the premier scholars of Aztec life, Jacques Soustelle, who has written, "Perhaps no people in history has been as much haunted by the grim presence of death as the [ancient] Mexicans." One of the principal aims

---

[181] Octavio Paz, *Piedra del sol* (Sunstone), English translation with original Spanish in *The Poems of Octavio Paz* (New York: New Directions, 2018).

[182] This passage and some of the points that follow are drawn from Paz's essay "Reflexiones de un intruso," in the magazine he edited, *Vuelta*, January 1987, 20–26 (author's translation).

of war, for example, was to capture enemies alive who might be sacrificed either on the altar or in a ritual ball game. Their hearts were cut out and offered to the gods of war and fertility.

As kinds of divinities themselves, the king and his queen were also expected to shed their own blood for cyclical renewal of the cosmos and the harvest. An elaborate system of rituals grew up in which the king practiced bloodletting on himself—among the Mayas, this was often from his penis. The queen shed blood into a basin, usually from her tongue, which was pierced and a rope passed through it. Thus, through the repeated ritual offering of blood—both their own and others'—was the original energy of the cosmos restored and the end of the world postponed. The sheer quantity of blood needed was striking as well: tens of thousands were sacrificed, so far as we can tell, at great festivals and at the consecration of major temples from Mexico to Peru. Amid the changes in style and personalities over the centuries, the underlying cyclical pattern of cosmic order remained pretty much the same.

An odd double standard permeates much of the writing about these matters. For example, if the Spanish kings of the period had regarded themselves as gods and required human sacrifice to preserve their world and rule, as all evidence shows the Aztec and Mayan kings did, a modern hermeneutic of suspicion would unmask the ideology of death behind the religious veneer. But even useful and lucid historical accounts, such as David Carrasco's *Religions of Mesoamerica*, highlight the astronomy, art, and other cultural achievements of native civilizations while treating the darker aspects as puzzling aberrations.[183] Carrasco goes so far as to rebuke the Spaniards, even the best of the missionaries, for thinking that

---

[183] David Carrasco, *Religions of Mesoamerica* (San Francisco: Harper & Row, 1990).

they needed to convert the natives from their traditional religions. The Spaniards saw human beings dismembered, decapitated, and sacrificed amid sacred serpents. The priests performing the sacrifices were forbidden to cut their hair or nails or to wash the gore from their bodies—a horrifying image that does not appear on any wall painted by Diego Rivera. Recalling the abominations denounced in the Old Testament, the Spaniards concluded that the Indians were worshipping demons. Modern readers may judge what, under the circumstances, their own reactions might have been, and whether the most multicultural observer would have felt obliged to "respect Indian belief" in the need to preserve natural cycles and harmony by such practices.

The Aztecs believed they were living in the era of the Fifth Sun and had very little sense of their own past or that of surrounding tribes. Mircea Eliade has shown with some force in *Cosmos and History* that this pattern of temporal cycles, and rituals to preserve it, are common to most archaic societies.[184] Those of us who live in the "historical," linear time of the West, which is the direct result of the unfinished story of the Bible, have great difficulty believing that history proper does not exist among most other peoples. Chronicles record the cycles of creation-destruction-creation bound up with war and bloodshed, reality and myth, but there is no history proper, either in theory or in practical life. History as we know it combines the directional time of the Bible with a critical sifting of evidence begun by the ancient Greeks. Ironically, it is the putatively Eurocentric culture that has discovered much of Native American history—a fact of some importance if we wish to measure the effect of Europe on Native American self-understanding.

[184] Mircea Eliade, *Cosmos and History: The Myth of the Eternal Return* (New York: Harper Torchbooks, 1959).

The Cost of Isolation

For Paz and other scholars, isolation from outside influences not only created troubling and stagnant social forms in Mesoamerica but doomed the Native Americans whom the Spaniards encountered. In addition to their technical advantages in weaponry, the Spaniards had cultural advantages. European ignorance in the face of Indian culture, of which we hear so much today, was comparable to Aztec ignorance about Europeans. While the Aztecs believed that these bearded men with six legs (i.e., mounted on horses) must be strange beings or gods, the Spaniards quickly obtained a general sense of the Indian religious, political, and social systems. Cortés, for example, immediately intuited how to use conquered tribes' resentment of Moctezuma's empire and how to appeal to human sentiments in his efforts to stop human sacrifice. At least for a time, Cortés and his men appeared to several subject peoples as liberators from political tyranny and from the burden of paying tribute to Indian rulers in human lives. In an odd, providential way, these highly unworthy Spanish vessels also became the bearers of a sort of liberation theology. Several thousand Indians joined the conquistadores in their assault on Mexico City.

By contrast, the Aztecs had no way of conceptualizing who or what the Spaniards were. As most readers of the early history of the Americas know, Moctezuma was terrified by an ancient prophecy that predicted the empire would be conquered by gods coming from where the sun rises. (By an odd historical coincidence, it appears the prophecy also specified the exact year, *Ce Acatl* or 1-Reed, that the Spaniards landed on the Mexican coast, though later events may have contaminated the original accounts.) Aztec thought allowed only two categories of beings: gods and men. And the men were divided only between those belonging to their own sedentary civilization and those outside

Columbus and the Crisis of the West

it, the barbarians. Because the Spaniards did not fit entirely into either category, the Native American tradition was of little help in confronting them. A similar handicap existed among the Spanish explorers, particularly a figure such as Columbus, who grappled with how to account for peoples previously unheard of in Europe.

Even before the arrival of Cortés, however, Indian culture had been crippled by a lack of contact with fresh influences. While Indian civilization produced some remarkable art and architecture over more than a millennium, no new impulses, such as had occurred elsewhere on the globe, led to the development of metals and the wheel, or to the breeding and training of animals for agricultural work. Whatever evils the Spaniards eventually introduced—and they were many and varied—they at least cracked the age-old shell of a culture admirable in many ways but also pervaded by repugnant atrocities and petrification. Anyone who wishes to defend the rights of surviving Indian tribes and to help preserve their cultures, two noble undertakings, must nevertheless not rely on a sentimental idealism about the value of all cultures. They should take care to learn what should and should not be retained from that heritage.[185]

---

[185] The present writer once made these arguments to a class at the U.S. Foreign Service Institute. One of the students, echoing what he had heard in other forums about minority issues, replied that the Indian culture "worked for them." This is, in a sense, true, just as the enslavement of the Israelites "worked" for the ancient Egyptians. Anthropological neutrality and a humanitarian belief in the value of all cultures—valid enough within limits—cannot replace our necessary judgment of what should and should not be permitted in civilized society. A sentimental belief in the equal dignity of all cultures leads inevitably, in the practical sphere, to defense of sacrificial murder.

Inevitable Tragedy

For Octavio Paz, the encounter between the Old and New Worlds in his country led to fatal tragedy: "For two thousand years, the cultures of Mesoamerica lived and grew by themselves; their encounter with *the other* was too late and in conditions of a terrible inequality. For that reason, they were demolished."[186] We may regret much of what occurred, but we should recognize that it would have taken superhuman prescience and virtue on the part of the Spaniards to help the natives evolve peacefully toward a culture combining the best of both worlds. This did not happen in North or South America, in British India or in French Vietnam. The encounter of two civilizations, especially when they are of widely differing cultural character, may involve more complexities than mere human intelligence and will can control.

The early record clearly shows as much. The most vivid eyewitness account of these first contacts on the American mainland is Bernal Díaz del Castillo's remarkably vigorous *Historia Verdadera de la Conquista de la Nueva España* (*True History of the Conquest of New Spain*). Díaz del Castillo was one of the conquistadores who came ashore with Cortés and is therefore viewed with suspicion by a certain type of historian. Why his narrative warrants more skepticism than any other history, however, is not clear. While Díaz del Castillo may not be a completely reliable source, he is far less biased than many of his detractors. He was moved to write initially, he says, precisely because of the false accounts of other early historians. Referring to one heroic chronicle of the conquest, written at a time when the numbers of Indians killed was regarded as a military achievement rather than an embarrassment, he remarks:

[186] Paz, "Reflexiones de un intruso."

When I had read it, I found that the whole was a misrepresentation, and also that in his extraordinary exaggerations of the numbers of the natives, and of those who were killed in the different battles, his account was utterly unworthy of belief. We never much exceeded four hundred men, and if we found such numbers bound hand and foot, we could not have put them to death.[187]

The simple but shrewd Díaz del Castillo tries, instead, to describe accurately what happened, as well as Cortés's real strengths and many weaknesses.

He also speaks credibly of the natives. Like many of his companions, Díaz del Castillo marvels at Aztec achievements and even regrets that, as he writes, many—particularly, the stunning buildings of Tenochtitlán—had been destroyed. But as a faithful reporter, he paints less flattering pictures too. Even in the small villages the Spaniards enter, human sacrifice is widespread. When Cortés is offered gifts of friendship by one tribe, he asks sincerely that they first give up these sacrifices, which he regards as worshipping idols. Díaz del Castillo explains: "For every day our sight was offended by the repetition of four or five of these horrid murders, the unfortunate victims being cut up and their limbs sold in the public markets, as beef is in the towns of Old Castille."[188] Each time the Spaniards conquer a new town and the inhabitants flee, they come upon the blood and bones of young men recently sacrificed.

---

[187] Bernal Díaz del Castillo, *History of New Spain*, trans. and ed. J.M. Cohen (New York: Penguin Books, 1983), is the most easily available translation. Cohen has condensed some passages and deleted others, somewhat distorting the text. The translation quoted here is the full English version by Maurice Keating (New York: National Travel Club, 1927), xxv.

[188] Díaz de Castillo, *History of New Spain*, trans. Keating, 105.

Díaz del Castillo reports these discoveries with the same regularity and matter-of-fact tone as he uses to report on architecture, food, and weapons. The modern person who would try to judge fairly the actions of the conquistadores and the Indians must first appreciate how appalling these practices must have been to have repeatedly horrified even these battle-hardened soldiers.

North American Tribes

Writers about Native Americans farther to the north often try to distance those tribes from Mesoamerican cultures or to blame Aztec influence for unsavory practices north of the Rio Grande. The Pawnee, for example, are known to have sacrificed a young maiden yearly, but a typical explanation is that the ritual "may well have derived from a Mesoamerican culture more than a thousand miles to the south."[189] No evidence for this "may well have" is cited, or available. Despite its relative infrequency among North American tribes, human sacrifice is assumed to have been imported. It is said to have jumped to or been preserved by the Pawnee, but not originated by them. Even ethnology occasionally seems slanted against southern peoples and to favor northern groups.

In fact, North American tribes rivaled their Latin American counterparts in possessing all sorts of rituals and cultural practices that are incompatible with modern notions of civilized society. In the previous chapter, we examined the shocking torture of captives by Iroquois, Algonquian, and northeastern tribes. Among the Plains Indians, Sioux men and women — the warm, gentle humanists in the highly popular film *Dances with Wolves* — offered sacrifices of their own flesh during their yearly Sun Dance, which lasted several

---

[189] Peter Iverson, "Taking Care of the Earth and Sky," in Josephy, *America in 1492*, 96.

days and was the most common and typical Plains religious festival. Usually one man, seeking a vision from the sun god, volunteered to be hung up from skewers passed beneath his skin and tied to ropes (a ritual accurately portrayed in an older film, *A Man Called Horse*). Still others would subject themselves to slightly lesser torments while staring into the sun as long as they could bear.

Each of these practices, of course, has an intelligible and purposive meaning within the Sioux system, and to describe them accurately should not be construed as an attempt to ridicule or discredit them. Rather, we need to become more fully aware of how profoundly *other* the beliefs and actions of Native American tribes really are. This crucial truth often escapes us when we are attracted to ways of life that seem to offer alternatives to the mechanical qualities and narrow rationality of modern life. People who would look askance at the ascetic practices of, say, Spanish Catholicism or English Puritanism often remain blissfully ignorant of the actual religious beliefs and practices of the Native Americans they admire. But without a serious effort to understand these complex and deep spiritual concepts, we cannot possibly comprehend native relationships to the land and the relations among different tribes, let alone native life *per se*.

Unfortunately, at present, facile acceptance of all aspects of Native American religion seems to be the rule. At Princeton University around the quincentenary, the course on Native American religion became the second most popular among undergraduates. Around 250 students enrolled each semester. David Carrasco, who taught the course, said that his greatest difficulty was getting students to be sufficiently critical in their approaches to the material.[190]

In this, the undergraduates were simply following a broad cultural trend that has only increased with later years. New Age religious

[190] See "On Campus," *New York Times*, 20 October 1991.

currents have appropriated and — almost always — grossly distorted Indian beliefs. Because belief, ritual, and lifestyle are so inextricably intertwined in Native American cultures, authentic indigenous spirituality has been seriously neglected in this process, while exploiters and hucksters have profited.[191]

The hope that Native Americans somehow possessed a lost and much-needed wisdom has been channeled into harmonic convergences, dial-an-Indian services, and sweat-lodge therapies. So commonplace is this element of popular culture that the porn star turned performance artist and sex therapist Annie Sprinkle, who became famous when the National Endowment for the Arts denied her a grant, blithely stated that her therapy includes "Native American techniques."[192]

Native American Feminism?

In that vein, Native Americans have sometimes been enlisted among natural feminists and touted as worshippers of a primal mother goddess. But here, too, multicultural hopes may not be able to withstand historical reality. Bernal Díaz del Castillo reports, clearly with some titillation, on how batches of young women, some of them the nieces and daughters of Indian leaders, are presented to the conquistadores as gifts. Before accepting these ladies, the Spaniards usually require them to be baptized, a strange precondition. What stands out over and above the particulars of these exchanges,

---

[191] For a sophisticated discussion of this phenomena, see Alice B. Kehoe, "Primal Gaia: Primitivists and Plastic Medicine Men," in *The Invented Indian: Cultural Fictions and Government Policies*, ed. James A. Clifton (New Brunswick, N.J.: Transaction Books, 1990), 193–210.

[192] Kim Masters, "Some Might Call It Art …," *Washington Post*, 9 February 1992, G-10.

however, is the basic difference in attitude toward women. Contemporary political alliances grouping minorities and women—what has come to be called "intersectionality"—cannot alter the fact that in pre-Columbian America, women were sometimes oppressed by the very groups we now promote as minorities. While women occasionally occupied important posts in Aztec or other native societies, they were oftentimes treated like chattel. And though the Spaniards may have tolerated this practice for less-than-savory reasons, they certainly would not have been able to give away their own wives and daughters in Spain, as gifts.

One of the facts most frequently cited by Columbus's critics in the current controversies is a passage from a letter written by his friend Michele de Cuneo:

> When I was in the boat I captured a very beautiful Carib woman, whom the said Lord Admiral gave to me, and with whom, having taken her into my cabin, she being naked according to their custom, I conceived desire to take pleasure. I wanted to put my desire into execution but she did not want it and treated me with her finger nails in such a manner that I wished I had never begun. But seeing that (to tell you the end of it all), I took a rope and thrashed her well, for which she raised such unheard of screams that you would not believe your ears. Finally we came to an agreement in such manner that I can tell you that she seemed to have been brought up in a school of harlots. [193]

Given everything else we've seen about Columbus, particularly his complaints to the Spanish monarchs about Spaniards' taking

---

[193] Samuel Eliot Morison, ed. and trans., *Journals and Other Documents on the Life and Voyages of Christopher Columbus* (New York: Heritage, 1963), 212.

indigenous concubines, this whole description raises serious doubts —and historians are divided about this one reference, from years after the event. If this is not Cuneo merely indulging in some macho braggadocio, Columbus would share in serious blame for subsequent Spanish mistreatment of native women. The case, however, seems weak and at a distance of centuries a slender reed on which to hang a very large charge.

Yet it is a crucial part of the historical picture to see clearly the status of women in parts of the pre-Columbian Caribbean as well. The Caribs, according to mainstream scholarship, not only were cannibals but made a habit of capturing women from the Arawak tribes—the peoples Columbus first encountered in the New World—and making them concubines. Women were segregated from the men to such an extent, moreover, that the two sexes spoke separate languages. Only the men spoke Carib; the women, even Carib women, spoke Arawak because of the large numbers of captive Arawak women among them. Though hotly contested by revisionists, no convincing evidence has emerged to discredit the general lines of this history.[194]

Nor were the Caribs an isolated instance of indigenous male domination in the New World. Modern Mexicans refer to La Malinche, the Indian woman who served as Cortés's interpreter, as *la traidora* (the traitoress). Yet if we practice some feminist interpretation here, her story may give us pause. A tribe allied with the Aztecs sold her into slavery some years before the Spanish landed on the American mainland. When the Spanish arrived, Malinche knew several Indian dialects and quickly mastered Castilian. It does not take a feminist hermeneutic to understand why this talented and independent woman may have felt less than full solidarity with the Aztec patriarchs when the conquistadores offered her a chance for liberation from their rule.

[194] See Alvin M. Josephy, *The Indian Heritage of America* (New York: Bantam, 1968), 264–265.

Columbus and the Crisis of the West

Well-defined gender roles were also common among the more simply organized North American tribes. Some ingenious recent scholarship has tried to show that, like good postmodernists, Indians either did not have our sense of the polarities of gender or that they recognized as many as six "genders."[195] This seems to be an obvious case of current cultural imposition on a far distant group of peoples. Constant warfare encouraged a natural division of labor between domestic and hunter-and-warrior occupations. Women were, in some groups, sexually free before marriage but after marriage became little more than domestic drudges. Matrilineal (not matriarchal) social arrangements existed in many tribes perhaps because of the need to keep track of descent where multiple wives and divorce were prevalent. Women in such societies sometimes had a say in choosing which male would lead the tribe or in deposing him for poor performance of duties. It was almost universally the men, however, who made decisions, including the crucial decision to go to war.

The modern feminist agenda finds very little fertile soil in traditional Native American societies. Indeed, the position of women in the Americas prior to European contacts was generally worse than it was in the so-called European "patriarchies." Nor do the hierarchies, castes, slavery, tribalism, and other evident features of various Native American societies support the conclusion that the New World provided a pristine alternative to the shortcomings of European societies. Though those societies are frequently lumped together as some evil monolith bearing down on native peoples, the Spanish, English, French, Dutch, and Portuguese who led the way to the New World actually represented a great multiplicity within a loose unity, which was Europe in 1492 and after.

---

[195] See Jay Miller, "A Kinship of Spirit," in Josephy, *America in 1492*, 309.

Renaissance Europe

In the postcolonialist world in which we live, Europe's relation to the rest of the world is being recalibrated not only in the political realm but in intellectual history. Long-suppressed or absent voices of non-European peoples are often rightly gaining a hearing. Frequently, these voices take on the tone of Caliban in Shakespeare's *The Tempest*, which is set, not incidentally, in the very Caribbean Columbus entered. In the postcolonial dispensation, Caliban now elicits more sympathy than he once did when he cries out:

> You taught me language, and my profit on't
> Is I know how to curse. The red plague rid you
> For learning me your language!
> (ii, 366–368)

Changed historical circumstances have also brought about reevaluations of what constitutes "civilization" and "barbarism," justice and rebellion.[196]

Curiously, America had a similar effect on Europe early in colonial history. Contemporary rereadings of history are the direct heirs of works such as Thomas More's *Utopia*, in which the fictional source is one Raphael, who is presented as having traveled with Amerigo Vespucci during his voyages. Another character in that book laments: "I don't know whose fault it was, mine, yours, or Raphael's, but we never thought of asking, and he never thought of telling us whereabouts in the New World Utopia is."[197]

---

[196] Cf. Garry Wills's comments on Aimé Césaire's play *Une tempeste* and revisionist productions of Shakespeare in "Goodbye, Columbus," *New York Review of Books*, 22 November 1990, 6–7.

[197] Thomas More, *Utopia*, trans. Paul Turner (New York: Penguin, 1961), 30–31.

Columbus and the Crisis of the West

Standing sufficiently far away in some vague location, Utopia — "No Place" — is able to serve as a blank slate on which More,
as a European, is able to build criticism of his own European society.
More wrote almost a century before Shakespeare, but even in the
early seventeenth century, the New World remained for Europeans
a useful *tabula rasa* for making seemingly objective comments that,
in reality, were self-criticism. Renaissance Europe did not wait for
the arrival of critics of Eurocentrism to begin feeling the effects
of other peoples.

In many ways, the new critique of Europe is desirable, when
it is well informed, because it corrects an intellectual imperialism
that Europe has exercised for too long over the histories of other
peoples. But the sheer violence of the present pursuit of abstract
justice often causes such corrections to introduce new intellectual
injustices, particularly in regard to the full record of European
influence. The previous chapter traced some religious and secular currents within Europe that sought just action from the very
beginnings of the European presence in the Americas. As Europe
expanded into all parts of the globe, it brought domination, torture,
death, and slavery of its own, but also bore other seeds that were
to exert some crucial influence for the good.

The mixture of all the world's peoples, which is now our native
condition, especially in the Americas, owes whatever success it has
had not only to European exploration but to European pluralism.
As the distinguished historian J. H. Elliott has observed:

> Divided into competing political units — and also, from the
> sixteenth century, into competing religious units — Renais-
> sance Europe was a pluralist society, with none of the mono-
> lithic central control that characterized the contemporary
> Ottoman and Chinese empires. While having no doubt of
> the superiority of its own religion and way of life, it was less

dismissive of the "barbarians" beyond its own borders than was the Chinese world.[198]

Elliott also cites as evidence of growing European universalism a principle that he found in the work of the theologian Francisco de Vitoria, who observed that the Indians' display of rationality had shown them to be "citizens of the whole world, which in a certain way constitutes a single republic." Explorers' records, too, indicate a certain curiosity about and tolerance for the new peoples they discovered. Europe was neither the simple vehicle of enlightened civilization nor the bearer of monolithic imperialism to the rest of the world. We might do well to notice the evidence of openness within the vigorous expansion that is overlooked in generally heated postcolonialist debates.

Needy, Materialist Europe?

Opposed to this view of Europe, however, is a hard ideological stance that virtually identifies Europe with several burgeoning modern pathologies. The well-known portrait of late-medieval cruelty and suffering in Johan Huizinga's *The Waning of the Middle Ages* is often combined with Marxist, neo-Marxist, feminist, and radical environmentalist critiques of capitalist culture to produce a vivid picture of a morbid and rapacious European continent. Europe's relatively poor soil, limited landmass, and consequent famines supposedly drove its peoples into terrifying exploits. Kirkpatrick Sale, for example, turns celebrated historian Ferdinand Braudel's analyses of European economic woes and ambitions into an entire historiography. Sale sees a uniquely needy Europe pillaging other wealthy, abundant, sedentary civilizations. Quoting Braudel, he

---

[198] J. H. Elliott, "A World United," in Levenson, *Circa 1492*, 650.

argues that "although other maritime cultures might have tried to compete on the seas, only Europe—mark the verb—'needed' the rest of the world, needed to venture outside its own front door."[199]

It takes only a moment's reflection to realize that his characterization of an entire continent is absurd. Many human "needs" stem from the indefinable combination of fantasy, enlightenment, enterprise, and curiosity that are inextricably part of human persons. Only a very few needs, such as shortages leading to starvation, can be measured in absolute terms. Famines have occurred in all parts of the world, and Europe is hardly unique in needing to remedy them. From what we know of tribal pressures and displacements among Eastern Woodland Indian tribes and Mesoamerican empires, Native Americans, too, were no strangers to that sort of "need" and conquest, nor were other indigenous peoples. What was unique about Europe, perhaps, was the belief that relatively long-distance, large-scale undertakings, necessitated by Europe's position as a rocky outcrop of coastline on the Asian landmass, were worth the effort.

Furthermore, those needs Europe did have for foreign goods did not quite result in the desperate quest that Sale's interpretation of Braudel suggests. Nowhere do the medieval and Renaissance courts of Europe give the impression of a feverish search for sustenance in wealth or goods. Portugal and Spain, the two principal exploring nations at the start of the period, are quite measured in their decisions about what they will and will not undertake. The Portuguese voyages down the coast of Africa seem to be a sign of a swelling enthusiasm nurtured by Prince Henry the Navigator, but no mad rush for resources to save a sinking continent. Columbus's own experience with his patrons—their doubts about his "enterprise of the Indies," their long delays and deliberations, and their meager assignment of only three ships to such a task—indicates

---

[199] Sale, *Conquest of Paradise*, 58.

the Spanish crown's solid but circumspect interest in potential trade (by comparison, the ill-fated Spanish Armada, only a few decades later, consisted of 130 ships). Columbus personally, as we discussed in chapter 2, was a unique blend of personal ambition and religious millenarism; thus his restlessness, and the energy of the whole European continent, cannot simply be attributed to strict physical need.

Energetic Societies

Careful scholarship paints a far different picture of the sixteenth-century culture that was about to reshape the world. George Holmes, editor of the *Oxford Illustrated History of Medieval Europe*, remarks in the conclusion of that volume that

> late Medieval Europe was certainly not a poor society. On the contrary we find evidence everywhere of high levels of income, greater sophistication in domestic comfort and artistic taste, and great vigour in both the economic and aesthetic spheres. Paradoxically it was a Europe reduced in population by the plagues but bursting with energetic life which began the conquest of the non-European world with the explorations of Vasco da Gama and Christopher Columbus.[200]

This is a far cry from the gloomy and frantic picture of a despairing 1492 Europe painted by the most radical revisionist critics.

The historian of late-medieval and Renaissance Europe John R. Hale has argued that Europe's lead in exploration arose not from weakness but from strength, cultural as well as material:

---

[200] George Holmes, ed., *Oxford Illustrated History of Medieval Europe* (New York: Oxford University Press, 1990), 354.

Columbus and the Crisis of the West

In spite of privileges exercised by kings, feudal lords, priests and guilds, the individual's freedom of action was less circumscribed than in caste-divided India, or in family-centered China, or under the priest-kings of Central and South America. Moreover, in spite of plagues and local famines, the standard of living in Europe was higher than elsewhere. Revolutions are the work not of the cowed and starving, but of those who have enough to want more: Renaissance Europe, having recovered from the ravages of the terrible Black Death plague of the 14th Century, was sufficiently comfortably off to want to become rich.[201]

These factors, combined with some of the dynamic this-worldly elements in Christianity, says Hale, are what prodded Europe to do what no other high civilization of the time attempted. Confidence, not need or desperation, in part explains European exploration, which brought to the rest of the world more than mere reckless flailing.

A certain worldly restlessness and sense of superiority showed itself in the Europe of this period. But neither of these characteristics is purely a fault. Hale points to the "almost senile complacency" of China at the time, whose earlier exploration in the Indian Ocean was hardly even exploration. The Chinese loaded seventeen thousand soldiers and great displays of wealth onto large fleets and expected that the inferior peoples, seeing these manifestations of Chinese culture and power, would simply desire to join themselves to the Celestial Empire. Facing this flotilla, heads of state understandably agreed to go to China and do homage to the emperor. Whatever faults Christian Europe manifested in its explorations of the world, it showed more humility than that. Europeans at least believed that they had to exert themselves to gain new resources

---

[201] John R. Hale, *Age of Exploration* (New York: Time, 1967), 16–17.

and win over converts to their ways. Compared with the Chinese sense of superiority, European self-assertion was almost modest.

Most critics of Eurocentrism have failed to notice another crucial fact. Unlike cultures as diverse as the Aztecs in Tenochtitlán and the Imperial Court in Peking, Europe in the Age of Exploration did not consider itself the center of the world. On European maps of the time, *Jerusalem* is both the spiritual and geographic center of the earth—a graphic reminder of what principles dominated even European conceptions of the globe: religious principles, not nationalist or economic ones.

Ultimately, how we judge Europe's energy since 1492 depends on whether we think certain human developments over the last five hundred years were or were not good. Machiavelli, for example, saw in the tensions and conflicts among Italian city-states the very well-springs of political vitality in early-sixteenth-century Italy.[202] These oppositions were to a great extent mirrored in complex European currents that help explain both that continent's turmoil and its vitality.

The Rigors of Modernity

Another major critique of Renaissance Europe charges that its complexity demonstrates a fragmentation caused by growing capitalism and materialism. Kirkpatrick Sale goes so far as to observe that "not for nothing is this the age that invents polyphony and counterpoint in music and double-entry bookkeeping in commerce, that knew such a babel of vernacular languages that Leonardo da Vinci at the time feared 'the generation of man will come to pass as not to understand each other's speech.'"[203]

---

[202] Peter Denley, "The Mediterranean in the Age of the Renaissance," in Holmes, *Oxford Illustrated History*, 243.

[203] Sale, *Conquest of Paradise*, 37.

Columbus and the Crisis of the West

Paradoxically, though, the same writer criticizes Spain—and the other budding nation-states—for incipient centralization of power and notes the sinister implications of Elio Antonio de Nebrija's compilation of the first Spanish grammar. When questioned by Queen Isabella about what use such a book might have, de Nebrija reportedly answered, "Language has always been the companion of Empire."[204] For some critics, then, Europe was both falling apart in dangerous fashion and consolidating power in dangerous fashion. But whether it was coming to speak too many languages or too few, it was embarking on a mission that would transmit all future evils to the rest of the world.

Just one indication of how simple-minded such assertions are may be glimpsed in the use Native Americans made of Spanish in the New World. Sam Gill, a brilliant student of Native American religion, remarks:

> During the seventeenth century, Spanish had become well established as a second language, providing a lingua franca among the many native peoples whose languages were unintelligible to one another; yet they retained their own languages and even made efforts to keep them free of Spanish words. Spanish became an instrument used by the Pueblo peoples against Spanish intrusions, in that it permitted them to better communicate among themselves. It helped support the growing sense of unity and common identity that replaced the antagonisms that existed prior to Spanish contact.[205]

This linguistic phenomenon reflects, perhaps better than anything else, the condition that Europe had uniquely experienced within

---

[204] Ibid., 18.
[205] Sam Gill, *Native American Religions: An Introduction* (Belmont, Cal.: Wadsworth, 1982), 22.

itself and was to bequeath, despite atrocities and imperialism, to the rest of the world: a new dynamic of particularity within unity.

A Beginning of a Reckoning

It is inevitable that the most influential culture in the past half millennium should receive the brunt of the blame for the world's evils. Oddly, however, it receives none of the credit for the good. The complexity of European society makes simple attribution of one trait to it without other contradictory or counterbalancing traits next to impossible. Papal power, for example, carried with it certain negative traits. But in Renaissance Europe, as in formerly communist modern Eastern Europe, a universal moral and spiritual authority was sometimes useful against political powers, whatever problems of its own it may have generated.[206] As we saw in the previous chapter, independent moral authority played no small role in taming—or at least trying to tame—the worst abuses in Spanish America.

Of course, the radical critique of the Europe of the last five hundred years contains many important truths. It often recapitulates the old European philosophical debate between the ancients and the moderns. To oversimplify somewhat, the ancients (including Jews and Christians) believed in a cosmos created and ordered by a divine principle that made it possible to identify correct personal and social modes of behavior. The Ten Commandments, the Christian appropriation of Aristotle, and the Stoic tradition of the virtues, among many other manifestations of Western thought, show a common belief in the order and limits of nature. The Enlightenment, scientific revolution, Industrial Revolution, modernism, and postmodernism all, to one degree or another, abandon that view

---

[206] Holmes, *Oxford Illustrated History*, 352.

for a more rationalist position that human intelligence can and should put nature "on the rack" to "relieve man's estate," in Francis Bacon's famous phrase.[207] The success of science—and the crisis in values attending that success—is the warp and woof of much current philosophical inquiry.

Today, while we generally feel that our scientific and techno-logical capacity is an advantage in many matters, we worry in-creasingly about the environmental damage and human aridity that seem to be unfortunate by-products of our material success. Anxiety about our own state makes us susceptible to claims about premodern societies, particularly little-known, non-Western ones. Few people would wish to return to medieval European society, a telling reluctance. For there is a vast price to pay for jettisoning the moderns wholesale. Though we may desire to minimize the ef-fects of industry on the environment and even to resacralize nature and culture, there is no simple return for us to premodern religious and philosophical traditions—whether from Europe or from non-Western cultures whose entire conceptual framework would quickly lead to the abandonment of modern modes of agriculture and the death by starvation of hundreds of millions of people.

Turning our backs on all of the modern tradition would also in-volve intellectual regressions. Many people blame medieval Europe or Puritan New England for the persecution of witches, for example, but witches were a common fear among Eastern Woodland and other Indian cultures as well. The Senecas believed in a kind of Manichaeism in which a good creator brother and a bad destroyer brother fight over the world. The False Face societies encountered by the early North American settlers performed "all sorts of acts on the model of the Bad Spirit ... in order to cure disease, fight

[207] Francis Bacon, *The Advancement of Learning*, vol. 1 of *Francis Bacon*, ed. Arthur Johnston (New York: Schocken, 1965), 44.

witchcraft, and remove disorder."[208] Unfortunately, our attraction to some Native American concepts of order and harmony does not allow us to select them at will from less congenial beliefs—such as the belief in witches. Native cultures were all of one piece. At this late date, we can hardly accept fighting disease and other evils with magic.

European Intellectual Contributions

Interesting questions arise from the debate that has erupted over the use of the term "discovery" to describe what happened in 1492. Native peoples, argue those who object to the term, already knew who and where they were and did not need to be "discovered." While this is true in a sense, it is also false in crucial respects. The Mexican historian Edmundo O'Gorman has shown that, for Europeans, America was not discovered but invented.[209] The ancient and medieval European conception of a single landmass encompassing Europe, Asia, and Africa had to give way to the empirical evidence provided by the voyages of exploration before the idea of America could come into being. Until then, probably sometime after Columbus's death in 1506, Europe was only adding data to its existing structure of beliefs about the world, not undergoing a revolution in geographical, philosophical, and even theological thought.

And across the Atlantic, Native American thought also had to undergo a revolution before being able to understand the true place of America in the world. Indians did *not* know who and where they were in important ways because they knew "the other" even less than did late-medieval Europeans. This is reflected in the difficulties we still have in naming the peoples inhabiting the New

[208] Gill, *Native American Religions*, 22.
[209] Edmundo O'Gorman, *Invention of America*.

Columbus and the Crisis of the West

World in Columbus's time and their modern descendants. For most purposes, "Native Americans" seems to have displaced "Indians" as a socially accepted term. "Indians" was the name Columbus gave to the peoples he thought were in the Indies. Columbus never knew that he had discovered America, nor was he to his dying day sure exactly what he had found on his voyages.

Terminology, as Native American leaders have emphasized, is not neutral in sorting out historical issues. But the questions are more complex than those leaders usually admit. "Native American," too, is a less-than-perfect, even misleading term, and not only because it invites confusion with all other people born and raised in the United States. America was named after Columbus's contemporary, the Florentine Amerigo Vespucci, and "Native American" suggests that the various peoples in these lands were all part of one easily identifiable cultural or racial entity defined in European terms. For the indigenous peoples themselves had no term for this diverse group and were not even aware of themselves and their land as constituting two of the continents of the world. That realization came much later and only because of the European presence.

While it is probably fair to deny that Columbus "discovered" America, it would be unfair to ignore the fact that he did something more far-reaching. He may not have proved the world was round for Europeans, but he did for Native Americans. And in so doing, he inaugurated the age in which, finally, all the world's people inhabited one world *and knew they inhabited it*, though that realization was slow to be accepted in many newly discovered lands. Europe does not have the right to define the history of non-European peoples, but—by virtue of its geographical and intellectual contributions—European thought necessarily became the framework within which even non-European histories would henceforth have to be worked out. Moreover, given Europe's pluralism—its distinctive multiplicity within a kind of unity that was, after a long struggle, to lead to recognition of universal rights and their embodiment in law—the multiculturalist effort to destroy Eurocentric thought is doomed at the outset. The wish to contest an allegedly monolithic European view of history with fresh voices and perspectives inescapably belongs to a very European mode of thought.

A Concluding Parable

Let us conclude with a parable:

In 1638, the French explorer and interpreter Jean Nicollet believed he might have finally discovered the water route to Cathay. Nicollet had "gone native," living for many years among the Algonquians of Allumette Island and the Nipissings and becoming conversant with their cultures and languages. He returned to the French settlement at Three Rivers on the Saint Lawrence because he remained a convinced Catholic and apparently did not wish to live without the sacraments.[210] A better early exponent of multiculturalism would be hard to come by in North America.

The Nipissings circulated stories that hairless people from far away were trading beyond the Great Lakes to the west. Since the time of Marco Polo, such anecdotes suggested to Europeans Chinese or Japanese dignitaries. Nicollet set out to find these people, having taken care to bring with him an embroidered robe of Chinese damask. When he landed on the western shore of Lake Michigan, he put on the robe and, holding a pistol in each hand, cut quite a figure as he marched into the village of Winnebago Indians at what is now Green Bay, Wisconsin. After three days of exploring, he

---

[210] This entire anecdote may be found in Francis Parkman, *La Salle and the Discovery of the Great West*, in vol. 1 of *Parkman: France and England in North America*, 725–726.

was sure from native accounts that only three days distant was the "great water" to Cathay. The Indians meant the Mississippi River.

Critics, of whatever stripe, who seek some transcendent deliverance from the evils of Western civilization in the American wilderness resemble Nicollet. However much they know about Native American and Western cultures (usually little, and probably far less than Nicollet), their quest is driven primarily by deep currents within the now-global culture inspired by Europe. The quest is not wholly misguided. After all, Cathay exists, as do solutions to many current Western problems. But to solve the problems, as to reach Cathay, requires true knowledge and a broader perspective than that provided by the most typical current critics. The Celestial Kingdom was not, and is not, to be discovered in the pre-Columbus Americas or anywhere on our troubled planet.

5

Events, Counter-Events, Non-Events

We understand the official celebration of the quincentenary (and its commercial variants) as an imperial liturgy not only retelling lies of the past, but building a consensus for more of the same, a two-tiered system of global and domestic economic apartheid.

—1992/Kairos USA[211]

The five hundredth anniversary of Columbus's first voyage evoked many radical statements that revealed a growing belief that the entirety of Western history—its very economics, politics, and culture, not just its darker sides—was steeped in injustice and repression so foul that it needed to be repudiated and replaced from the ground up. And in the particular instance quoted above—and not only there—the wholesale rejection came from a quarter nominally both Western and Christian. This, it is clear, represents a departure from the old Christian belief that all are sinners, that prudent steps are necessary in public affairs to keep legitimate aspirations for justice from turning into injustices, and—perhaps most significant of

[211] 1992/Kairos USA describes itself as "a partnership movement of local and national groups and churches" whose contact person is at the National Council of Churches headquarters, 475 Riverside Drive, New York, New York. The statement was reprinted in *Sojourners* 20, no. 8 (October 1991): 27.

all—that it is only on the basis of Western and largely Christian values that such claims have any foundation. The great John Henry Newman, writing in 1825 as the British were growing into one of the dominant world powers, wrote, "The Christian world, so called, what is it practically, but a witness for Satan rather than a witness for Christ?"[212] But his plea was for a Christianity and the civilization to which it had given rise to become what it should be, not to destroy itself on the basis of a radical and senseless misapplication of its own best principles.[213]

Radical Critiques

On 12 October 1992, along the coast of the island of San Salvador, the best guess as to where Columbus made first landfall in the Americas, the sun rose on a strange ceremony. A group of ecologists conducted a funeral service for "the natural environment of the Western Hemisphere" and mourned the destruction of native peoples and species that has occurred since 1492. While this event probably reached a high-water mark for New Age emotionalism over the quincentenary, it is by no means uncharacteristic of the kinds of public events that marked 1992—and have grown in scope and ambition ever since. Facts such as the continued existence and appreciation of native peoples in North and South America despite mistreatment and the immense fruitfulness and healthiness of "the natural environment of the Western Hemisphere" seem to count for nothing in such blindly ideological events.

[212] John Henry Newman, *Parochial and Plain Sermons*, I, 10, "Profession without Practice" (San Francisco: Ignatius Press, 1987), 88.

[213] It could be argued that the provision in the U.S. Constitution (1787) that would allow laws against slavery after 1808 and the British Slave Trade Act of 1807 are the kind of reforms that, in every age, a civilization not bent on mere suicide will seek to carry out.

In fact, far from being an eccentric countercultural act, the proposed funeral service received sympathetic treatment and advance publicity in one of the central documents issued by the U.S. government's Smithsonian Institution in anticipation of the Columbus commemorations.[214] In the United States, a radical environmentalism drove no small part of the large-scale negative reactions to the quincentenary. But the plight of surviving Native Americans and residual racial prejudice, especially against African Americans, has increasingly become part of the mix.

Prior to the quincentenary, Winona LaDuke, a well-known Native American and feminist activist who spoke frequently on college campuses, explained the "intersectionality," as it would come to be called a few decades later, of environmental and racial injustices:

> The ecological agenda is what many indigenous people believe can, and must, unite all peoples in 1992. That agenda calls for everyone to take aggressive action to stop the destruction of the Earth, essentially to end the biological, technological, and ecological invasion/conquest that began with Columbus's ill-fated voyage 500 years ago.[215]

In 1992, this seemed an extreme view to many people, but such apocalyptic views did not remain confined to a small and embattled minority. Even then they formed part of mainstream American institutions and have become even more common since.

---

[214] Cited in Steven King and Liliana Campos Dudley, "Nature's Future," in *Seeds of Change: Five Hundred Years Since Columbus*, ed. Herman J. Viola and Carolyn Margolis (Washington: Smithsonian Institution Press, 1991).

[215] See Winona LaDuke, "We Are Still Here," *Sojourners* 20, no. 8 (October 1991): 16.

Columbus and the Crisis of the West

Official Views

As we saw in chapter 1, the most extensive and sober government-sponsored events commemorating 1492 featured similar impulses. For example, the Smithsonian's primary quincentenary exhibition, *Seeds of Change*, which, for the most part, restricted itself to recording the human and environmental effects, good and bad, produced by the mixture of New and Old Worlds, also sounded an ominous warning. In the book accompanying the exhibit, Frank H. Talbot, the director of the National Museum of Natural History, expressed the hope that it will "encourage the urgently needed redefinition of our relationship with our world and its peoples."[216] It would be difficult to deny that, as the twenty-first century has developed, that redefinition has happened.

Herman J. Viola, coeditor of the book and director of the quincentenary programs at the museum, explained the vision behind the activities. Viola was a generally sound scholar (his book *After Columbus: The Smithsonian Chronicle of the North American Indians* is a useful guide to Native American history), but like many commentators, he tended to make extreme statements when he addressed broader issues. About the environment, for instance, he claims: "What had taken nature thousands of centuries to create was largely undone in less than five, beginning in September 1493, when the Admiral of the Ocean Sea returned to America at the head of an armada of seventeen ships."[217] Even those of us deeply concerned about environmental damage may hesitate to describe the past five hundred years as having "largely undone" nature. Though this may have been only a slip, it was a telling one about background assumptions from the director of such a prestigious public event.

[216] Viola and Margolis, *Seeds of Change*, 9.
[217] Ibid., 12.

The bulk of the exhibit was devoted to clear, well-documented explanations of changes around the world generated by Europe's first contacts with the Americas. Corn, tomatoes, potatoes, peppers, peanuts, yams, turkeys, and various other foods were indigenous to the Americas. Their introduction to Europe, Africa, and Asia altered eating patterns, politics, and culture. Corn provided additional calories for people and livestock in Africa, and both corn and potatoes helped Europe feed itself more easily. Potatoes grew well even in northern Europe's rocky soil and could be left in the fields until needed, enabling the northern nations to become stronger and challenge the traditionally dominant countries of southern Europe. The slowly improving diet of the European nations in general, it is believed, helped them become more populous and more assertive around the globe. In a paradoxical way, then, America's crops fed European expansion.

Similarly, introduction of European animals and plants reshaped the Americas. Wheat, apples, and grapes have certainly flourished here; pigs and horses, which had become extinct in the hemisphere after the last ice age, were reintroduced by the Europeans and changed the culture of the Plains Indians and other tribes for good. We now find it hard even to imagine the Plains Indians without the horses that they integrated so majestically into their traditional culture. Sugarcane brought to the Caribbean, unfortunately also brought with it Africans to work the fields there because they were resistant to European and African diseases, as the natives of the Caribbean were not. So sweeteners and slavery fed one another.

This information, and much more of sound historical value to all America's ethnic groups, was registered in the exhibit. (The taped guide with the English-accented voice the Smithsonian favors for august occasions, however, paid Hispanics little respect by its apparent belief that "con-kwist-a-dor" is the proper Spanish pronunciation of the term for Cortés and his men.) What was problematic about the show was the frame into which this picture was set—the introduction by Talbot and Viola, and the even more dubious concluding chapter by radical ecologists Steven King and Liliana Campos Dudley. The latter pair endorsed not only the San Salvador funeral service for nature but a wide spectrum of environmentalist political nostrums of doubtful credibility.

They all but canonized Chico Mendes, a Brazilian environmentalist murdered by Brazilian developers. Mendes may have been pursuing defensible aims and was brutally slain, but, as a member of the Brazilian Communist Party and a committed revolutionary (his son was named for the Sandinistas in Nicaragua and his daughter for a Brazilian terrorist), he carried other baggage along with him. Though these facts are well known, none is mentioned in the Smithsonian volume.[218] That the conclusion to a U.S. government–sponsored publication used such materials uncritically indicates just how pervasive the radical environmentalist agenda had become. Indeed, official America showed little inclination to celebrate "imperial" liturgies in memory of 1492, but quite the contrary, a stance that has grown only more prominent in the following decades.

The Art World and 1492

Indisputable facts at least anchor most natural history. The officially sponsored artistic displays, however, were not nearly as securely tied to historical reality. The other major government-supported exhibit, *Circa 1492: Art in the Age of Exploration*, which had a brief

---

[218] Kenneth Maxwell traced these connections in two long articles: "The Tragedy of the Amazon," *New York Review of Books*, 7 March 1991; and "The Mystery of Chico Mendes," *New York Review of Books*, 28 March 1991.

run in the fall of 1991 at Washington's National Gallery of Art, seemed allergic to aligning itself in any way with the historical facts surrounding Columbus. As the exhibit catalog took pains to emphasize, the show was "not about a man called Columbus....[but] about the extraordinary age in which he played a part."[219] *Circa 1492* simply assembled quite striking works from several cultures that were directly involved in the upheavals of 1492, or—in the case of Japan, China, and India—would have been involved, had Columbus arrived at his intended destination in Asia.

The problem with such an approach is its burial of the truly significant historical event that gives meaning to the exhibit beneath a falsely distorting and multiculturally neutral "Age of Exploration." And yet despite the enormous number of works he gathered together from different cultures, Jay A. Levenson, the managing curator and editor of the exhibit catalog, still feared sinning against the principle of equal representation:

> A survey that included, in acceptable depth, every significant culture that existed in the world of 1492 would be beyond the scope of any exhibition or catalogue. Difficult choices had to be made in each of the major sections of the show, and if a particular culture is not represented, that is likely to be because it is less central to the theme of that segment of the exhibition rather than because of any shortcomings in its artistic creations.

To mollify the excluded, Levenson poured out further multicultural libations:

> We have specifically tried to present each civilization on its own terms, not as it might have appeared to visiting

---

[219] Brown, foreword to Levenson, *Circa 1492*, 9.

Columbus and the Crisis of the West

Europeans of the period. Homogeneity was not a feature of the world of 1492, and under no circumstances could a single theme have done justice to the amazing variety that characterizes the cultures that are represented in the show.[220]

The intended lesson of raw celebration of "diversity," of course, was that we have much to learn from the multiple actors and mutual interchanges of that period, which was true. But it was false in its flight from recognizing as a simple historical fact that one particular culture—and one particular individual—was central to the very reason for remembering the date at all, and the many good things amid the many bad that flowed from that particular culture, Western civilization.

Unfortunately, to avoid privileging even this European perspective, the curator presented the lesson so indirectly that the entire exhibit illuminated neither art nor history. Instead, it vaunted hundreds of separate objects thought to illustrate a general social or political thesis. "Object" is the appropriate term here. Aztec ceremonial knives or Taíno throat ticklers used to induce vomiting in ritual purifications, for example, are not, strictly speaking, *objets d'art*. The historian Simon Schama wrote of this incoherent assemblage:

These problems of selection and scale are only symptoms of a deeper failure to understand what it means to historicize. Columbus's conspicuous banishment from the exhibition exemplifies the kind of approach that is willing to sacrifice the considerations of historical agency to a kind of milquetoast universalism. The mere presentation of contemporaneity, after all, explains nothing. Instead, the whole invidious, conflict-ridden mess of history disappears within the embrace of synchronicity. In the weightless historical space called *Circa*

[220] Levenson, *Circa 1492*, 19.

1492 no particular persons or powers actually bring about events. Indeed, there are no events; there are only phenomena hazily defined, formed and reformed and deformed with the shifting winds and tides of the zeitgeist, now medieval, now renaissance, now scientific-empirical-capitalist. [221]

This weightlessness and the refusal to allow any potentially controversial history to peek through the multicultural facade, Schama laments, characterizes "histories that are consciously designed as reparation."

Official Wariness

For the quincentenary, then, the two major public displays mounted by America's official cultural and historical institutions were far less an imperial liturgy and far more the kind of revision-cum-reparation favored by the critics of Columbus and his legacy. In fact, other than a brief remark during a Public Broadcasting Service (PBS) television special in which the mayor of Columbus, Ohio, ventured that the admiral symbolized all that was good and decent and honest about the United States, it would be difficult to find an official statement unambiguously praising Columbus in the entire country. This is a remarkable fact when you consider that without the Genoese navigator, there would have been no United States—and no global "universalism" with which to frame the previous half millennium.

In the late 1980s, the U.S. government did set up a Christopher Columbus Quincentenary Jubilee Committee that was to plan somewhat more traditional celebrations and events for 1992.

---

[221] Simon Schama, "They All Laughed at Christopher Columbus," *New Republic*, 6–13 January 1992, 33.

But the whole enterprise soon ran aground. John N. Goudie, a Cuban native and Miami real-estate broker appointed by Ronald Reagan to begin the preparations, became embroiled in shady financial dealings and eventually was questioned by the Congressional Subcommittee on Finances. Goudie contended that much of the two million dollars originally given to him (a small sum to be supplemented by private contributions) had been badly spent because of his ignorance of how the government works rather than through malfeasance. Nevertheless, he prudently invoked the Fifth Amendment thirty-two times during his congressional testimony.[222]

But even without the mishandling of funds, it is doubtful that Goudie would have promoted a general celebration of Columbus. Garry Wills interviewed him before the controversies and found him chary of using the term "discovery" and pliant to outside pressures: "Russell Means [an Ogala Lakota activist and leader of the American Indian Movement] complained about the word jubilee," Goudie said, "but I told him it is the Jewish word for a time of remembrance when one can redress wrongs."[223] Whether a jubilee under Goudie would have satisfied Means or other radical critics of Columbus became impossible to know. The financial mismanagement and Goudie's removal as the committee's head created such turmoil that the program was vastly reduced and weakly implemented.

On the more scholarly side of government activity, the Library of Congress, under the leadership of the distinguished historian James H. Billington, published a well-written and thoroughly researched guide, *Keys to the Encounter*.[224] Though the text strove to avoid what

---

[222] Bill McAllister, "Columbus Jubilee Panel Gets Few Answers," *Washington Post*, 22 November 1991, A23.

[223] Wills, "Goodbye, Columbus," 6.

[224] Louis De Vorsey Jr., *Keys to the Encounter: A Library of Congress Resource Guide for the Study of the Age of Discovery* (Washington: Library of Congress, 1991).

its author, Louis De Vorsey Jr., eccentrically calls a "Europocentric" view, it effectively points curious readers toward solid historical investigation and the wealth of source materials available at the Library of Congress. As Billington rightly emphasized, encounters between civilizations cannot be understood without encounters between researchers and sources: "The knowledge therein can only be mined when someone actively seeks it out."[225] This otherwise obvious truism was worth repeating when so much about 1492 and after had come to be assumed.

The Organization of American States (OAS), the heirs of the Spanish and indigenous civilizations that created the New World, also planned some quincentenary activities, but of a very cautious and low-key nature. For the most part, the OAS was content to record the events and controversies within various member states. But such direction as the organization's efforts took may be gauged from a summary remark made by James Kiernan, the head of the OAS quincentenary programs: "Columbus sailed to find the Indies and started a process that was more catastrophic than the separation of the continents in the Pleistocene age."[226] Clearly, the OAS had no intention of sponsoring any forthright celebrations of Columbus and was ready to regard the history of its own nations as cosmic evil.

Television Histories

One of the few serious public attempts to analyze the Columbus history emerged from a collaboration between PBS and the National Endowment for the Humanities (NEH). Previous projects jointly

[225] Ibid., vii.
[226] In a television debate with the author, C-Span II, *Close Up America*, 5 July 1991.

undertaken by these two semi-independent government agencies did not always have happy results. NEH had funded some wildly propagandistic leftist specials during the 1980s. *The Africans*, for example, drew particular ire for its one-sided history, and not only from conservatives. But the PBS-NEH *In Search of Columbus* arrived at a fairly straightforward presentation of its material, which was skewed only slightly to avoid overly controversial topics and to make some ritualistic bows to several contemporary constituencies.

Perhaps the main reason for the project's overall success was the choice of Mauricio Obregón, a longtime Columbus scholar and collaborator with Samuel Eliot Morison, as the principal researcher and narrator. Obregón was too serious a historian and too forceful a personality to have any simple readings of Columbus thrust upon him. He lucidly described Europe in the fifteenth century and Europe's relations with other civilizations. If the seven-hour series tacitly settles many questions about Columbus that might be regarded among scholars of the period as forever beyond our knowing—an occupational hazard for all television histories—the argument at least never contradicted the evidence. Obregón's sheer enthusiasm for the subject and his meticulous research carried the storyline into interesting shoals and estuaries that more partisan approaches overlook.

Obregón traced, for example, the importance of trade for Islam, both as an economic activity and as a vehicle for Muslim evangelization. Mohammed himself, he reminded viewers, was a trader. Viewed against this Islamic background, Europe's search for new markets and new converts does not appear as unusually sinister in the world or as much a precursor of a rapacious "capitalism" as some critics believed then, and still do. We also get a glimpse into the psychology of trade in the period. Like Columbus, the Muslim traders were very secretive about their sources of supply. Information of this sort was worth a great deal of money. The Muslims were crafty enough, for instance, to keep secret the locations of the only two islands on earth where cloves could be found — cloves being worth their weight in silver at the time.

Obregón also toured other civilizations of the late fifteenth century. China, after a brief burst of exploration to determine if any serious enemies might attack from the sea, decided the answer was no — and settled into a self-satisfied isolation. Japan, one of Columbus's intended destinations, was so wealthy and sophisticated that a shogun around the time of Columbus's first voyage was able to build a temple decorated completely with gold leaf, the famous Golden Temple of Kyoto. African kingdoms that the Europeans contacted also came into sharper focus. Before the arrival of the Europeans, the Ashanti in West Africa had already created extensive gold mines and were trading in slaves from the interior without moral scruple. (Approximately eighteen million Africans were sold into slavery by other Africans, primarily to Islamic nations and other places bordering the Indian Ocean. Another huge number, about nine million, made up the Atlantic slave trade.)[227] Both these factors influenced European attitudes toward native peoples and the Africans themselves in the coming decades: wealth could be gotten from these contacts without too much delicacy about the human means used to extract it — at least for unscrupulous men.

In sum, the series accurately reflected the qualities — positive, negative, and ambiguous — of the world's various civilizations in 1492. In his treatment of Columbus *per se*, however, Obregón sometimes equivocates. He brings to the story many fine touches and beautiful photography, but like many other more-or-less-official commentators, he avoids facing the toughest issues head-on. The

---

[227] *Encyclopedia Britannica Guide to Black History*, https://web.archive.org/web/20070223090720/http://www.britannica.com/blackhistory/article-24156.

failed settlement at La Navidad and Columbus's poor governance of rebellious natives and Spaniards, as well as his loyalty and continuing kindness to Guacanagarí, are quickly passed over. The viewer is left somewhat confused, therefore, when Obregón tells him in the final segment that Columbus "failed miserably as a governor"—which was true. As a result, the encounter's potential for good and the roots of very definite evils were left obscured by what can only be called squeamishness about provoking controversy.

Also, Obregón often permitted a multicultural din to drown out important observations. He is clear, for example, that the diseases introduced into the New World produced "perhaps the greatest human disaster of all time, it is one that no one—not even Christopher Columbus—can be faulted for." Yet many people who have not made the slightest effort to know the truth assume that the succumbing to disease of millions of indigenous—as people have in every historical period—is somehow the West's or Columbus's fault, even somehow a deliberate genocide. On the subject of well-known Spanish atrocities, Obregón draws together some useful judgments. He speaks of the "long and distinguished history of sword and cross being opposed" (i.e., Christians often, if ineffectively, opposed brutal conquest by other Christians). And he had the eminent historian of the Spanish Empire J. H. Elliott explain how remarkable it was in history that the Spanish were "the first to denounce atrocities by their own compatriots." He also gives the Spanish New Laws of 1542, which outlawed slavery and limited the *encomienda*, their proper due.

The force of all this is diminished by other voices, which generally came from indigenous and African American protesters. And while the opinions of these spokesmen were certainly understandable, they were not always firmly grounded in history or even very widely held by the people the leaders claim to speak for. Surveys taken of native populations in Latin America have shown a more mixed picture. Large majorities of Indians are grateful for the arrival of Christianity and European culture, though there is also some regret over what was lost from their indigenous cultures. The situation in Latin America, of course, differs from that in the United States, where tribes were almost obliterated by disease and violence. In Latin America, the indigenous peoples melded somewhat with Spaniards, and the series showed quite well how, in culture, religion, and racial features, a country like Mexico truly became a new nation, fusing new and old.

A large question was not answered in the series—and still remains decades later: Why should Columbus, a man who was primarily an explorer with little interest in conquest and mayhem, take the blame for what Spaniards and English colonists, of a very different disposition, did decades and centuries after he had passed from this world? And why is the subsequent history of the New World, with its problems, but also with its growing embodiment of equality, liberty, and prosperity for all—along with its openness to self-criticism about the past and the present—also not to be classified as part of the legacy?

The dissenting voices were generously allowed to accumulate in the series final episode, which weighed the overall merits and defects of the encounter. Only after those protests were heard did Obregón himself step forward and announce what was certainly a courageous position under the circumstances. He concluded that, taking into account the overall record, we should not only remember or commemorate Columbus but should *celebrate* the man who boldly inaugurated the new age in human history.

The Buried Mirror

The Buried Mirror: Reflections on Spain and the New World, a Discovery Channel television series sponsored by the Smithsonian

Columbus and the Crisis of the West

Institution and the Spanish Quinto Centenario España Foundation, also took a basically evenhanded approach to the history of the Americas. Hosted by Mexican novelist Carlos Fuentes, it provided a remarkably balanced account of how two civilizations coalesced into one new civilization across vast religious, cultural, and material divides. Fuentes, who made a career of denouncing U.S. imperialism while being lavishly supported as a visiting scholar at various U.S. universities, nevertheless managed in this instance to tell us of the good and the bad on all sides.

Like his fellow Mexican Octavio Paz, mentioned in the previous chapter, Fuentes admires native cultures but does not indulge in nonhistorical idealizations. The fabulous remains of high civilizations in the Americas impressed him with their serenity and sheer scale. For him, such achievements exist on a plane comparable to that of ancient Mesopotamia or Egypt. While most of these Mesoamerican civilizations disappeared or regressed long before Columbus, Fuentes makes the unusual observation that their collective history—the "buried mirror," like the mirrors found beneath the earth at some Mayan archaeological sites—help us to see some of our own features.

European and native civilizations present both parallels and contrasts. Spain hacked an empire out of the Americas with gunpowder and the sword, but the Aztecs and Incas had also created empires, with the weapons available to them. The Aztecs used "tyranny, tribute, fear, and *la guerra florida* [the flowery war]" to gain the endless supply of prisoners they needed for human sacrifice. Fuentes went so far as to characterize the Aztec gods as "a whole pantheon of fear," spiritual forces to be appeased or employed to combat threats posed by nature.

The difference between Moctezuma and Cortés is that the former was ruled by fate, the latter by will. Perfectly illustrating Machiavelli's conception of *virtú*, Cortés was able to make use of good fortune in his conquests. By contrast, Moctezuma was virtually helpless in the face of the strange new onslaught. For Fuentes, the conquistador's child by his interpreter and mistress, La Malinche—a child who was the first known mestizo on the mainland and therefore the first Mexican—symbolized the beginning of a truly new civilization. After that birth, fate and will, resignation and vigorous action would be interwoven in the fabric of Mexican culture.

In the Spanish conquest of the Incas in Peru, Fuentes discerns a similar process at work amid that region's notoriously dirty politics and strife. By taking advantage of a civil war then going on between the sons of a recently dead Incan emperor, the unscrupulous adventurer Pizarro was able to conquer and impose his rule with only 180 Spanish soldiers. The Incan emperor was considered a god, the descendant of the sun. When that god was killed by Spaniards, the stage was set for a new empire to rise on the foundations of the old.

Fuentes returns often to Spain's unusual and constant examination of the moral questions connected with the conflict. Though he recognized that this did not prevent the worst atrocities, he rightly pointed out that similar scruples never troubled the minds of other colonizing nations. About Christianity in particular, he makes a remarkable observation: missionaries believed they had the religious obligation and right to convert Indians, he says, and a majority of them accepted the *encomienda* and other Spanish coercions as prerequisites to proper evangelization. Nevertheless, he notes an epochal shift in native cultures owing to Christian influence:

> One can only imagine the astonishment of the hundreds and thousands of Indians who asked for baptism as they came to realize that they were being asked to adore a god who sacrificed himself for men instead of asking men to sacrifice themselves to gods, as the Aztec religion demanded.

Columbus and the Crisis of the West

Such positive developments are often overlooked out of defer-
ence and sensitivity toward surviving Indian communities. Fuentes
himself, in spite of the overall fairness he brought to the material,
glossed over another problem. Showing Indians who currently
practice a syncretism of Christianity and worship of old indigenous
gods, as many continue to do, he repeats the often-enunciated plea
that Indians are asking us only to "respect their values." It is, of
course, a good thing to respect one another's values when those
values are worth respecting, but such pieties run up against some
hard facts. We certainly cannot respect ancient Indian ways in
their entirety because, like European cultures, they contained some
horrible things. And even existing practices may give us pause.

People who point to Indian values as a remedy for our evil
exploitation of the natural world are often squeamish about in-
humane treatment of animals. How many of them, then, would
feel comfortable watching the Indian rite — filmed by Fuentes's
crew — of cutting the throats of young animals and sprinkling
the blood libation collected in basins on the lintels of mines and
houses? Here, as elsewhere, "respecters" of native cultures choose
to emphasize the nicer elements from them that already have some
standing in the mainstream Western culture.

Fuentes was guilty of worse lapses. After masterfully explaining
some stone carvings and statues from Aztec times, he commits the
error of aestheticizing them. Depictions of horrifying deities and
terrible events, he says, no longer have religious meaning for us,
and therefore we can regard them as striking art objects. This approach may calm the consciences of people who like Aztec "art"
but who do not wish to take the trouble to learn about the ancient
cultures. It draws on the modern Western aesthetic fascination with
the primitive. But for anyone who thinks art has an intimate and
dynamic connection to life, ignoring the conceptual dimension of
Aztec "art" is tantamount to ignoring the Napoleonic invasion of

Spain when we look at Goya's *Desastres de la guerra* or forgetting Hitler's Luftwaffe when we see Picasso's *Guernica*. Fuentes himself was quick to mention the social contexts when he later commented on the two European works. The different approach to native objects not only willfully diminishes them as human creations but falsifies the nature of the works themselves.

Despite these lapses, however, Fuentes created an informative, affectionate, and well-proportioned survey of American and European history and future prospects. Anyone who would see in the serious work of the longtime leftist Fuentes, or in that of the Columbus scholar Mauricio Obregón, nothing but "imperial liturgies" must contemplate history through very thick ideological lenses indeed.

Lighter Fare

The only other major government-sanctioned public acknowledgment of the quincentenary was a special issue of *Newsweek* produced in conjunction with the Smithsonian's *Seeds of Change* exhibit. Probably because the journalists who did most of the writing are not very inclined to accept romantic pieties from any quarter, the overall outline of events in those pages is extremely well balanced, despite its popular nature.

The issue concluded with Raymond Sokolov, a former food critic for the *New York Times*, asking us to celebrate the culinary consequences of 1492. Putting aside the cultural anxiety over the quincentenary, Sokolov noted that all of us—Europeans and Asians, Africans and Native Americans—eat far better today because the globe has been united. Western technology has exponentially increased the availability of food, more than enough to feed our now huge global population. And then there is the variety. The Chinese have made good use of hot peppers and peanuts; Europeans have grown fond of them, too, along with tomatoes, corn, and potatoes; and Native Americans now enjoy chicken, pork, beef, wheat, and various delicacies. In his book on the subject, Sokolov decided to observe a "Kirkpatrick Sale Day" by experimenting with pre-1492 menus of both Europe and the Americas—unappetizing concoctions like dry bread crusts and pond-scum cheeses—and demonstrated how much better it is today to savor the "progressive dinner in which the whole human race takes part but no one need leave home to sample all the courses."[228]

In *Newsweek*, he suggested that we stop criticizing Columbus: "He is only a convenient scapegoat for our own self-hate and our own very modern doubts about the value of our culture. We and Columbus may have a lot to apologize for, but we also deserve plenty of credit."[229]

Oddly, *Newsweek*'s special issue conveyed information much more effectively than did the contemporaneous *National Geographic*'s *1491: America before Columbus*. While the articles in this special supplement showed aspects of life in North America before the arrival of the Europeans, they focused on only a small portion of that life. Clearly, a few pages could not do justice to the hundreds of American Indian tribes, but the inadequacies are more fundamental than that. What is covered is reduced to *National Geographic*'s usual categories of the visually beautiful and the alluringly exotic; missing is the grit and richness of human reality.

The issue tells us that Native Americans had vivid creation myths that gave life meaning; they lived closer to nature than we do on both land and sea (some were politically incorrect and hunted

---

[228] Raymond Sokolov, *Why We Eat What We Eat* (New York: Summit Books, 1992), 15–16.
[229] Raymond Sokolov, "Stop Knocking Columbus,'" *Newsweek*, special issue, Fall/Winter 1991, 82.

whales and clubbed seals in the Pacific Northwest); and they were somehow in better balance with their surroundings than we are. But nowhere do we get a picture of what such societies truly were: human communities where tragedy and difficult choices, good and evil and the terrors of death had to be faced and explained. These portraits bear about as much resemblance to their subjects as a *Reader's Digest* story bears to contemporary American life.

In addition to intoning the usual pieties, some of the Native American sentiments expressed in the magazine yearned for historical impossibilities. One woman interviewed in the *National Geographic* spread, for example, lamented the loss of her tribe's traditional songs and rituals, as would anyone living with a reduced cultural heritage. But she goes on to register the tragic contradictions of neolithic cultures in tension with modern life: "I am a Christian; I am not sorry the missionaries came. But I wish they had known how to let their news change peoples' lives from the inside, without imposing their culture over our ways."[230] But to be a Christian means precisely that some "ways" are changed, both in attitude and practice, forever. Tragic or not, this is certainly unavoidable.

Religion and Culture

The quandaries of religion and culture were profoundly coupled with serious historical material in the 1991 Canadian film *Black Robe*. *Black Robe* tells the absorbing story of Father Laforgue, an early-seventeenth-century Jesuit missionary to the Hurons who makes a fifteen-hundred-mile canoe trip up Canada's Saint Lawrence River. Exciting and frightening opportunities presented themselves to red and white alike in those early contacts. For the most

---

[230] *National Geographic* 180, no. 4 (October 1991): 53.

part, however, these opportunities failed to come to full fruition because of disease, misunderstanding, and profound cultural differences. (We appreciate the difference guns made in native life, but we underestimate, for instance, the importance of even steel knives and hatchets to peoples previously without metals. Natives eagerly traded with the Europeans for them and for woven cloth to replace their animal-skin garments.) The sheer struggle to survive natural and human predators in a harsh environment discouraged all parties from following anything but the most proven ways.

Religion in particular offered a chance for mutual interchange. Though unrecorded in the film, the Jesuits came to have great appreciation for the natural piety of the natives. As we saw in chapter 3, the Jesuit *Relations*, the widely read yearly reports priests sent back to their superiors in France, recognize symbolic similarities between Christian sacraments and native rituals, as well as parallels between their stories and those of Scripture. In spite of what they regard as moral shortcomings among the Indians, the black robes saw a possibility for grace to build on nature among woodland tribes. But since whites and Indians alike sought to exploit one another, as we see clearly in *Black Robe*, only something like a religious and cultural confluence would have prevented the sad history that ensued.

Whatever their aesthetic merits, most recent films about European encounters with natives (the film *Dances with Wolves* being the most popular example) show far less accurate and serious history than *Black Robe*. In fact, they simply reverse the old movie stereotypes of cowboys and Indians. Before, peaceful white settlers bravely confronted a harsh nature and savage tribes to open up an immense land. Now, callous whites disrupt a bountiful nature and nature's aboriginal children, whose lives, by a kind of mirror-image wish fulfillment, become everything that modern urban life allegedly is not—vigorous, free, in harmony with nature. Everything "white," including white religion, merely degrades people already living noble lives. It's no wonder that, a few decades later, "whiteness" and "white privilege"—despite their obvious reverse racism—could be accepted as legitimate, even "woke," moral categories.

Black Robe, by contrast, took a stark and independent approach to its subject. It was the best popular representation of the encounter between indigenous peoples and Christianity among quincentenary events. Not only did it include real religion in the story; its generally authentic portrayal of both Europeans and natives has little to do with Eurocentrism or with what we might call aboriginal chic.

To begin with, despite the stunning beauty of its North American woodlands setting, the film never glosses over the hard reality of primitive life. In winter, Indians sleep in cold shelters with open fires that fill the air with smoke. Food is a constant worry, and disease a perpetual specter for which native remedies and medicine men are not sure defenses. This world, as a dying native leader confesses to the priest in the film, is a harsh one; those who live closer to nature than we do know clearly that, for human beings, the physical environment is a sometimes good, sometimes bad relation.

No easy opposition between white and red operates in *Black Robe* either. Some whites are relatively benign; others are not—even to one another. Indians are shown killing and torturing other Indians, as they regularly did throughout tribal societies long before the arrival of the white man. Nor are we given neat divisions between good and bad tribes, as in *Dances with Wolves*. Having escaped from a hostile tribe after a bout of torture, an Indian explains to the priest that his tribe is just as brutal. (Perhaps a slight anachronism creeps in here since no native, without the perspective on tribal ways afforded by contact with another culture, would have seen anything much wrong in the perpetual tribal feuds except the inconvenience.)

That such tortures no longer occur in the twentieth century can be attributed, as the film implies, only to the slow and uneven influence of European culture and religion. Tribal society and religion dictated that captives in war had to be treated cruelly as a sign to surrounding tribes of unattackable fierceness. Tribes such as the Huron, who accepted Christianity after a fashion and who may have relented to a degree in their use of torture, were simply wiped out by more ruthless tribes, such as the Iroquois. Suffering genocide was a fearsome price for the Hurons to pay for their turn to softer ways. These converts and their martyred missionaries set native cultures, in fits and starts, on a far less bloody course for which we all—white and red alike—should be deeply grateful. Unfortunately, this gradual improvement was later marred by the atrocities of white men themselves.

Native religion receives sympathetic treatment in *Black Robe* but not the blanket acceptance now common in most works of popular culture. The Europeans are half intrigued, half repelled by native belief in dreams and wood spirits. Native Americans clearly have belief systems encompassing this world and the next. At the same time the native shaman cuts a rather silly figure as he tries to ward off the evil spirits he thinks the priest brings with him. And we overhear the Iroquois discussing the sacrifice of one of their captives to a war god the next day. (In fact, the Iroquois sometimes went raiding as far as the Dakotas in search of victims for such sacrifices.) While these are small touches, and perhaps not sufficient to correct some widespread misconceptions, they are of crucial importance in accurately presenting native belief and practice.

Tunnel Vision

Just how unusual and necessary even this small critical treatment is may be appreciated by comparing it with the situation on most college campuses today. Princeton's highly popular course in Native

American religions, mentioned in chapter 4, is typical of courses around the country. And as at Princeton, professors elsewhere also complain not of student resistance to native ideas but of their uncritical embrace of native religion. We can probably imagine the type of student that usually studies Native American religion today—a student who thinks of native spirituality as a multicultural antidote to civilization. If it got the attention it deserves, *Black Robe* might be a useful antidote to that false multiculturalism.

Unfortunately, even the few people who have seen *Black Robe* do not always comprehend its lessons. Some see it as a chronicle of the Jesuit priest's slow recognition of the validity of Indian culture.[231] This interpretation is simply wrong; we never see any such thing. The French Jesuits learn that the natives have many admirable qualities and that life among them is more complex than their training in France prepared them for. Yet many young people, apparently assuming that this exceptional creation is just one more item in a monolithic popular culture, interpret *Black Robe* as a kind of homage to Native American wisdom and nobility.

Perhaps more worrisome is the pox-on-both-your-houses approach of urbane critics such as the *New York Times*'s Vincent Canby, who view the whole story as a pointless disaster for both sides: the Jesuits were ineffective, and the Hurons were wiped out.[232] That reading assumes a superiority to and distance from the historical actors that is not warranted. In one astonishing scene, Father Laforgue demonstrates to his Algonquian guides how writing works. He takes down a sentence, walks over to a French colleague, and asks him to read it aloud. The Indians draw

---

[231] Peter Steinfels, "Beliefs," *New York Times*, 26 October 1991, A25.
[232] Vincent Canby, "Saving the Huron Indians: A Disaster for Both Sides," review of *Black Robe*, directed by Bruce Beresford, *New York Times*, 30 October 1991, C15.

back in some fear at this inexplicable witchcraft. Yet without the individuals who were willing to carry that witchcraft to unknown peoples at great personal peril and inconvenience, the descendants of those Native Americans would have been in no position to read Vincent Canby in the *New York Times*. Though they might be the better for that particular incapacity, would they be better off isolated from the rest of the world's knowledge and cultures by being unable to read?

Lacking writing, most natives would now not even be well acquainted with their own past. The complaint that whites have written the histories of the Americas has a basis in truth because Europeans were the only people involved who *could* have written the history at all. The Mayas had a writing system, the Aztecs a few pictorial "books," but nowhere in the Americas were there written histories as we understand histories. In fact, as in other parts of the world, European historical interests have retrieved or preserved much of native culture that would have been lost.

Though scholarly interest may seem small consolation for peoples who have suffered unjustly at the hands of Europeans for five hundred years, past injustice should not be compounded by distorting what remains of native cultures to suit the purposes of various interested parties living now. Anyone—even a Native American—who looks fairly, from a now partly Western perspective, into the history of the tribes that existed when the first Europeans arrived will conclude that resurrecting them as they were would not be a good idea. Neither would resurrecting every aspect of seventeenth-century European culture be very attractive. But many disaffected Westerners are turning to Native Americans as the last available candidates for utopian dreams. The terrible disfigurements of Native American history that those utopian impulses will produce should concern Native Americans as much as anyone.

Another American Path

The myth of the noble savage is likely to mark popular culture for about as long as his counterpart, the ignoble savage, did earlier. What we still fail to appreciate in our common American past is the agonistic nature of all human movements. Should the Europeans who came to the Americas simply have left them as they were? Or, even under the best of circumstances, would the natural evangelical nature of Christianity have made that seem intolerable and a grave lapse of moral responsibility? Mel Gibson's 2006 film *Apocalypto* portrayed the bloodiness of Mesoamerican culture and religion — the accuracy of that portrayal was disputed by some scholars — but there's no question it was one of the very few efforts to bring some of that material into popular culture.

Accusations that white Eurocentric thought has distorted the study of Native American cultures usually arise when these issues come up. Another sin to be identified, however, has been the simple assumption that we already *know* what the native peoples were. Even careful anthropologists, who have devoted their lives to studying peoples they deeply love, are seen as guilty of either subtly or crudely imposing meanings by the very tools of their scholarly trade and assigning value to native phenomena. By definition, then, the only impartial and correct views of Native American cultures must come from Native Americans themselves.

On the face of it, this is an odd claim that would be made in few other cases. We may well believe, for example, that the British understand something about their own culture that we Americans, despite a closely related culture and language, do not. Monarchy certainly seems to mean something to them that, after all explanations have been made, still remains a mystery for us. But that does not stop us, or anyone else, from criticizing English stuffiness, bland cuisine, and addiction to interminable cricket matches. The British themselves often return the favor. When we turn to native cultures, however, a sort of *noblesse oblige* seems to intervene. Not only do we fail to treat Native Americans as moral and intellectual equals, as real people, but a condescending attitude arises that distorts the very examination of native culture. In any culture—be it the culture of the United States or the former Soviet Union, of South Africa or Canada's First Peoples—we know that positive and negative qualities will be mixed in differing proportions. Good and evil traits are indigenous to every human society.

Yet Native American cultures seem to be excluded from this universal rule. When many contemporary scholars, politicians, activists, clergy, journalists, and just plain folks turn to these cultures, an odd thing happens. Suddenly, the tradition of intellectual and journalistic professions to question everything vanishes, and we are overwhelmed with pleas to "respect" certain cultures without debate. Whereas, for some people, the disparity between the average incomes of men and of women in the United States is an abomination, and calling attention to the deep structures that perpetuate it is a duty, pointing out the low position of women, incessant tribal warfare, torture of captives, and enslavement that existed in most precolonial North American Indian cultures—and most cultures everywhere—is disrespectful.

Such facts have been horribly used, of course, to justify the white man's mistreatment and genocide of the red man. Merely to raise these issues is to run the risk of placing oneself outside the bounds of civil discourse. After all, whatever the Native Americans did to one another, doesn't it pale in comparison with what whites did to them? Furthermore, because Native Americans now are often in sad shape, wouldn't additional criticism simply be cruel? Doesn't moral seriousness require us to be more concerned about respect for Indian traditions than to bring up old issues that may well feed stereotypes?

Answering yes to the three questions just posed is taken as a sign of sophistication and transcendence of Eurocentric categories. But is it? Is it not rather a failure akin to the failure to appreciate ancient Israel's warring kings, or Japan's shoguns, or India's moguls? Instead of "paying respect" to other traditions—the respect of presenting them and trying to understand them in their fullness—doesn't this patronizing attitude reduce them all to bland caricatures, props for contemporary quarrels?

It need not be so. Seriously studying native cultures with sympathy need not lead to one-sided readings of history. In fact, at Berkeley, where a "diversity" requirement introduced students to previously unfamiliar material about the history of native America, students came to appreciate historical complexities and paradoxes. In one class, Berkeley students discussed Joel S. Martin's *Sacred Revolt*, a study of Muskogee Indians and their resistance to white influences around 1800.[233] Like many other Indian groups, the Muskogee had slaves and patriarchal social structures. A woman in the class complained that the text underemphasized how "women were being oppressed while a black student objected to the facile disposal of the question of slavery by saying that slaves were treated better in Indian villages than on white plantations."[234] Such reactions indicate that attempts to face past injustices need not lead to the creation of new intellectual injustices.

But the concern should spread beyond trendy feminist and racial preoccupations. The Muskogean Natchez of the U.S. southeastern woodlands lived in a rigid society of four castes, practiced human sacrifice, and killed the wives of upper-caste ("Great Sun") males out of grief when they died, a kind of Natchez suttee.[235] Knowing

---

[233] Joel W. Martin, *Sacred Revolt: The Muskogees Struggle for a New World* (Boston: Beacon Press, 1991).

[234] Reported in *The Chronicle of Higher Education*, 11 March 1992, A16.

[235] Peter Nabokov and Dean Snow, "Farmers of the Woodlands, in Josephy, *America in 1492*, 140–141. Nabokov and Stone follow the

these facts and their connection to Indian culture and belief systems should lead us to look outside or beyond what is of contemporary salience to even broader questions, to "the other" in all his glory and horror. What good effects have new modes of thought brought to many of the Native Americans themselves? This kind of multiculturalism, however, would have no time for sentimental pieties about respect for indigenous ways that do not warrant respect.

Elementary-School Distortions

If Berkeley students could see only part of the problem, what about students not as mature? They are often subjected to one-sided presentations they can hardly be expected to notice, much less resist. In the fall of 1991, for example, an issue of *Scholastic Update*, a typical grade-school-level newsletter on current events, decided to stimulate discussion about the Columbus anniversary under the familiar rubric "Separating the Man from the Myth."[236] In a sense, *Scholastic* does present different views, but it also leaves the overwhelming impression—and at this age impressions, not critical thought, are more formative of future opinions—that Columbus was a brute who does not even have the honor of being the first European to arrive here.

Typical of many similar efforts to separate myth from reality, the discussion includes very little about Columbus and his actions. He

---

usual North American practice of denying that human sacrifice could have been indigenous to North American Indians: "Along with some other Caddoan and Muskogean-speaking groups of the Gulf Coast region, the Natchez practiced human sacrifice—more evidence of the diffusion of Mexican traits into their territories." Evidence of sacrifice we have; evidence of diffusion from another culture is another matter and has to be demonstrated, not posited.

[236] *Scholastic Update* 125, no. 2, September 1991.

appears only in a sketchy three-page overview that crudely sets out some of the historical material. The rest of the issue is devoted to how different countries, such as Spain, Mexico, and the Dominican Republic, feel about 1992; how young Native Americans feel about themselves (they want and do not want to be part of white culture); and how all of us should feel about the environmental crisis. The magazine asserted (falsely) that the Spaniards entirely wiped out the Aztecs and the Incas. It also lingers over one reporter's visits to the Yanomami, a still-intact tribe in the Brazilian Amazon that has become an international cause célèbre almost on a par with the undisturbed rainforest itself. The Yanomami have been so isolated that they remain susceptible to "European" diseases and disruptions. They are described as displaying a profound knowledge of their environment in one paragraph, but this appears in another:

> The Yanomami believe that their god, Omame, deserted them when the white men invaded their soil. Kopenawa, another Yanomami leader, offered an explanation for the onslaught of malaria in the region.
>
> "Omame put the minerals below the earth because it is cold," he said. "Then came the miners and [they] took out the minerals. When the minerals came out into the hot air, it [sic] turned to poison and spread many diseases. The miners don't know they are spreading poison to the world. The world will end, will die."

After reading this mythological account, intelligent American schoolchildren may be puzzled about the pious assertions on another page that Indians are serious caretakers of the earth who "can't do it alone anymore."

The single page in *Scholastic Update* devoted to "debate" does not even attempt to engage issues. It merely allows space for certified and predictable voices to be heard: Houston Baker (black),

Columbus and the Crisis of the West

Mario Cuomo (Italian), Antonia Hernandez (Mexican American woman), Wilma Mankiller (chief, Cherokee Nation), and Patrick Buchanan (presumably, pugnacious Eurocentrist). Students learn elsewhere in the newsletter that Indian groups will be sending ships from New York City to Spain to claim it as Native American territory, that protests are planned against the replicas of Columbus's ships sailing to San Salvador for October 1992 and stopping before and after in other cities, and that 1992 has been declared the Year of Indigenous Peoples—by indigenous peoples.

Absent other information, even an adult would have a hard time knowing what to think about Columbus after reading all this. A twelve- or thirteen-year-old will be left with little historical information with which to separate the man from either the myth or the anti-myth.

National Leadership in Education

It is hardly surprising that *Scholastic Update* should have spurned Columbus himself and approached 1492 from the angle of current ethnic tensions, however, since that is precisely what many of the most prestigious educational and professional organizations in the country advocated. The National Council for the Social Studies (along with almost thirty signatories drawn from educational, scholarly, and professional organizations) prepared a brief position statement in 1991 for use by educators: *The Columbian Quincentenary: An Educational Opportunity* contains some very good suggestions set in a less-than-ideal framework. (The document was "developed by the National Council for the Social Studies, October 1991." Cosignatories include organizations such as the American Anthropological Association, the National Education Association, and the World History Association.) The council makes two major recommendations. The second suggestion—that students should be provided with "basic accurate knowledge about Columbus's voyages, their historical setting, and unfolding effects"—has an unobjectionable, even laudable aim. Unfortunately, it follows on the heels of the more dubious recommendation that teachers "help students comprehend the contemporary relevance of 1492"—in short, not to read history but to read current issues into history.

Were it not for the fact that the contemporary relevance has already been determined, even the latter aim might be a relatively benign or enlightening undertaking. But we know that historical objectivity now often succumbs to other interests when Europe figures centrally in a story, as it does in this one. In fact, the statement admits that "the world as we know it would not have come to be were it not for the chain of events set in motion by European contact with the Americas." Yet out of fear that "public hyperbole," meaning uncritical adulation of Columbus, will dominate the anniversary, the council issues several cautions.

First, Columbus must be understood in the context of a contemporary multiethnic and culturally pluralistic United States with ties to all other parts of the world. While this America should be regarded as "one of history's first universal or world nations," however, it should not be seen as having anything that places it above other nations or cultures. Here, the council crosses into the ghostly world of global education. As currently practiced, global education does not so much teach facts in order that students in the various parts of the world may understand one another. Rather, the goal of global education is to lead students to some sort of disembodied, neutral point of view vis-à-vis all the nations and cultures of the world. In this vision, the United States becomes nothing more than a respectful receptacle of various other cultures that, of course, in their turn, have great intrinsic value. American culture as such is suspect.

Columbus and the Crisis of the West

Second, the council advises teachers to provide students with a fuller account of the history of the Americas prior to 1492. That history should not be regarded as a virtual blank, but a story of highly developed agricultural systems, centers of dense populations, complex civilizations, large-scale empires, extensive networks of long-distance trade and cultural diffusion, complex patterns of interstate conflict and cooperation, sophisticated systems of religious and scientific belief, extensive linguistic diversity, and regional variations in the levels of societal complexity.

All this, as I have argued in previous chapters, is quite true and a much-needed corrective to past neglect. Yet, set as it is in the council's framework, the directive gives the impression that "white" Europeans simply ignored a wealth of historical information available in native form. But it bears repeating: were it not for the white Europeans who cared enough to re-create much of it, this history would have remained all but unknown to native populations and others alike. The fact that political appreciation of such knowledge lagged behind scholarship should not blind us to the basic openness of European culture and its interest in the cultures of the others.

So strong is the council's desire for all parties to have an equal role in this story, however, that the obvious lead of Europe, conceded at the document's beginning, is denied in the subsequent enumeration of groups that have made up the Americas. Native Americans and Africans, we are told, were not merely passive victims of Europeans—a true statement within limits. But then the limits are entirely ignored:

> All parties pursued their interests as they perceived them— sometimes independently of the interests of others, sometimes in collaboration with others, and sometimes in conflict with others. All borrowed from and influenced the others and, in turn, were influenced by them. The internal diversity

of the Native Americans, the Africans, and the Europeans contributed to the development of modern American pluralistic culture and contemporary world civilization.

If this is true, one begins to wonder, why are Native American and African American groups complaining? Of course, in a very general way, everyone "contributed" to what is now America, but the desire to credit everyone equally here blurs the fact, evident to any dispassionate historian, that, for both good and bad, Europe is central, no less for its sins than as the unique source of the concepts of pluralism, human rights, and democracy that we value in the Americas.

The peoples of the Americas caused the Europeans to do some rethinking (see chapter 3), and the National Council for the Social Studies might have done well to include that history in its observations and recommended bibliography. Its failure to do so exacts a heavy toll. Interpreting the "contemporary relevance of 1492" in current political, ethnic, and racial terms only obscures the origins of the very ideas that seek to guarantee liberty and justice to all. Those origins are lost and falsely seen as having emerged almost impersonally from the bare contact of different peoples. The council was no worse in this regard than many other groups examining the quincentenary, but its responsibility is greater. It encourages teachers to leave students exactly where they started—vaguely oriented toward a dream of universalism but lacking any idea of the sources of the precious legacy of freedom, however flawed and incomplete, they have inherited.

Later Developments

Nearly three decades after the quincentenary events and counterevents outlined here, the situation has hardly changed at all, except that the burst of historical interest in 1992 has settled into a kind of historical orthodoxy about the unremitting evil of "white," Western culture. Given how steeped in one-sided historical assumptions educational institutions were in 1992, from the earliest grades to graduate studies, it is no surprise that some of the fiercest—and least informed—critics of the West and Columbus in the twenty-first century are the young "white" products of that education and almost equally unaware of the Western principles and freedoms that undergird their protests. That self-denying stance, along with a belief that only people of absolute moral purity—and a purity as defined by current Western elites—can be valued is a recipe for utter disaster. As both our best religious and secular traditions have always taught, all people are imperfect and sinners, every one of us. To reject everyone who is less than perfect is tantamount to declaring your independence from the human race.

During the unrest of 2020, not only did statues of Columbus fall, as if he were the precursor of the Confederate generals whose statues were also toppled; Americans—and people from Ireland to Australia, Canada to South Africa—began what can only be termed a kind of historical cleansing. Washington and Jefferson, both slave owners, had their monuments threatened in America's capital as if they had never done anything memorable. Abraham Lincoln, once the Great Emancipator, also came under fire for his sometimes expressed belief that blacks should return to Africa and his efforts to establish Liberia there. Mahatma Gandhi had a low view of blacks during his years in South Africa, as did Winston Churchill in his own early days, and they too became all but exclusively identified with those failings. Karl Marx had a low view of blacks as well but somehow the many monuments to him in Europe remained undisturbed.

During the anti-racism protests and rioting of 2020, one of the most often cited books about the reasons for the unrest was

Robin d'Angelo's *White Fragility*. In a passage intended to wake "whites" from their unconscious racism, she writes:

> To get a sense of the white racial frame below the surface of your conscious awareness, think back to the earliest time you were aware that people from racial groups other than your own existed. People of color recall a sense of always being aware, while most white people recall being aware by at least age five. If you lived in a primarily white environment and are having trouble remembering, think about Disney movies, music videos, sports heroes, Chinese food, Aunt Jemima syrup, Uncle Ben's rice, the Taco Bell Chihuahua, Columbus Day, Apu from *The Simpsons*, and the donkey from *Shrek*.[237]

The appearance of Columbus in a list of what most people might find to be relatively harmless features of American society reflects the ways in which the man himself and everything he symbolizes (Columbus Day) had come to be taken for granted in certain cultural circles as irredeemably evil. The fact that the crude and humorless list of suspect cultural elements is wildly skewed — do "white man" Homer Simpson and his family get any less comic treatment than the East Indian Apu? — does not diminish the shift that had taken place at a popular level. Columbus and all his works and pomps were now assumed — no further need to argue — to be no longer a heroic or even historic bit of the story of America and the West worth preserving. They were part of the guilty Western *id* beneath a placid "white" consciousness, a pathology that needs to be brought to the surface and eliminated. It was no wonder

---

[237] Robin d'Angelo, *White Fragility: Why It's So Hard for White People to Talk about Racism* (New York: Penguin Random House, 2018), 34–35.

that statues of the explorer began to fall to mobs in Milwaukee, Baltimore, and other American cities.

For reasons that are not entirely clear, in the same period, Padre Junípero Serra, a Spanish Franciscan, became one of the most controversial religious figures associated with the development of the New World. Serra came from a dirt-poor family on the island of Mallorca and was taken into the Franciscan seminary at Palma because of his sheer brilliance in his studies. He made rapid progress and eventually became a professor of theology and philosophy. As a Franciscan, Serra was dedicated to a life of poverty and study and was in many respects an idealistic intellectual who in early manhood caught fire at the idea of bringing both the gospel and a better way of life to the indigenous people of the Americas. He left Europe for Mexico, but the already settled ways of Spaniards and Indians there were not challenging enough for him. At just over five feet tall, he was nonetheless a powerhouse. He formed a series of around a dozen missions—from San Diego in Southern California all the way up the coast through Los Angeles to just north of San Francisco. The very names of these settlements attest to the fundamentally religious nature of his efforts.

His many remarkable feats were often carried out in the midst of the usual challenges of dealing with not only indigenous peoples but brutal Spanish soldiers as well. Further, he is known to have made trips back to Mexico City to get legal protections for native peoples. All of this earned him recognition as a figure central to the creation of the state of California. In the years around the Columbus quincentenary and the decades that followed, objections to his mission system—by which he hoped to save souls and nourish bodies by introducing farming and ranching—grew wildly, culminating, during the turmoil of 2020, in the toppling or removal of statues honoring him. The charges against him usually refer to physical punishments within the missions—which was a common feature in all premodern societies—even though there is no recorded instance of his unjustly punishing anyone. Some accounts—reaching lazily for contemporary categories of offenses—claim that native animals and plants were damaged or destroyed in California because of his efforts. But in fact, the wine industry, fruit cultivation, and other crops in California are also the result of his efforts. Yet he has been attacked as if all he had done was establish a series of concentration camps.

It can be debated, of course, whether his vision of peaceful agricultural missions and his methods of evangelization were appropriate to the indigenous population. But he believed that Christianity and a settled form of life would be of benefit—as opposed to postmodern assumptions that Indian belief systems and cultures were fine as the Spanish found them. Anyone with a heart will feel some ambivalence about the whole history. But the vitriol directed toward Serra—Sacramento's monument to him was ripped down by mobs as if he were a genocidal monster—is simply wrong. If even the best intentioned of poor Franciscans, who had risked his life to preach and help people, is to be driven out of our public spaces for such flimsy reasons, it is past time to think about who we are and what we truly value.

6

Democratic Vistas

Heaven have mercy on us all—Presbyterians and Pagans
alike—for we are somehow dreadfully cracked about the head.

—Herman Melville, *Moby Dick*

In early 1992, the City Council of Berkeley, California, declared unanimously that October 12 would no longer be celebrated as Columbus Day but as Indigenous Peoples' Day. One leader of Resistance 500, the task force heading the coalition that sought the change, explained the vote in terms that would be attractive to many Americans in the approach to the quincentenary: "It's moving from a philosophy of war, imperialism, and exploitation of peoples and lands personified by people like Columbus and the conquerors to a philosophy of living in peace and harmony with neighbors and different cultures."[238] Though the Berkeley declaration begs several difficult questions and surely reflects no serious attempt to become acquainted with the history of Columbus or Native Americans, it was a trendy—almost predictable—political move. By making it, the Berkeley city council propagated the kind of received wisdom that should, instead, be examined carefully if we wish to understand the civic dimensions of the controversies over 1492 and the

---

[238] *The Daily Californian*, 14 January 1992.

past five hundred years. Nearly thirty years later, as America was riven by riots in the summer of 2020, not only predictably radical Berkeley, but jurisdictions all over America—mainstream middle-class suburban places—declared they would substitute Indigenous Peoples' Day for Columbus Day.

Something, clearly had happened in the meantime. If the Berkeley council and its later imitators had decided simply to highlight the need for mainstream America to accord greater recognition to Native American citizens, and for finding a better *modus vivendi* among our diverse peoples, it would not have generated much interest or disagreement. In recent decades, Native Americans—like many other U.S. minority communities—have found a new acceptance within traditional majorities. The minorities proudly celebrate their many contributions to the common culture and see those achievements reflected in textbooks, politics, and the media.

In the 1990 census, a much larger number of people identified themselves as Native Americans than ever before, and by the 2010 census, the numbers were greater—almost 2 percent of the total population, nearly five million people, depending on how the categories were set up. Futures censuses are likely to continue the trend. Why this is so remains unclear, but ethnic pride and, paradoxically, social advantage in an increasingly open United States seem to be two important factors. Though minority leaders have at times abused this openness and provoked some backlash by taking extreme, aggressive positions that most of their own people do not support, by and large popular opinion about minorities is probably at an all-time high in U.S. history. The desire to mark that status on the calendar and remind us all of the social failures yet to be remedied, then, does not come as much of a surprise.

But the most emblematic and disturbing aspect of the Berkeley decision is that it *replaced* the Columbus holiday with the indigenous peoples' celebration—a step that represents not an addition but an intentional repudiation of traditional European culture. Furthermore, as the Resistance 500 members' explanation made evident, this step stems from the belief that native peoples were greatly superior to Europeans in their capacity to live in harmony with one another and with nature. Rightly or wrongly, a sizable group of Americans—Native Americans, other minorities, and "whites"—today feels that we have lost our social links with one another, are radically at odds among ourselves in exclusive ethnic groups, and are even at war with the natural environment.

Use and Abuse of "History"

Unfortunately, several widespread notions about traditional Native American life are literal fictions. Just one indication of how they may be artificially contrived surfaced in early 1992 when the nineteenth-century Indian sage Chief Seattle was invoked on Earth Day. For some time, the chief has been identified as a visionary and an eloquent speaker who commented on the issues many middle-class Americans now find most worrisome—the environment and social tensions. Accordingly, the organizers of Earth Day 1992 (22 April) encouraged religious and political leaders to read a letter Chief Seattle had supposedly written in 1854 to U.S. president Franklin Pierce. Among other concerns in the letter, the chief proclaims the earth to be our mother and complains, "I have seen a thousand rotting buffaloes on the prairies left by the white man who shot them from a passing train." The entire letter confirms widespread current beliefs about the relations of Indian and "white" man, Indian wisdom and "white" rapacity.

The principal problem with these beliefs, however, is not even that they are gross generalizations and often have no basis in fact.

Columbus and the Crisis of the West

It is that even people who know the truth ignore it, for ideological purposes. In this case, Chief Seattle never wrote those words. His home was six hundred miles from the nearest buffalo, and the letter is dated fifteen years before the railroad arrived in the Northwest. But even though Earth Day USA officials had heard reports that the letter might be inauthentic, they decided to send it out to religious leaders anyway as "attributed" to Chief Seattle.

And indeed it had been attributed to him in an odd way—by a modern "white" religious institution. The words in the fictional letter were created by Ted Perry, a Texas scriptwriter, for a 1971 film produced by the Southern Baptist Radio and Television Commission. The commission wanted to give a warning about the environment and thought it would be appropriate to have Chief Seattle make the plea. Unfortunately, many viewers assumed that the film's moving environmental sentiments had been pronounced by Seattle himself, and several institutions publicized them through various channels as his—a mistake that angered both Perry and historians of Northwestern indigenous peoples.

Though this comedy of errors may be unusual in degree, such contemporary use (or misuse) of a revered Indian figure as a ventriloquist's dummy is by no means unique. General public ignorance about specific Native American groups makes it easy to attribute to them just about any notion that seems progressive without much fear of contradiction. How popular sentiments toward Native Americans will be affected when the truth eventually becomes known is another story. Just as Columbus found himself embroiled with people who believed that wealth could be easily gotten in the New World, those who oversell the Native American heritage may be inviting deep disillusionment.

As these revelations about the letter were coming out, *Brother Eagle, Sister Sky*, a children's book on the environment based on Chief Seattle's spurious sayings, was number five on the *New York*

Times best-seller list. Questioned about that volume's authenticity, its illustrator told the *New York Times*, "Basically, I don't know what he said—but I do know that the Native American people lived this philosophy, and that's what's important."[239] Which native peoples lived what philosophy, or even the barest outlines of the chief's real views, does not seem to interest people who have already been conditioned to believe—without any evidence or historical study—what Native American cultures were in the past and what they mean in the present.

Chief Seattle, who gave his name to the city in Washington, was pure Native American (father Suquamish, mother Duwamish). A mighty warrior, he essentially eliminated the rival Chimakum tribe in a battle on what is now the Quimper Peninsula. Like other native chiefs, he owned eight Indian slaves—in time-honored Northwest Indian tradition—until Lincoln's Emancipation Proclamation. He was also an adult convert to Catholicism, probably in his fifties. Though he earned a reputation as a bold raider against surrounding tribes, he had some deep and sensible things to say about relations between red and white men, for which he should be honored. But the president of the company that published *Brother Eagle, Sister Sky* appeared to have no interest in any of this, dismissing charges of inaccuracy by saying, "For want of a tape recorder [presumably to have properly recorded Chief Seattle's original words] maybe we have a book that will change children's view about the environment." Giving those same children false and misleading information about a Native American leader and his culture did not seem to trouble her, as long as it served a cause that a certain segment of white society regarded as a contemporary good.

[239] Timothy Egan, "Chief's 1854 Lament Linked to Ecological Script of 1971," *New York Times*, 21 April 1992, Al, A17.

Columbus and the Crisis of the West

Multitudinously Native

As part of the rich variety of native cultures in the Americas, more than three hundred Indian tribes existed within what is now the United States alone. Even using the word "tribes" to describe these diverse groups cannot begin to convey the range of peoples and social forms between North America's two coasts. As mentioned earlier, near present-day Saint Louis, for example, Mound Builders raised enormous structures, probably temples, in the midst of a large, fixed urban complex. Contemporaneous with the Cahokian Mound Builders, whaling peoples on the Northwest Coast, nomadic tribes in the interior, and numerous other nations dwelled in these lands. The complexity of this country's Native American history far exceeds any one person's capacity to know.

Several immovable obstacles, moreover, stand in the way—primarily the lack of written native languages. We must rely almost entirely on oral traditions and archaeological evidence, where available, to reconstruct Native American history. Often these two sources do not confirm each other. Later accretions to oral histories and gaps in the physical evidence introduce uncertainties everywhere. The written testimony of European settlers helps but inevitably contains inaccuracies and downright misunderstandings, though it is receiving renewed attention.[240] Given the vigorous economic, political, and military interaction of native peoples, all these instruments, even combined, still leave much to be desired. It is as if we had to reconstruct several centuries of Italian Renaissance history, not from the documents of the warring city-states,

---

[240] See Daniel T. Reff, "Anthropological Analysis of Exploration Texts: Cultural Discourse and the Ethnological Import of Fray Marcos de Niza's Journey to Cibola," *American Anthropologist*, no. 93 (September 1991).

but from the anecdotal accounts of Arab traders who had contacts with Genoa or Venice, Florence or Naples.

In addition to this fragmented situation, the more politicized assertions regarding the abilities of Indians to live harmoniously with one another and with nature, which may be supported by evidence from one tribe, can be quite easily contradicted by evidence of different practices in other tribes. The Natchez Indians, as we have seen, had social hierarchies and slavery; the Sanpoils, who lived on the Columbia River, practiced absolute equality and pacifism: pacifism, of course, was a rarity among indigenous peoples. The Sanpoils were highly unusual and fortunate in that they were able to preserve their equality and pacifism between two very different types of societies: those on the Northwest Coast with rigid social structures and those on the Great Plains marked by bellicosity.[241] Yet, in a sense, Carlos Fuentes was right to claim that all these peoples act as a "buried mirror" in which we may see our own mixed and partly obscured features more readily (see the previous chapter).

Iroquois Democracy and Imperialism

Contradictory traits sometimes show up within the same indigenous group. The Iroquois had probably the most highly developed Native American political association in North America, and much has been written of their achievements. DeWitt Clinton called them the "Romans of the West" because of their "martial spirit" and their "rage for conquest." The so-called Iroquois Confederation — the nascent civic structure of the Seneca, Onondaga, Oneida, Mohawk, and Cayuga — arrived at peaceful and relatively democratic

[241] James A. Maxwell, *America's Fascinating Indian Heritage: The First Americans: Their Customs, Art, History and How They Lived* (Pleasantville, N.Y.: Reader's Digest Association, 1978), 283.

relations within the Five Nations. In 1987, the U.S. Congress formally proclaimed that the Iroquois played an important role in the development of American democracy. As a result, American schoolchildren are taught today that the Iroquois Confederation was a model for the American Founders when they began to consider how to organize the newly independent former colonies.

Controversy is widespread among historians over whether this is a historical fact. A few — very few — passages show that the Founders were, of course, aware of the confederation. In his remarks on the need for a union, Ben Franklin probably best captures the spirit of how most of the Founders felt about the question:

> It would be a very strange Thing, if ... Nations of ignorant Savages should be capable of forming a Scheme for such a Union, and be able to execute it in such a Manner, as that it has subsisted Ages, and appears indissoluble; and yet a like Union should be impracticable for ten or a Dozen Colonies.[242]

Franklin's combination of disparagement ("ignorant Savages") and admiration (suggesting "a *like* Union") reflects the vague interest typical of his times. Not until the 1840s did anyone investigate the structure of the confederation. Consequently, its role in shaping the Constitution in any serious way is doubtful, to say the least.[243]

In any case, outside the constituent Iroquoian groups, the confederation practiced what can only be called an imperial policy toward other peoples. Francis Jennings, an appreciative student of Indian cultures, has written that the Iroquois, because of their

---

[242] Quoted in Elisabeth Tooker, "The United States Constitution and the Iroquois League," in *Invented Indian*, ed. James Clifton. Tooker's entire essay is a valuable review of the claims and counterclaims.

[243] Schlesinger, *Disuniting of America*, 97.

political structure, considered themselves the wisest of Indians and "rationalized their role of hegemony over other tribes. It was for the latter's own good—not an unfamiliar argument among imperialists."[244] The British called the heavily fortified Iroquois villages "castles"—a further indication of the kinds of relations that existed among tribes long before the white man added his own evils.

E pluribus plures

Ethnocentrism in the Americas was not unique to Europeans and Iroquois either. We are appalled at the abuse, physical and verbal, that Europeans visited upon Native Americans, and no amount of historical reconstruction can ever excuse behavior that the Europeans themselves should have recognized was an outrage—and not a few among Spaniards, French, and British did. Yet Native Americans visited a great deal of abuse on one another as well, as their languages reveal. A culture claiming to be sensitive to all sorts of "hate" speech and subtle forms of racism might find it interesting that most Indian groups regarded only themselves as full human beings and regarded members of other tribes as inferior in customs or understanding. The Algonquians called the Iroquois army the "Nation of Snakes." Jennings points out that, owing to this habit of identifying other tribes by derogatory names, we do not always possess even a good idea of the actual names of certain groups, and not only because of the lack of written records: "Clarity is not helped by the ethnocentricity of the tribes. They did not hesitate to refer to their hostile neighbors with pejoratives equivalent to 'stinker'

---

[244] Francis Jennings, *The Ambiguous Iroquois Empire: The Covenant Chain of Indian Tribes with English Colonies from Its Beginning to the Lancaster Treaty of 1744* (New York: W. W. Norton, 1984), 94.

and 'cannibals.' "[245] The Taínos, whom Columbus encountered in his first contacts and who he thought were living in natural harmony, had a lower class from "the place of people without merit," as they called it.[246]

At one time, settlers justified their actions toward natives by citing native atrocities toward one another. Both the Dutch and the British, for instance, bought land from Indians who had recently driven off other Indians—a native usurpation that set a bad example for some Europeans only too ready to believe that "primitive" peoples had no rights to land or other rights.[247] The record of intertribal warfare should never have been used in that way. It is the moral equivalent of saying that because some Frenchmen steal from one another, it is all right for Englishmen to steal from Frenchmen. The whole exercise is a moral muddle that shows bad faith on the part of the excuse makers. What the historical record does indicate, however, is that Berkeley and other proponents of "living in harmony with neighbors and different cultures" have not really looked into Native American cultures; they've patronized them instead of learning about them.

Even Columbus's gentle Taínos had earlier "displaced" the Guanahacabibes and found themselves enmeshed in the long-standing warfare among Caribbean tribes.[248] But modern Columbus critics continue to invoke—out of sympathy, not knowledge—peaceful "indigenous peoples," as if these were a consistent and common entity rather than a collection of distinctive groups with divergent mores and interests, often in sharp conflict with one another.

---

[245] Ibid., 25.

[246] Miguel León-Portilla, "Men of Maize," in Josephy, *America in 1492*, 153.

[247] Sale, *Conquest of Paradise*, 98.

[248] Nash, *Red, White, and Black*, 81.

In fact, it is only fair to point out to modern admirers of tribal systems that they carry within them some of the very problems that contemporary critics of America find most annoying. Tribal systems, almost by definition, exist by sharply delineating those within from those outside the kinship system, though kinship among most Native Americans is a primarily social, rather than biological, concept. Tribes often adopted captured members of other tribes, including "whites," to replace their own members who had died or been killed in battle. After a particularly severe decline in population, for example, the Iroquois adopted the entire Tuscarora tribe. A tribe usually consisted of all those who were born into it or had formally been inducted into it. Yet the entire cultural formation of those within, of whatever biological background, distinguished them from those without. The Iroquois tribes stopped perpetrating cannibalism on one another after forming their confederation but continued it, along with torture, against captives from other tribes. Those who find modern mainstream America horribly exclusive and its treatment of various groups outrageously inequitable might benefit from some exposure to comparative ethnology[249] — and reflection on how far we have come from our own past.

Furthermore, while open to integrating others in certain circumstances, tribal practices at their core represent the very opposite of cultural openness. Outsiders were accepted in many groups, but only insofar as they accepted and participated in the monolithic culture of the tribe. The cultural pluralism that we value so highly did not exist within any tribe. And the various tribes in North America, taken together, made up a diverse group only in that each

---

[249] See, for example, Anthony Pagden, *The Fall of Natural Man: The American Indian and the Origins of Comparative Ethnology* (Cambridge, U.K.: Cambridge University Press, 1982).

preserved itself as a separate entity, mostly in opposition to others, within a certain land area. In this there is not much of a lesson for a contemporary America seeking the meaning of E pluribus unum. Rather, it would seem to caution us that the current equivalent of tribal animosities, fostered by separate social entities who do not wish to be part of any larger whole and who are willing to defend their separatism militantly, threatens the generally peaceful fabric of American civic life.

The Many Forms of Myth

Another way of looking at current attempts to find a lost paradise in native America, however, is to recall the enduring myth I cited in the introduction. Since the beginning of the European arrival, Americans have been tempted to think, as David Noble has shown, that they can escape from the "the terror of historical change to live in timeless harmony with nature."[250] That myth used to conjure up biblical images of the Garden of Eden, but after two hundred years of national existence, many Americans see both Judaism and Christianity as too deeply intertwined with the past to help much with historical terrors. Instead, they turn to Native Americans and their cultures for a prehistorical—i.e., nonhistorical—and therefore unsullied set of beliefs and behaviors that can fill the gap in the old "white" European psyche.

But that need can be met, as we've just seen, only if Native Americans are not scrutinized too closely. Native America, as its defenders sometimes claim, has a history as well. And like all human history, Indian history, though fascinating, as are all human

---

[250] David W. Noble, *The Eternal Adam and the New World Garden: The Central Myth in the American Novel Since 1830* (New York: Grosset & Dunlap, 1968), ix.

things, cannot be studied in any depth without disenchantment: there was no utopian garden; there were numerous epic and tragic events. Even a superficial reading of indigenous epics, prophecies, and songs reveals as much. Furthermore, Native American myth provides little guidance for alleviating contemporary American woes. Understanding the various stories and rituals of widely differing Indian tribes may lead us to appreciate the human wisdom and often witty invention encapsulated in their oral traditions. But in the modern world, there is an unbridgeable chasm between them and us. Just as we may appreciate certain truths formulated in ancient Greek myths about Athena, Aphrodite, Zeus, and Hera, so we may learn from stories about Raven, Coyote, Fox, and Changing Woman—but only with the most willing suspension of disbelief. For most of us these tales can be only broadly edifying and hardly offer otherwise unattainable solutions to contemporary crises.

The very term "myth" already relegates the phenomenon it describes to a status somewhere between truth and fiction. There are "true" fictions after a fashion, but when we deal with ultimate questions, we want to know more than whether a given system provides moral or spiritual light; we want to know whether it fully represents reality. Because the stories of creation in Genesis and in a few Native American myths cannot be falsified by any scientific discovery, they are universal and enduring. But other creation stories—such as those in which the earth rises from the movements of a turtle stirring up sand from the bottom of primordial waters or (with the Aztecs) solidifies from the blood of the gods—exist in another realm. The modern Western anthropological stance, which seeks to give equal value to all cultures, has limits; these stories are not in the same category as Genesis, any more than are the stories in the early Western tradition. In Homer, black-winged Night joins with the Wind and lays a silver egg from which emerges Eros, double-sexed, golden-winged, having four heads, and the source of motion in the universe.[251]

This is a Western story in which we may no longer "believe" except in the most esoteric sense and only after considerable modern literary exegesis.

Frank recognition of myth as myth is important in the Columbus controversies. General claims about the value of Native American spirituality rarely acknowledge the filtering process that separates from its full original context what we consider to be useful for us now. Belief and practice were highly integrated in native societies, and preserving one part of the system absent others is no easy matter. In violence-prone modern urban America, few people who praise native cultures would be willing to reinstate North American male puberty rites intimately tied to hunting and warfare. Nor would many people concerned with the status of women be likely to embrace the corresponding female rituals:

> Puberty rites for girls usually correlated with their biological maturity — the onset of menstruation. Isolated from their communities, these girls had to observe many personal restrictions, such as not touching their own flesh lest they mar their beauty; drinking only through a straw to prevent causing an excess of rain; avoiding the food and belongings of men, especially hunters, lest they weaken them; and practicing benevolence, humility, and proper demeanor.[252]

Though it would be unfair to suggest that these elements exhaust any native group's conceptions of male and female roles, the problem we

---

[251] See Robert Graves, *The Greek Myths*, vol. 1 (Middlesex, U.K.: Penguin Books, 1964), 30. See the following pages for similar creation stories.

[252] Sam Gill, "Religious Forms and Themes," in Josephy, *America in 1492*, 290.

face is clear. Whenever we sentimentally pit Western ways against allegedly pure native practices, we pick and choose from among them those that are in harmony with the needs of the present. We usually do the selecting, moreover, on the basis of a value system that most of us would consider universal, not simply the product of Eurocentric thought but certainly derivative from it.

Double Standards

It is curious that the critiques of militarism and power, fixed gender roles and social taboos, which are vigorously applied to delegitimize Western cultures, are almost never directed toward native societies that were clearly as enmeshed in these universal human questions as we are. An odd tendency runs through much scholarly writing on Native Americans. On the one hand, we are led through complex facts about their societies to show us that they, too, had developed social forms often, it is implied, superior to our own. On the other hand, many facets of these societies are tacitly accepted, or explained, in ways that would never be permitted in the discussion of any Western system.

One typical anthropologist, for example, praises the communitarianism of native societies in which persons "took their identity from membership in various groups and had little or no independent status apart from society. Hence, the self was not a unique entity, but rather the intersection of family lines, social positions, and spiritual bonds, all intended to serve the whole community."[253] While this degree of connectedness to a community may sound attractive to modern Americans who find society too fragmented and individualistic, is a self that is solely the product of society and subordinate to it something we

[253] Miller, "Kinship of Spirit," in Josephy, *America in 1492*, 327.

wish to embrace without further discussion? The social fit is so perfect that we may even grow suspicious that perhaps what is being described is not so much what *was* but what we in large, industrialized, urban societies would *wish* a vigorous life to be in face-to-face communities close to nature. The writer quoted above seems to confirm such suspicions when, after spending most of a long essay emphasizing the ties to a responsible and benevolent community, he suddenly—without explanation and in contradiction to massive historical evidence—announces that "all the [North American] societies tolerated a wide range of personal freedom and gender variations."[254] What happened to indigenous caste systems, socialization, and slavery? And what about the self that was "not a unique entity"?

The impression from much literature on Indians is that they are a blank sheet of paper on which to write various contemporary *desiderata*. Thinkers who would denounce priestcraft and oppression in medieval Catholicism, for example, seem to have no trouble defending native shamans, who directed entire communities, on the grounds that they acted out of traditional knowledge and benevolence. But some of their behavior may give us pause. Much like an ancient Christian catechumen, a Keresan boy growing up in a pueblo was gradually introduced to the mysteries of his religion. But there the similarity ends. Anthropologists report blithely that the penalty for revealing to women or children that men dress up as the kachinas, or tribal gods, was beheading. While all these historical studies involve countless complexities, even this brief examination clearly makes us realize that Indian cultures do not provide a simple reservoir of social or religious value upon which we may draw without careful discernment. And this realization should help us better understand the early

[254] Ibid., 337.

North American settlers' errors and misreadings of native culture and intentions.[255]

Corporate Relations

We are constantly being told that other cultures contain vast deposits of wisdom and that we need only discover them. In fact, it might be truer to say that we should approach all such promises of lost riches with caution. We know now, for example, that most Algonquians and Iroquois along the Atlantic coast, with whom the first settlers came into contact, viewed intergroup relations as basically corporate. We tend to project onto these social arrangements idealistic portraits of solidarity within and unity outside the group. While some individuals — red and white — occasionally established personal relationships with members of the opposite group, group mentalities, misunderstandings, and reciprocal atrocities greatly hampered good developments. Indiscriminate white retaliation for red acts is now familiar to even grade-school children; the converse is not.

In the early North American contacts during the sixteenth century, Indians would hold any white responsible for the transgressions of any other white. A climate of suspicion and awareness of slights also grew. Natives unfamiliar with markets thought French and other European arguments about price fluctuations were nothing more than excuses for cheating. They tended to regard their own tribe's ways as the best, and their attitudes toward Europeans, despite admiration for European technical accomplishments, were frequently condescending. Indians familiar with the land felt vastly superior to the palefaces who were unable to feed themselves or hunt very well. All told, it is astonishing that, in the early contacts,

[255] Ibid., 321.

Columbus and the Crisis of the West

Indian-white relations were as good as they were—in more instances than we are inclined to remember today.[256] Proponents of precontact native cultures would do well to consider how corporate approaches to mutual interaction made conflict with Europeans virtually unavoidable, and how facile invocation of group grievances in contemporary society may be returning us to far-from-ideal indigenous conditions. The rioting, looting, and racial revenge that occurred in Los Angeles in 1992 after a controversial jury decision in the Rodney King case show how easy it is to slip back into indiscriminate corporate retaliation. And the riots, looting, assaults on police, and wild charges of racism after the murder of George Floyd in 2020—quite apart from the justified anger and authentic protest—confirm that one injustice can easily lead to many more only distantly connected to the initial fault.

Harsh Introductions

"Early contacts" is a concept worth examining in itself. Most Americans, if asked, would probably date the beginnings of the United States from either the English settlement at Jamestown (1607) or the Pilgrims' at Plymouth (1620). Yet both dates neglect a long history of contacts between Europeans and natives that had already shaped relations here decades before the founding of permanent colonies. When Captain John Smith arrived, he found that the Indians of the Chesapeake Bay had—and were accustomed to—French goods shipped down from Canada. Jacques Cartier's explorations had taken place in the 1530s, and French influence had grown ever since.

---

[256] On these issues and many other details, see T. J. Brasser, "Early Indian-European Contacts," in vol. 15 of Trigger, *Handbook of North American Indians*, ed. Bruce G. Trigger (Washington, D.C.: Smithsonian Institution Press, 1978), 78–88.

Hoping for advantageous trade relations, Chief Powhatan in Virginia even invited Smith to abandon Jamestown and move the settlement to territory Powhatan controlled.[257] Early contacts in North America, then, consisted of gradually expanding interaction between Indians and Europeans—often stimulated by native desire for goods, trade, and military advantage over traditional enemies—not a sudden and crushing eruption of the latter among the former.

Witness Chief Massasoit's welcoming of the Pilgrims at Plymouth. The Indian Squanto, who introduced the English and acted as an interpreter, was a Patuxent who had been kidnapped by an English sea captain and sold into slavery in Spain (in violation of Spanish law) in 1614. He escaped from Spain to England with the help of another English captain and returned to his native land in 1619 to find that his people had been wiped out by an epidemic. As he sailed along the New England coast toward what would become Plymouth:

> What Tisquantum [Squanto] saw on his return home was unimaginable. From southern Maine to Narragansett Bay, the coast was empty—"utterly void".... What had once been a line of busy communities was now a mass of tumbledown homes and untended fields overrun by blackberries. Scattered among the houses and fields were skeletons bleached by the sun. Slowly Dermer's crew realized they were sailing along the border of a cemetery two hundred miles long and forty miles deep. Patuxet had been hit with special force. Not a single person remained. Tisquantum's entire social world had vanished.[258]

---

[257] Ibid., 84.

[258] For a vivid portrait of the whole period, see Charles C. Mann, *1491: New Revelations of the Americas before Columbus*, 2nd ed. (New York: Knopf Doubleday Publishing Group, 2011), 61–62.

Columbus and the Crisis of the West

Despite all this, he promoted and succeeded in establishing good relations between Pilgrims and Indians for some time. One analyst of these relations has written:

> For nearly fifty years, the simple treaty of 1620 signed by Massasoit, a sachem representing, it was believed, the entire Wamponoag Federation, and Plymouth's governor John Carver worked splendidly. By the treaty, both parties pledged that they would not "doe hurte" unto the other, a pledge that was maintained throughout extremely provocative and risky times. Then in the 1660s came the cultural disturbances that led to King Philip's War—the war that totally ruined the peaceful accommodations of two generations of native and English diplomats.[259]

In the current controversies about larger issues and longer-term injustice against Native Americans, these fragile first accommodations that might have developed into a more pacific mixed culture are often overlooked, just as Columbus's relations with Guacanagarí are overlooked.

Two generations of peaceful relations was no small achievement. While goodwill or cultural understanding may not have been sufficient on either side to have made the long-term history turn out differently than it did, a rich and fluid situation clearly existed at the time of the first permanent settlements, and opportunities were sometimes taken. Unlike the Spanish, the English never devoted themselves to sustained theological and ethical reflection on the status of natives, but even a thoughtful pursuit of mutual advantage might have led to a far different outcome.

---

[259] Russell Bourne, *The Red King's Rebellion: Racial Politics in New England 1675–1678* (New York: Oxford University Press, 1990), xii.

Wilcomb Washburn, a longtime resident scholar at the Smithsonian Institution, rightly denounced the violent acts of Puritans and Virginians against natives, but remarks:

> None of the Indian wars of New England was inevitable—even in the psychological sense … and certainly not in an economic sense…. Peaceful coexistence between Indian and White was, therefore, possible. Although it did not occur, it was not because of underlying imperatives but because both sides—particularly the English—blundered into confrontations that exploded into full-scale war…. In Virginia also peaceful coexistence was possible but did not occur…. All the wars of Virginia could have been avoided and the conspiracies made unnecessary if English conduct toward the Indians had equalled the standards of honorable dealing that the Virginia Company and the royal government sought to uphold.[260]

This assessment is more than mere late wishful thinking. Several alliances and treaties, and the slow evolution and increase in mutual trade and understanding, could indeed have yielded a better result. And that the Virginia Company and the British crown—like Spain and Rome—sought "honorable dealing" should not be neglected because of what people actually did in hard circumstances. The view that European arrogance and blindness, or the gap between the neolithic natives and the English, made war and destruction inevitable rests on no firm historical basis.

What Indian Opinion?

One of the little-told stories about contemporary controversies over the Native American past is the division of opinion within

---

[260] Wilcomb E. Washburn, "Seventeenth-Century Indian Wars," in vol. 15 of Trigger, *Handbook of North American Indians*, 99.

surviving indigenous groups themselves—something we would take for granted in any other U.S. ethnic group. James A. Clifton, an anthropologist who played a role in legal and political battles over tribal rights and entitlement, has recorded some of the complex cleavages that exist among Indians today.[261] Quite often these Indian cleavages mirror cleavages within the rest of American society. While retaining a strong tribal identity, some groups such as the Klamath in Oregon, says Clifton, are prosperous and underwent a relatively smooth process of integration into the mainstream culture. Other groups, such as the Southern Ute of Colorado, have maintained a separate identity on a self-administered reservation but have flourished, largely owing to skillful management. Public discussions of Native American affairs rarely include these success stories.

More familiar to the popular consciousness is another type of group Clifton has studied. The Prairie Potawatomi Indians, for example, are very poor and deeply divided internally, making it virtually impossible for them to formulate or pursue a coherent tribal policy. In their efforts to get political and economic relief, they become involved in endless legal struggles that disregard their particular history and anthropology. Clifton summarizes their aims: "obtaining absolute political autarchy while perpetuating absolute fiscal independence."[262]

The tribal situation perhaps least understood in the public mind, however, is illustrated by the Menominee in Wisconsin. The tribe voted years ago to accept a terminal financial settlement and to disband itself as a formal entity under government support. But as the mood among Indian leaders throughout the nation changed (as it has periodically in the past) and pressure built for all indigenous

---

[261] See in particular Clifton, introduction to *The Invented Indian*.
[262] Ibid., 5.

groups to reassert their identities, the Menominee were moved to consider "retribalization." Clifton, who was then administering a VISTA-like program in Wisconsin, was confronted with three large Menominee factions:

1. Restorationists: "mainly educated middle-class, off-reservation women ... the protégées of the liberal wing of Wisconsin's Democratic Party, spurred on also by flotsam on the rising tide of militant paleface feminism."

2. Terminationists: "all elder, mainly male, upper middle-class managers and entrepreneurs ... aided and abetted by the conservative wing of Wisconsin's Republican Party."

3. Warriors Society: "mainly young, urban, lower-class males and the women who adored them ... covertly coached in their deftly played confrontational tactics by a political splinter group—Wisconsin's tiny band of zealous Trotskyites ...joined by a perfectly weird medley of the other protest groupies who invariably show up when storms brew in Indian Country."[263]

Predictably, Clifton's efforts to be nonpartisan led conservatives to accuse him of aiding communist Indians, led liberals to reject him for failing to turn over all funds to approved groups, and led one pistol-toting Warrior (wearing the garb, unknowingly, not of a local group but of a distant and alien Southwestern tribe) to threaten him with death. Lost in these factional and theatrical machinations, of course, were whatever common desires and needs might have remained among the tribal people themselves.

This regrettable experience shows the political manipulation to which contemporary Indian claims are routinely subjected and also bears witness to the variety of native reactions to white presence. While a vague Pan-Indian agenda might be said to exist as a result

[263] Ibid., 8.

of overwhelming white pressure, it is not as easily identifiable as some might think. The most radical agenda should certainly not be accepted as representing the true and only "Indian" voice.

Quite clearly, Indian issues are now as much enmeshed in power politics as they are in the pursuit of justice. No matter how native views may vary, only the high-minded, ecofeminist Native Americans imagined by the Berkeley City Council—rather than, say, their lowly relations in profit-minded tribes permitting reservation gambling casinos—are allowed legitimately to claim the name Native American in elite circles. Clifton writes of the typical organization concerned with Indians today: "To meetings of these now come churchmen, statesmen, feminists, environmental activists, and academics—as suppliants, soliciting coalitions, seeking favors, checking their approval ratings."[264] There is no calculating the effects this atmosphere has produced on campuses and in publishing houses—to say nothing of social media and society at large.

Multitudinously American

Questions about Native Americans' status in modern society, in fact, reflect a much more complicated set of issues now troubling the United States in particular and the Western world in general. The very terms we have begun to use to describe ourselves suggest widespread uncertainty. Before the fall of the Berlin Wall, Marxists used to refer to the modern West as "late industrial" or "late capitalist." With the demise of Marxism and socialism as viable theories, other labels have become more prominent: "post-Enlightenment," "post-bourgeois," and—most inclusive of all—"postmodern." It is in this intellectual and social environment that the repercussions

---

[264] Clifton, introduction to *Invented Indian*, 16.

of the 1492 controversy are felt most profoundly. The more extreme activists ostensibly serving the Native American cause often dismiss proposals for reparation, recognition, and reform in favor of profound rejection of, and revolution against, contemporary American life. They seem to use the label "Native American" only as a means of achieving goals having little or nothing to do with traditional native interests and probable futures.

Life in modern industrialized societies with pluralistic rather than monolithic cultures has raised fundamental questions about our relations to nature and to one another. At one time, it was assumed that the outcome of modernization was inevitable progress. The sociologist Max Weber, however, famously spoke of the "iron cage of modernity," in which traditional bonds would be summarily broken and individual belief, behavior, and social ties would be radically rationalized. But events in the late twentieth and early twenty-first centuries have revealed that the iron cage is a sociological fiction. Modern societies, for all their standardizing and uniformizing tendencies, have not destroyed ethnic, religious, or familial identities. Even the totalitarian power of the former communist societies was unable to stamp out such deep human loyalties, which survived and emerged with renewed force after those systems collapsed.

Clearer still, however, is the growth of a pervasive sentiment that insists that these loyalties *not be allowed* to disappear. It is important to note the precise role that these natural human institutions are being asked to play. Unity amid particularity is now our global native condition, and, logically, a recalibration of the time-tested *E pluribus unum* should be our goal. But in the conditions of late modernity, radicals who see no good in modern economics, politics, or culture will not, of course, be satisfied with this traditional vision, no matter how it is extended to new groups. As the great culture historian Jacques Barzun has noted:

Columbus and the Crisis of the West

Today the full realization of the Western world's practical concerns would not reconcile and make happy its chief denouncers. It might make the poor and disfranchised happier, but one may wonder for how long, since those already free from want, tyranny, ignorance, and superstition declare themselves the most oppressed and miserable of men and willingly risk what they have in order to smash the system.[265]

And Barzun was writing before the emergence of even more radical "identity" and "intersectional" movements. The postmodern disenchantment runs deep, even with those things that would formerly have been considered indisputable, precious, and historically unique achievements. Barzun again: "Like representative government, like capitalism, like traditional religion, the culture that the West has been painstakingly fashioning since Columbus has ceased to serve and satisfy."[266]

One response to this situation—a response traced in detail in the preceding chapters—is to seek to escape to some premodern age or non-European context, untouched by Columbus and what he wrought, because our Western legacy is held, usually on as scant acquaintance as our knowledge of indigenous peoples, to be responsible for all our present miseries. Native cultures, largely unknown, have the advantage of at least never having exerted much influence on our societies. Some people regard the neolithic inhabitants of the precontact Americas as a potential *deus ex machina*, a deliverer from the world we have created for ourselves.

But this "solution" comes at a high price and not only to those who benefit from the current arrangements. It places an enormous burden on native groups, who are not allowed simply to become a

---

[265] Jacques Barzun, *The Culture We Deserve* (Middletown, Conn.: Wesleyan University Press, 1989), 175.
[266] Ibid., 173.

more respected voice in the American mosaic. They must redefine the whole set of human relations with other humans and with the natural world. Unfairly, living Native Americans are made to choose between assimilation to the mainstream culture and symbolic death, on the one hand, and separation and marginality for the foreseeable future, on the other. Unlike other ethnic peoples on these shores, Native Americans are considered most authentically themselves only when they live as they did five hundred years ago—and denounce the present.

This inflexibility may advance certain agendas within the mainstream culture, but it is of questionable value to Native Americans. For those who seek the good of both Native Americans and modern culture as a whole, the best relationship—barring some fresh currents of thought on our way toward a new epoch in world history—can only be something of a dialectic. The mainstream culture will, without doubt, continue to dominate the development of native communities. But native communities are in a better position than at any time in their history to resist where they will and to make such contributions as they can to mainstream culture. The struggle is unequal, and native contributions will not go unopposed, and they may even be ignored. But in this they will be no different from German, Jewish, Italian, Polish, African, Hispanic, Korean, Vietnamese, and a host of other influences on American society.

The alternative is the ghetto. Any group may choose isolation as a means of retaining cultural purity, of course, but the inevitable accompaniment of that choice is marginalization. A freely chosen condition cannot also then be a case of complaint and group claim against the rest of society. In our world, such claims will simply not be heeded. If the past five hundred years of atrocities, openness, misunderstanding, freedom, slavery, emancipation, and struggle for civil rights have taught us anything, they should have taught us that the United States—more than any other society in history—has at least been willing to grapple with the pursuit of justice for a wide variety of peoples. That process is not complete and perhaps can never be completed. But as millions around the world have demonstrated in recent years in their wish to immigrate, the promises of American-style democracy and society offer greater hope for all peoples than any other known system.

One undeniable impulse behind the promotion of Indian culture under the aegis of redefining 1492 is a perceived lack of spirituality in modern life. Joseph Epes Brown describes the difference between our lives and those of Native Americans in which "religion"

is not a separate category of activity or experience [but] is in complex interrelationships with all aspects of the peoples' lifeways. Shared principles underlie sacred concepts that are specific to each of nature's manifestations and also to what could be called sacred geography. In addition, a special understanding of language in which words constitute distinct units of sacred power. Sacred forms extend to architectural styles so that each dwelling ... is an image of the cosmos. Mysticism, in its original and thus deepest sense, is an experiential reality within Native American spiritual traditions.[267]

As is clear from this quotation, however, the interest in Native American spirituality actually reflects a Western sense of discontinuity with the fullness of our own cultural and religious background. The ideal describes something akin to a Holy Roman Empire and its sacred social order, art, and architecture.

Much of the current revisionist agenda, properly understood, comes close to endorsing deep currents in the very mainstream

[267] Quoted in Kehoe, "Primal Gaia," in Clifton, *Invented Indian*, 197–198.

European culture the multiculturalists abhor. When Robert May-nard Hutchins and Mortimer Adler were criticized for not includ-ing masterpieces from the East in their Great Books series, for example, they argued that they had to draw a limit to the volumes somewhere. But then they pointed out—quite rightly—that the works many people suggested for inclusion (out of a kind of proto-multiculturalism) were far more similar to ancient and medieval European literature than their modern proponents might have suspected.[268] The same is true, *mutatis mutandis*, of the pitting of certain indigenous, or supposedly indigenous, cultural elements against the modern Western world. The protest is, in its most profound moments, a Western objection to the disappearance or attenuation of several religious and philosophical currents within the West itself.

Native American culture may not have much to say directly to our current crises, but it may at least remind us of some essential things. It would be far better for us, better physically and better spiritually, to do Corn Dances or Rain Dances on Saturdays or Sun-days than to spend so much time at shopping malls, for instance. A certain exuberance about nature and about the spiritual, properly understood, would open some windows in our climate-controlled world.

Life in the twenty-first century is in many of the deepest hu-man ways hard, and sources of light seem few. Since the future is unknowable, we naturally turn to the civilizations of the past for enlightenment. When we do so, however, we must be ready to look honestly at the record. With respect to Native Americans, to do

---

[268] Robert Maynard Hutchins and Mortimer Adler, eds., "East and West," in *The Great Conversation*, vol. 1. of *Great Books of the West-ern World* (Chicago: Encyclopedia Britannica, 1952), particularly 70–71.

anything less is to practice the final imperialism: redefining the historical facts to fit our own categories. There are no perfect societies in America's or any other region's past, and any attempt to realize such a fiction is a flight both from truth and from responsibility.

Such flights are understandable. As anthropologists have discovered, primitive cultures prefer cyclical visions of nature and human life because they promise escape from the terrors, tragedies, and epic demands of history. In modern societies, we have not entirely outgrown that impulse. An ominous feature of the more radical of such flights, however, is the sharp alienation from our common American culture that they represent. If Columbus was a wicked and rootless wanderer because he found no home in late-fifteenth-century Spain, what are we to say of his modern detractors who can find absolutely nothing good in their own science, technology, religion, social arrangements, and industry? Or to adapt an observation made by one of the primary creators of that bad Old World culture, if the critics cannot love their neighbors, whom they have seen, how can we rely on their love of the noble savage, whom they have not seen?

But perhaps the profoundest lesson we may hope to learn from contemplating 1492 is that it is important for every people to have a vigorous culture. A multiculturalist will admit this in every case save one, that of so-called Western culture. Like it or not, Western culture with its own particularities and its openness to light from the outside is the cultural matrix upon which the world has become, if not unified, then set on a path of something like universal mutual intercourse. No other culture in the world has—or probably could have—undertaken that task.

The Western tradition is debased, cut off from or in uncertain relation to its own roots. But those roots are what make an authentic multiculturalism possible at all. Indeed, with its inheritance from Israel, Greco-Roman culture, Christianity and medieval kingdoms, and much more, "the West" is by nature multicultural.[269] At its best, the West has integrated what is good and true into itself without losing its momentum. As we look back at the last five hundred years and more of world history, we should appreciate that even today's declining Western culture—and not some monolithic political or theological system—presides over all our cultural futures in the third millennium. Columbus succeeded in his vision of universal evangelization at least to that extent. And that's something for which all people may be, properly, grateful.

---

[269] See Rémi Brague, *Eccentric Culture: A Theory of Western Civilization*, trans. Samuel Lester (South Bend, Ind.: St. Augustine's Press, 2006).

Chapter 7

What Is "Western" Civilization?

A dynamic force seems to be drawing first Western society,
then the rest of the world, toward a state of relative
indifferentiation never before known on earth, a strange
kind of nonculture or anticulture we call modern.

—René Girard, *Violence and the Sacred*[270]

So what is this "Western civilization" that is entwined with the
Columbus story, and where did it come from? The term does not
refer to any simple geographical location and did not exist until
relatively recently. According to the *Oxford English Dictionary*, in
1907, G. K. Chesterton was the first to use the expression "Western
man." How the notion came into existence explains a good deal
about what the West represents. For many people, "the West"
simply means Western Europe and countries of European origin,
such as the Americas, Australia, and New Zealand. But the non-
European parts of the West, particularly America, have added to
and altered the original cultural base. Much of what is characteristically American was forged against European influences, long
before there was such a thing as opposition to "Eurocentrism."

---

[270] René Girard, *Violence and the Sacred*, trans. Patrick Gregory (Baltimore: Johns Hopkins University Press, 1979), 189.

Columbus and the Crisis of the West

Yet America also undeniably remains an offshoot of Europe. In addition, Western ways are spreading to other parts of the globe. Paradoxes of this kind make it necessary to inquire more carefully into exactly what we mean by "the West."

Whatever else it may mean, Western civilization is the primary culture in America and Europe. Yet this simple statement has begun to raise all sorts of protests. Many individuals and groups dominant in our society identify Western civilization with racism, slavery, imperialism, colonialism, sexism, environmental destruction, and other equally repulsive traits. Even more troubling, they do so without much acquaintance with the rich, varied, open, and questing nature of what is best about the West—or a realistic appraisal of the likely alternatives. Most of these attacks depend on moral or intellectual intuitions that, elsewhere, have little, if any, importance. So anyone who thinks Western institutions to be of value finds himself at an odd, embattled crossroads. He may agree with the quite Western principles used to criticize some Western failing, but he senses danger—and no little inconsistency—in the way such principles are blindly turned against their very source.

A civilization is not something we simply inherit or ever finally possess. Each generation, individually and collectively, needs to make a continual effort to appropriate it anew because a civilization is not passed along to us at birth. A civilization is an elaborate structure of ideas and institutions, slowly built up over time by the intelligence and effort of countless individuals working alone and together. If we fail to understand and live out that complexity, which tries to answer to the complexity of human life itself, we can easily fall back to a less human existence. It has happened often in history. At present, we need a profound cultural recovery, yet most high school and college students are not introduced to the basic historical knowledge necessary for that recovery to begin. And although modern America continues to embody many principles of the West, it would be a grave mistake to identify our deeply confused country with Western civilization. America's manifest troubles cause many to question the virtues of Western civilization even before they learn what it is or to what degree contemporary America reflects it.

At a minimum, any comprehensive account of the West would have to look at ancient Greece and Rome, the contributions of Judaism and Christianity, the Middle Ages (including the Age of Discovery), the Renaissance, the Reformation and Counter-Reformation, the Enlightenment, and the current anti-Enlightenment mood in its several postmodernist forms. And this does not even begin to weigh the various ethnic and national contributions to the larger civilization. Such a survey would require book-length treatment, at a minimum, and several detailed studies to paint an accurate portrait.[271] But just to list these complementary and conflicting currents should warn us that the West cannot be reduced to a few simple slogans. Only the decline in the serious study of the past has allowed critics to make public claims that this complex history may be reduced to an organized conspiracy of "white" men engaged in protecting their own interests.

In the anti-Western reading, the Greeks spawned the whole problem. In any balanced view, ancient Greece produced a series of great geniuses in rapid succession, unparalleled in human history, and later became the tutor of ancient Rome. Christianity and the Jewish tradition from which it arose first spread to a larger world in Greek. Though Greek language and thought all but evaporated in the West for almost a thousand years—from before the fall of Rome to the early Renaissance—many labored to preserve as much as they could from the ancient Greek heritage. And when the Greek

---

[271] I have tried to present some of this material in an earlier volume: Robert Royal, *The God That Did Not Fail: How Religion Built and Sustains the West* (New York: Encounter Books, 2006).

language became known again, people would turn back, century after century, to study Greek political thought, philosophy, art, architecture, and science. Columbus himself was still using ancient Greek geographies and related materials as he planned his first voyages.

Why? Not because the Greeks were the oldest Dead White European Males.[272] Europe (in the current sense of the term) did not yet exist when Greece flourished. Ancient Greek culture became part of later European culture because a variety of peoples in very different social circumstances simply found Greek achievements great. So did the high medieval Arabic civilization, which produced some interesting commentaries on Greek philosophy, even before the West. Further, Greece did not think of itself as "European," and by the time Europe arose, Greece lay on its margins. There were many reasons why Greek achievements could simply have been lost or left out of Europe.

Ancient Greece straddled Europe and Asia. The father of history, Herodotus, was a Greek born in Halicarnassus, on the Greek-inhabited coast of today's Turkey. Nonetheless, he began the tradition of distinguishing East and West in his *Histories* by characterizing the Persian invasion as a battle between Greeks and barbarians. That dichotomy has drawn intense criticism, and not only from people who have never seriously considered the question. In *A Study of History*, the great British historian Arnold Toynbee (1889–1975) berates Herodotus for contributing to European haughtiness toward other civilizations. He points out that, at the time, the Easterners were far less barbaric than the so-called Westerners.[273] Writing in

---

[272] For a sophisticated commentary on this notion, see Bernard Knox, *The Oldest Dead White European Males, and Other Reflections on the Classics* (New York: W. W. Norton, 1993).

[273] Arnold Toynbee, "'Asia' and 'Europe': Facts and Fantasies," Ix, C (I) Annex to *A Study of History*, vol. 8 (New York: Oxford University Press, 1954), 708–729.

the first half of the twentieth century, Toynbee thought it urgent to deflate what he called "Modern Western assumptions." But were he writing today, he might feel the need to correct an equally exaggerated denigration of the West.

Europe's borders were always uncertain. In the East, it has been difficult to say whether Turkey, Russia, and "Eastern" Europe are really European. In the West, Spain, as European a country as any, spent more than seven hundred years under Islamic domination, a period as long as the time that separates us from the Magna Charta. And England and Ireland have been regarded — and sometimes regard themselves even now — as not really part of continental Europe. Yet despite all uncertainty about its physical borders, "Europe" has an unmistakable cultural as well as a geographical meaning.

Aristotle once wisely remarked that we should not expect greater precision in defining a subject than the subject itself allows. And in the *Politics*, he observes of East and West:

> Those who live in a cold climate and in Europe are full of spirit, but wanting in intelligence and skill; and therefore they keep their freedom, but have no political organization, and are incapable of ruling over others. Whereas the natives of Asia are intelligent and inventive, but they are wanting in spirit, and therefore they are always in a state of subjection and slavery. But the Hellenic race, which is situated between them, is likewise intermediate in character, being high-spirited and also intelligent.[274]

Today, of course, we do not put much confidence in *géographie moralisé*. But for all the objections that can be raised against Herodotus or Aristotle, their intuitions proved historically right. The Greek ideal of liberty differed from that of surrounding peoples. For the

[274] Aristotle, *Politics* 1327b.

Columbus and the Crisis of the West

Greeks, the virtue of self-control makes us fit to rule and to obey the rule of law; order in the soul answers to order in the world. This idea has flourished in the West as it has nowhere else. Indeed, it was only as the inhabitants of the "cold climate" of Europe centuries later made that idea their own that the West was set on its characteristic course.

Today, the most common attacks on Greece come from familiar quarters. Feminists claim that the low status of Greek women overshadows other achievements. Black writers make similar arguments about Greek slavery. And leftists of various stripes argue that Plato and Aristotle represent the ideology of a privileged class rather than the first steps toward discovering universal human nature and ethics. A grain of truth lurks in each of these charges, but, as with many criticisms laid against the West, the failure to see other truths and give them the correct relative weight renders such contentions largely null.

For the great Greeks were not uniquely evil in these matters. All ancient societies showed differences in the status of men and women and great economic disparities among classes. As we have seen in previous chapters, slavery existed in almost all premodern societies: in pre-Columbian Mexico and Peru, among native peoples in the Caribbean and North America, and in Asia and Africa down to this day. A less ideologized approach would be more curious about how Greece opened up the path toward a political freedom correlated with human excellences. There are complicated historical reasons why we have now come to think women are equal to men, slavery is an abomination, and opportunity should be available to all. But Greek thought about liberty, extended later to all human beings, is a crucial part of the story. That needs to be understood and defended from unconsidered attack—along with other Greek achievements in science and philosophy, poetry, drama, architecture, and art—because they begin a new chapter in human history.

What Is "Western" Civilization?

The heart of the accusations against ancient Greece, when they are not merely ideological slurs, lies in Aristotle's belief that some were "slaves by nature." The first book of the *Politics* makes this case that those who do not or cannot control themselves are destined to be controlled by others. This is a serious argument in any age that should not simply be dismissed because of our qualms about the word "slavery." The American Founders and some of the greatest thinkers throughout history warned of the inevitability of tyranny if popular virtue dries up. This argument has resurfaced at various points, not least during debates over the status of Native Americans and blacks in the New World. But we will be misreading Aristotle and blinding ourselves to the liberation that studying other ages may bring if all we get from "slaves by nature" is a reflection of our own preoccupations with race, class, and gender.

Aristotle claims *some* of us are slaves by nature; but in a sense we are *all* slaves by nature — slaves to our ignorance, passions, and untutored capacities. Elsewhere in Aristotle we see the need constantly to pursue education and self-discipline to overcome our natural slavery. And it is no accident that as our attachment to that view of civilization weakened, our view of education shifted. An errant pedagogy has arisen that makes the ignorant passions of the student the measure of what should and should not be learned. As a result, even when people spend long years under instruction they usually wind up in a kind of learned barbarism.

In a curious development, some Afrocentrists have claimed that Greek philosophy was stolen from the Egyptians — which is to say from Africa. Whether the idea of slaves by nature, slaves being an integral part of ancient Egyptian society, is part of the African wisdom they do not say. Yet the very Greek thought denounced as embodying Western racism, sexism, and classism by one set of scholars is being coveted by another for its Africanness. A single ideological standard lies behind this superficial double standard:

Greece and the West are bad, while the non-West, especially Africa, is good. Whatever good Greece may have achieved, therefore, originated in Africa. To anyone familiar with the ancient world, though, ancient Egypt was African in much the same sense that modern Egypt, with its Islamic and Mediterranean background, is African; i.e., it's nominally on that continent and not simply black. Even leaving aside the lack of evidence for the African origin of Greek philosophy, this Afrocentrist thesis is built on seriously flawed scholarship.[275]

To be sure, we cannot defend everything even about as great a moment in Western history as ancient Athens. Slavery was a serious evil, and we cannot deny that Greek thinkers looked down on manual labor. Combined with some later currents in the Christian religion, however, this shortcoming was remedied.

Christianity grew from humble beginnings: fishermen, tentmakers, artisans, slaves. That would have long-term effects. When Saint Benedict set up his monasteries after the fall of Rome in the sixth century, one of his rules for the monks was *laborare est orare*, "to work is to pray." This sanctified work, including sheer manual labor, as no previous culture had ever done. In the Middle Ages, guilds and other corporations put themselves under religious patronage. At the time of the Reformation, it became increasingly common for laymen under Lutheran and Calvinist influences to think of

---

[275] Facts have not stopped some overingenious characters such as Martin Bernal in his *Black Athena* from confusing Greece, Egypt, and black Africa. The antidote to this ideology-driven misreading of the ancient world is the kind of cool reasoning to be found in Mary R. Lefkowitz's *Not Out of Africa* (New York: Basic Books, 1996). See Martin Bernal, *Black Athena: The Afroasiatic Roots of Classical Civilization* (New Brunswick, N.J.: Rutgers University Press, 1991); see also Mary R. Lefkowitz and Guy MacLean Rogers, eds., *Black Athena Revisited* (Chapel Hill: University of North Carolina Press, 1996).

their secular occupations as part of their religious vocations. The ancient philosophers, trying to elevate the human spirit, were right to put work and commerce on a lower plane than the highest things. But the fact remains that human work and the economic dimension of liberty were underemphasized in ancient Greece, until Christianity slowly came to reform all that.

It has been necessary to linger over the charges leveled against this major stage in Western history because, today, if we don't know how to get outside current intellectual obsessions, we will not be able to study the tradition with profit at all. There may be benefits in considering alleged sexism, racism, and class interests in the West. But if we look to unparalleled cultures such as ancient Greece for enlightenment only to find reflected there the concerns of contemporary campuses and the media, we will learn only what we already think we know. We do not need Greece, or the Renaissance, or the Enlightenment if we want merely to engage in self-adulation for our supposed superiority to the past rather than to receive with gratitude the gifts the past offers.

History enables us to make intelligent comparisons. We may thus find, say, male-female income disparities among us. But before we indulge ourselves in outrage against the very sources of our liberties, we should compare them with African female genital mutilation, Chinese foot-binding, Indian widows and suttee, the general repression of women in Islam, and a host of other practices that were never tolerated in the West. Let us turn, then, to examining more fully the emergence of the West and its significance for us.

As we have seen, Aristotle thought the peoples living in "Europe" were free, but only in a wandering barbarism lacking political order. Something between his time and ours created a unified Europe. To a Greek, strange as it may seem to us, an identifiable Europe need never have been at all. Europe, as may be observed on ancient maps, is merely a peninsula of the large Asian land-mass. Greece under Alexander the Great amassed an empire that extended all the way to India; in Europe, it founded small colonies and traded. Only later did Europe gain a unity of both a general political nature and a spiritual, cultural, and moral cast. The two institutions most responsible for the emergence of that Europe were the Roman Empire and the Roman Catholic Church.

The Roman Empire presents an even more mixed picture than does ancient Greece, a reminder that, historically, quite unworthy vessels are often the bearers of great human goods. Gladiator and animal fights in the Coliseum, the brutal persecutions of early Christians, the crude crucifixions of criminals, and the vast slave populations all confirm that, paradoxically, something quite uncivi-lized in Rome coexisted alongside civilizing tendencies. Without Rome, for example, the Greek influence on the West might have remained as distant as Persia's. The Rome of the Caesars was a conduit for Hellenistic civilization, and Rome itself — minus its obvious brutality — would become the standard of civilization in Europe for more than a thousand years.

The Romans were a practical people; their philosophers, poets, and artists, with notable exceptions, were inferior to the Greeks. As a result, Roman culture was largely a borrowed affair. The char-acteristic Roman professions were soldier, engineer, and governor. The Romans energetically took control of the lands around what they came to call *mare nostrum*, i.e., "our sea," the Mediterranean. Under the genius of Julius Caesar, Rome conquered Gaul, parts of Germany, Britain, Asia Minor, and beyond. The greatest Roman poet, Vergil, gives a picture in his epic the *Aeneid*, not of Rome as it really existed, but of an ideal Rome, founded by an Aeneas who undertook the journey from Troy to Italy. During a visit to the underworld, Aeneas hears from his dead father a humble and realistic description of Rome's missions:

Others will cast more tenderly in bronze
Their breathing figures, I can well believe,
And bring more lifelike portraits out of marble;
Argue more eloquently, use the pointer
To trace the paths of heaven accurately
And accurately foretell the rising stars.
Roman, remember by your strength to rule
Earth's peoples—for your arts are to be these:
To pacify, impose the rule of law,
To spare the conquered, battle down the proud.
                    (*Aeneid* 6, 848–857; Fitzgerald trans.)

The word translated as "strength" here is *imperium*, "empire." Earlier, Vergil's Jupiter promises the Romans something later writers saw as similar to what Jahweh promised the Israelites: "For these I set no limits, world or time/ but make the gift of empire without end." It is almost as much a religious as a practical vision, and that is why in the *Divine Comedy*, Dante, the greatest Christian poet, looking back at Roman history, chose Vergil as his guide in the next world, all but the parts that enter specifically Christian territory.

Furthermore, the line "To pacify, impose the rule of law" might be better translated as "To add the habit of peace to peace itself." In the centuries to follow, the rule of law, the law of nations, and natural law, all notions that got a strong boost in Rome, would become mainstays of Western thought about matters within and among states. These are issues too complicated to go into at any length here. But listen to Marcus Aurelius, the Stoic emperor of the second century, who expresses his gratitude to one of his brothers for teaching him to value "the conception of the state with one law for all, based upon individual equality and freedom of speech, and of a sovereignty which prizes above all things the liberty of the subject."[276] Marcus Aurelius would have been a great figure in any age. Still, it is not merely chance that almost two millennia later, this is still the common moral language — Roman language — among Western nations.

In the making of the West, the ideal Roman type worked slowly behind the quite unideal day-to-day reality. We find a Roman impulse toward justice and the unifying of various peoples that helps us understand why the American Founders thought a good deal about Rome, particularly because of the history of squabbling between individual city-states in the ancient and medieval worlds, and tendered us the Latin motto, *E pluribus unum*. Rome's penetration into much of the known world through roads, bridges, effective administration, and the Latin language would not be surpassed in Europe until the seventeenth century. That physical and political drawing together, that unique mixture of the practical and the ideal, prepared the ground for the spiritual and cultural unification of Europe.

This brings us to the question of the third great early formative influence on Europe: Christianity and the Jewish background from which it arose. It has long been a blind spot in historiography, at least since the Enlightenment and, in ways, going back to the Renaissance, to think that the Middle Ages were merely a dark interlude between the ancients and their rediscovery. In this reading, crusades, inquisitions, forced conversions, and superstition form the trajectory of Western religion. This is both wrong and crippling in any attempt to understand the rise of the West.

By the time the Roman Empire in the West fell apart and was overrun by the barbarians, much of Europe had been brought together within Roman culture. But North Africa and large parts of

---

[276] Marcus Aurelius Antoninus, *The Communings with Himself*, trans. C. R. Haines (Cambridge, Mass.: Harvard University Press, 1970), 11 (I, 14).

the East had been brought within the same culture, and they would not have a history similar to Europe's. The division that occurred, one that persists to this day, was between the Latin West and the Greek East. Europe underwent a series of changes that enabled it to emerge from the period of loss of learning and centuries of barbarian invasions as something that we would identify even today as Western Europe. But in the High Middle Ages, people thought of themselves not in a geographical sense but rather in cultural terms as part of "Christendom." If we overlook Latin Christianity, out of either a prejudice against religion or a misplaced fear that telling the truth offends against pluralism, we will have no way of understanding the emergence of Europe and the West.

There was a missionary fervor in Christianity that made it by nature expansive. Christians created an international network of church authorities quite separate from their civil counterparts. Despite all the disagreements, apostasies, and turmoil within the churches, this authority and the slow missionary work of monks — sometimes in collaboration with secular rulers, sometimes in opposition to them, drew the European peoples into a real unity.

The parallel authorities seemed to reflect Christ's instructions to the apostles to "Render unto Caesar's the things that are Caesar's and to God, the things that are God's" (Matt. 22:21). That basic idea has had a varied career in the past two thousand years. We are used to thinking the separation of church and state a modern idea, but its roots run deep in the West. Edward Gibbon remarked in *The Decline and Fall of the Roman Empire* that "the various modes of worship which prevailed in the Roman world were all considered by the people as equally true; by the philosopher equally false; and by the magistrate equally useful."[277] This is a clever formula, but

---

[277] Edward Gibbon, *The Decline and Fall of the Roman Empire*, vol. 2, ed. J. B. Bury (London: Methuen, 1900), 28.

every one of its assertions is demonstrably false. And as Christianity spread, such minimal truths as it expressed would no longer be the case. The emperors, for instance, often tried to use Christianity and sometimes succeeded, but something new had appeared that resisted complete manipulation.

Two main ways of relating God and Caesar emerged in the empire. In the Roman East, God and Caesar became closely identified, especially around the new capital, Constantinople. Bishops might be appointed and church councils called by the emperor. Here lie the roots of what is sometimes called "Caesaropapism"; and while that Eastern Christianity had and continues to have great contributions to make to culture, it followed closely the ancient idea of the city and its gods as inextricably bound up together. One reason the countries of Greek Christianity—Greece, the non-Latin Slavic nations, preeminently Russia—are ambiguously "European" is a different understanding of the relationship of the spiritual and the temporal that began in the late empire.

In the Western part of the Roman Empire, something else happened. Bishops and other church officials became alternative sources of authority. They were not necessarily opposed to the new Christian empire. Indeed, sometimes in figures such as Saint Ambrose, the great bishop of Milan, training in the old imperial bureaucracy was combined with vigorous pursuit of the new Christian dispensation. Ambrose's pupil, Saint Augustine, one of the greatest geniuses who ever lived, explains brilliantly how, though the two are inextricably bound to one another in this world, the City of God differs from the City of Man. Rebutting charges that the Christian religion had softened the old pagan virtues, thus enabling the barbarians to overrun Rome, Augustine instead claims that Christ empowers people able to act virtuously as mere pagan philosophy could not. Furthermore, Augustine believed, Christian humility purified the very virtues of paganism, which, though real virtues, had been placed at the service of Rome's *libido dominandi*, a lust to dominate.

There is good historical evidence to believe Augustine was right. The Church was carrying out a practical task, running health and support groups, slowly winning people over to differently oriented lives all over the West. For example, acting on the Mosaic law, it succeeded in eliminating the widespread ancient acceptance of male homosexuality. Plato and Aristotle, and some of the later Roman Stoics, had already arrived at the view that it would be best for any society if sex occurred only between a man and woman in marriage. But given the morals of the ancient peoples, such views might have never gone further than sophisticated philosophical circles. It took the Christian church to shift social mores both among the elites and throughout the general population.[278] Along with homosexuality, the ancient practices of suicide, infanticide, and slavery slowly diminished in the West.

During what we used to call the Dark Ages, not only do we see the origins of church-state separation and a new morality; we also begin to see representative institutions that balance various interests in society. Medieval kings and lords answered to lesser nobles and the people in ways that later kings, when a new concept of divine right was emphasized more than it had been in the medieval view, would not. In any event, we need a renewed appreciation of medieval political and spiritual contributions to the modern world to understand ourselves and the world in which we live, because by the twelfth and thirteenth centuries, it is possible to detect the geographical, spiritual, moral, and political outlines of modern Europe.

The later Middle Ages also began the recovery of ancient wisdom through Latin translations from earlier Arabic translations of

---

[278] On this point, see my "Plato Does Colorado: Were the Ancient Greeks Modern Gays?," *Crisis*, March 1995.

Columbus and the Crisis of the West

Greek thinkers whose works were lost after the fall of the Western Empire. During the Italian Renaissance, the Western Europeans were reading philosophers and the New Testament in Greek again with enormous consequences for European science, art, literature, and religion. That they could think of themselves as one people recovering their classical and Christian heritage was due to the medieval synthesis they and many since have ignorantly spurned.

The ancient division of the world into Europe, Asia, and Africa began to take on concrete importance during the Renaissance for several key reasons.[279] First, the need to find other routes to the spices and wealth of the East drove the Portuguese down the West African coast and around the Cape of Good Hope to India, thus giving Europeans a palpable feel for these ancient regions they had earlier grasped in only the vaguest way. Second, the discovery of the Americas and their conquest by European powers both strengthened Europe's global power and sharpened its sense of its identity as different from these new peoples. Finally, the division of the West into Catholic and Protestant during the Reformation weakened the idea of a unified Christendom, though European peoples clearly felt themselves part of one culture. Thus, Christendom was becoming Europe at the same moment that Europe, by its overseas adventures and other developments, was turning into a global presence that ultimately would be better described by the less restricted term "the West."

Let us turn briefly now to Europe's world expansion for the light it sheds on some of the controversies that have arisen over the modern history of the West. Around 1500, Europe "discovered"

---

[279] For the best brief statement of this view, see Peter Burke, "Did Europe Exist Before 1700?," *History of European Ideas* 1, no. 1 (1980), 21–29. Denys Hay's *Europe: The Emergence of an Idea* (Edinburgh: Edinburgh University Press, 1957) remains one of the best studies of the medieval contributions to the notion of "Europe."

the Americas and began opening up the first truly global inter-change among the various parts of the world. Critics dispute this way of putting it: peoples in the Americas and other parts of the world, they say, already knew where they were and had no need to be "discovered." But this is false. None of the civilizations in the Americas, not even the relatively high cultures of the Aztecs and Incas, had the slightest notion of the rest of the world or their place in it. The same was the case for the ancient civilizations of Asia. It may be true that, during exploration, Europe introduced assumptions (and spread colonialism) to the great annoyance of latter-day anti-Eurocentrists. But this is only to say that Europe was the first to attempt a kind of global understanding where previously there had been none at all. All current attempts to give a different reading of the past five hundred years of history, like it or not, must begin with the European achievement of global scope.

This is particularly upsetting to many theorists. The "postcolo-nial" theorist Edward W. Said, for example, argued that since 1500 "Eurocentric culture relentlessly codified and observed everything about the non-European or peripheral world, and so thoroughly and in so detailed a manner as to leave few items untouched, few cultures unstudied, few people and spots of land unclaimed."[280] The odd thing about this statement is that Said thinks this European curiosity about non-Europeans is somehow sinister. A Palestinian culture critic and classical pianist, who has been welcomed by a wide Western audience while teaching at a prestigious university in the United States, where he uses the very tools of Western historical scholarship to appeal to the Western inclination to-ward egalitarianism, is in an odd position to denounce alleged Eurocentrism.

---

[280] Edward W. Said, *Culture and Imperialism* (New York: Knopf, 1993), 267–268.

Columbus and the Crisis of the West

Europe's interest in other cultures is unparalleled in human history for many reasons. European culture is a multicultural amalgam of the two ancient classical civilizations and the Eastern culture of the Bible, which was wholly non-European. In addition, as we still see today, the national cultures of Europe complicate the picture further. Instead of regarding Europe as an evil monolith, the champions of multiculturalism might do well to recognize that their very interest in diverse cultures stems directly from multicultural Europe. In many instances, the interest accompanied missionary work. As we have seen in earlier chapters, for example, the Franciscan Bernardino de Sahagún wrote the history of the Aztecs in Nahuatl, the Aztecs' own language. The Aztecs themselves had not written it since they had neither true writing nor a critical sense of history; the Jesuits among the Canadian Indians learned about native languages, cultures, and religions in order to better evangelize. Of course, there were quite brutal and deplorable European clashes with other cultures, but why would we expect anything else of thousands of people operating in different cultures and continents beyond the reach of the law over hundreds of years?

There is a reason such disciplines as anthropology, ethnology, and archaeology are European creations. Even when they introduced prejudices or false judgments or distorting paradigms about other cultures, the early Europeans did so unintentionally and against their own scientific principles. It is common these days to claim that, even if the Europeans began such a process of worldwide understanding, Europe and its culture are no better—indeed usually they are characterized as a great deal worse—than the cultures of the indigenous peoples with whom they came into contact. This wrongheaded assertion stems from a conflation of the two meanings of the term "culture." The first meaning connotes the neutral description of a society attempted by anthropologists or sociologists, an approach developed by the West—a perfectly legitimate and valuable study, if we avoid the error of believing that our neutrality toward cultures for scientific purposes means we cannot judge them in more broadly human terms.

The second meaning of "culture" signifies the cultivation of each object or human activity to the highest perfection. Music, painting, manufacturing, child-rearing, and cooking all have internal standards that enable people in every culture to distinguish better from worse. We may not like a particular culture's cuisine, just as we may not have an ear for jazz. But people engaged in that form of cooking or music will have quite definite ideas of better and worse within that field. Once cultural practice discovers excellence, we may disagree about new developments, but we never decide that, after all, Salieri was greater than Mozart. All peoples sense that certain elements of their culture are more vital, richer, deeper, and more expressive than others. Cultural hierarchies do indeed exist within cultures, and to deny that is to blind ourselves to a proper appreciation of what others think about themselves.

It is more controversial to apply this principle across cultures, but we may do so circumspectly. Cultures are complex wholes and can only with difficulty be compared, but a society identical to pre–Civil War America that did not include slavery would have been superior to the one that existed. We can make similar judgments across cultures, but often do not today because they may lead to politically incorrect conclusions that some non-Western societies are not preferable to the West. For instance, we have all heard of Aztec sacrifice of captives by cutting out their still-beating hearts at the summit of their impressive pyramids. Witnessing these atrocities drove some of the quite callous early Spanish conquistadores to sheer outrage. But the sacrifices were not a mere barbarism; the cosmology of ancient Mesoamerica, Mayan, and Aztec, saw the world as having been created by the blood of the gods. As mentioned earlier, for the Aztecs human sacrifice was necessary to keep the world in balance; the blood of humans reinvigorated the cyclical processes of nature. This might also alert us to the complexities that may be concealed under apparently good environmental attitudes when someone tells us that another culture believed in "balance with nature."

Now, what are we to say of this? Shall we say, as some do, "It worked for them," or, "We cannot judge among cultures"? No one says that about American slavery or European colonization. Of course, we can always do what the multiculturalists do today and evade these sorts of judgments by pointing to some Western atrocity or refusing to criticize any non-Western culture at all. But this is to abdicate what, even in the eyes of most critics, is the core of human life: moral judgments about good and bad behavior.

Where do we get the principles for such judgments? Obviously, we have a very complex inheritance that involves Greece, Rome, and our biblical roots along with more recent developments. Today we often apply principles of international law developed during the Age of Discovery.[281] And despite the old European inclination to romanticize or demonize the noble savage, who, looked at closely, is sometimes a complex, fallen creature like the rest of us, some Europeans also tried to think clearly about this new situation. As we have seen, it is widely accepted that Francisco de Vitoria, a Dominican friar, laid the foundation for international law in his reflections on the ethical questions raised by the European encounter with Indians.[282] Vitoria's revulsion at Pizarro's conduct in the conquest of Peru first stimulated his thinking about Spanish conquests in the New World, but he was soon carried by the very force of his thought to examine a whole gamut of issues relating to the widely differing and previously unknown peoples.

[281] See chapter 3.
[282] See Scott, *Spanish Origin*.

What Is "Western" Civilization?

Vitoria's positions develop the best of the prior Western international-law tradition in the face of a new challenge. Those reflections led, in turn, to further elaborations of international law back in Europe. And this history of ethical reflection on the New World probably influenced John Locke—a key source of thought of the American Founders—who had an extensive collection of books and documents about the European discoveries.

When we think of Indians today, our view of them as a weak, essentially benign group of peoples badly treated for centuries must inform our historical judgment. They suffered many outrages that they should not have. But the peoples and cultures of the New World before the spread of European influence differed widely from one another and did not always display characteristics that anyone would wish to defend today. If these cultures had been left alone and were still intact today, most of us would think that humanity and reason required intervention, for good Western reasons. It is only ignorance—of history and anthropology—that permits a sentimental view of people who have, without question, been badly treated.

It is against this background that we must view the modern history of the West. It can always be objected that despite this rich heritage and the labors of philosophers, theologians, and statesmen to achieve a humane world, the West has been a miserable failure by its own standards. Anyone who has read of the wars of religion in the sixteenth and seventeenth centuries, the conflicts between nation-states in the eighteenth century, and the sometime brutal European colonization of non-Western areas may believe that the West cannot be taken as any kind of model. Furthermore, the West very nearly destroyed itself in the twentieth century with two ferocious world wars and a Cold War that, given the power of nuclear, biological, and chemical weapons, could have poisoned or destroyed human life on earth.

Columbus and the Crisis of the West

All of this raises important questions about principles and practice. One of the things Americans in particular want to avoid is any temptation to think of ourselves as somehow outside history. A wise European pointed out not long ago that only in America would people seek a "more perfect union" since Americans "by their very nature, have never been satisfied with mere perfection."[283] It deserves to be said that this dissatisfaction is the source of much of what is good about America; we neither settle for things as they are, nor, at least until recently, have we become cynical about the possibilities of human life. And that is why as the hegemony of Europe gave way to the American Century—probably sometime around Chesterton's invocation of Western man—America became the leading example of the globalized European culture now called the West.

One way we express perfectionism, however, is through a curious kind of a historical pragmatism. English-speaking democracies have been prone to think they can get things done without worrying very much about justifying theories. We like to compare ourselves with continental Europe, which got itself into trouble over the past few centuries by following various systematic ideologies. The French Revolutionary tradition, we enjoy pointing out, fell prey to various theoretical fanaticisms that have terrorized the world. Socialism and communism were variants of that tendency; Nazism with its mad "scientific" racial theories was another. But just because wrong theory has led to hell does not mean that no theory will lead to paradise.

The English-speaking democracies today are themselves falling prey to a pragmatic tyranny precisely because they are drifting further and further from their Western roots. We never had, for example, the sharp clash between religion and political liberty

---

[283] Barzini, *The Europeans*, 11.

that some of the continental nations did; indeed, we used to see the religious and moral traditions of the people as the bulwark of public life. That is no longer the case. The engagement of our courts in the ethnic cleansing of all such traditions from the public square would have seemed inadvisable, and perhaps impossible, to Augustine and Washington alike. Pockets of resistance remain within civil society, but, given the crisis of education (including religious education), it remains to be seen if these age-old sources of our liberty will last. The vast influence of the media, so-called popular culture, and state education monopolies tie all of us in a knot difficult to escape. As we try to recover the high Western culture, we have to make immense efforts to restore this popular culture as well. And we cannot do that by appeals to pragmatism; we need to begin speaking in popular language about Western principles, which, with proper encouragement, most Americans would practice.

It has become common lately to ridicule the notion that the West is in decline. Optimists, or historical skeptics, say that people always have the sense that some prior age was better or more secure. They point to undeniable achievements and the most spectacularly successful political and economic arrangements in human history and bid us to be of good cheer. We may be grateful for all these things and count them among the achievements of the West. But the spiritual, moral, and intellectual grounding on which they were built is slipping away from us, despite our material success. To say this is not to accept some inevitable, fated decline. One of the central principles of the West is the belief in free will. Since the ascent or decline of a civilization can only be the sum total of the rise or decline of individual wills and minds, what each of us thinks and does can make all the difference in whether we continue to lose our heritage or whether we rediscover it and make our materially satisfying world spiritually and intellectually fulfilling as well.

Columbus and the Crisis of the West

One final characteristic of the West that is quite evident to people around the world, is our development of science and technology. Why these arose in the West alone is another complex story involving primarily Greek curiosity, biblical views of an ordered creation, and the independent institutions needed to pursue research—namely, universities, which were the creations of the Church in the High Middle Ages. Once those elements were in place, the various revolutions of recent centuries in the subject matter of science were, by comparison, relatively small changes.

The West used to boast of these achievements, as great testimonies to human ingenuity and patience that gave the West the tools needed to dominate the world. More recently, critics have seen the West's social and material dominance as different expressions of evil: We have lorded it over other peoples, they say, even as we have destroyed nature. Even the Bible, the crucial element of our moral heritage, has been indicted. "Be fruitful and multiply and have dominion over the earth," in Genesis, it is said, is the evil root of the West's will to power.[284] Combined with the European sense of superiority, we arrived at a potent formula for the exploitation of nature and other cultures.

Sorting out these claims is difficult because there is a way in which modern science and technology have broken the bounds of our ethical sense. We see in early modern figures such as Francis Bacon the belief that it is acceptable to "put nature on the rack for the relief of the man's estate."[285] Something brutal *was* released with the new science, yet it does not seem absolutely necessary to its practice. On the positive side of the ledger, millions, even billions,

---

[284] The *locus classicus* of this view is Lynn White Jr., "The Historical Roots of Our Ecologic Crisis," *Science* 155 (March 10, 1967): 1203–1207. Though thirty years old, White's essays continue to provoke debate over biblical sources of callousness toward nature.

[285] Bacon, *The Advancement of Learning*, 44.

of people have been freed from the age-old scourges of famine and disease by that same development. Today, the only reason large groups of people starve is because of politically induced famine. We are capable, in an ecologically sustainable way, of feeding and providing for not only the billions of people now alive but those who will be born in the coming decades to increase the population to perhaps half again its current size. Turning our back on technology in our circumstances would be both imprudent and inhuman.

Some population alarmists do not shrink from recommending human diebacks, but that is not an option for most of us. Besides the sheer human suffering it would bring, what kind of world would we create if in addition to killing children in the womb and hastening death among the aged and infirm, we begin callously to allow perfectly healthy people to die out of some abstract notion of what ecological balance requires?

There is within the Western technological paradigm something far more worrisome than the ecological questions: those problems are already largely being resolved and, with the exception of the controversial questions about greenhouse gases and the ozone layer, there seems no doubt we can cope with the problems we have created.[286]

More worrisome, however, is that within the West technological ideology has come to separate us from the deeper bases of our culture. We see in medical ethics, human life issues, and contemporary attitudes toward nature a reductionist view that no longer preserves the fullness of the West. Human beings are regarded as a collection of chemical reactions resulting in certain impulses. Sex,

---

[286] See Jesse H. Ausubel, "The Liberation of the Environment," *Daedalus* 125, no. 3 (Summer 1996), which is entirely devoted to explaining how most of our environmental questions will be solved.

therefore, becomes a mere matter of hormones over which we have no control. Crime is the result of an interplay between genetics and environment. We cannot reject insights into human action that the sciences may bring us. But the old Aristotelian notion of the patient formation of virtue—and the very belief that we are spiritual beings who can rule ourselves and therefore attain a certain dignity—finds few cultural institutions willing to encourage us in this always difficult task. The consequences for relationships between men and women, families, children, and the social order have been devastating. We, of course, need to fight various battles in politics, law, and the culture, but without that Western notion of human nature, none of the rest will really matter.

One reaction to the narrow, rationalist view of human beings that has been with us since the Enlightenment is to deny the validity of reason. We cannot here explore the complexities of postmodernism, deconstruction, post-structuralism, and many other movements that are often used to bully us into thinking the Western tradition a guilty conspiracy. In theory, these movements are attempting to open up a falsely closed view of human life. The problem is that they do so, not by conceptualizing a truer one but by a radical skepticism, a Nietzschean drive toward self-creation that denies all value in the world and locates it only in what we ourselves create. That is to substitute for one inhuman theory another even worse.

We also need to recognize how the inhuman has entered our free economy. Plato once warned that if we forget the knowledge of the good life, shipbuilding will still provide us with ships, shoemaking with shoes, the others arts with their various products, yet without the science of the good life that all things are to be used for, we will find all the other arts have failed us.[287]

[287] Plato, *Charmides*.

What Is "Western" Civilization?

Western civilization cannot be found in some textbook or database. It has no website. It is not a course that you take and then forget, like so many others. Today, many people with advanced degrees do not understand civilization—indeed, may barely have heard of it. We are still quite early in our lives as a global species—only five hundred years separate us from Columbus and the first Westerners who set out around the world. Whether a universal civilization will emerge from this situation is impossible to say; whether it is even desirable is almost as difficult to say. We need a long reflection on unity in diversity before we come to that. But the multiculturalism of such a global civilization is likely to be quite different from the one the multiculturalists envisage, if only because the West has set the terms for much of the debate and continues to attract many to itself from other cultures.

Despite its many shortcomings and occasional atrocities, this Western dominance is providential. No better champion of justice, fairness, liberty, truth, and human flourishing exists than the complex and poorly known entity we call Western civilization. The West, in the broadest sense of the term, produced both the New Testament and the Marquis de Sade, Francis of Assisi and Hitler. Yet its rise has, in the main, been a blessing to the human race. The West's weakening or demise would pose a threat to many human virtues. Recovering and extending Western principles remain our best hope for a more humane world. For in these matters, there is no serious rival to the West.

Appendix

The Europe That Gave Us Columbus

As Orson Welles famously remarked, playing the unscrupulous Harry Lime in the film *The Third Man*: "In Italy for thirty years, under the Borgias, they had warfare, terror, murder, and bloodshed, but they produced Michelangelo, Leonardo da Vinci, and the Renaissance. In Switzerland they had brotherly love. They had five hundred years of democracy and peace, and what did they produce? The cuckoo clock." Lime's history was more than a little vague and self-serving (Welles himself seems to have been titillated by this dangerous truth since he added it to Graham Greene's original script for the film). Fifteenth-century Italy in particular, and Europe more generally, drew their vitality from a lot more than Borgias and Machiavellianism. But it is a paradox of history that social turmoil often offers rich soil for human achievement.

The world we know began in the fifteenth century. Not the world, of course, in the sense of human life or human civilizations, which had already existed for millennia, but the world as a concrete reality in which all parts of the globe had come into contact with one another and begun to recognize themselves as part of a single human race—a process still underway and far from complete, even in the Age of the Internet. The spherical globe we had known about since the classical world; in the Middle Ages, readers of Dante took it for granted. Yet it was only because of a small expedition by a few men driven by a mishmash of personal ambition, religious motives, and the desire for profit that an old mathematical calculation was turned into a new human fact. Or, as a historian sixty years later accurately characterized the discovery of the New World, it was "the greatest event since the creation of the world (excluding the incarnation and death of Him who created it)."[288]

In our own confused way, we continue to pay homage to that achievement. In 2015, NASA put a satellite into an orbit a little less than a million miles out into space at what is called "L," the libration point where the gravity of the earth and the sun exactly balance one another. Equipped with a telescopic lens and video camera, it provides a twenty-four-hour-a-day image of the surface of the earth; the new satellite is called DISCOVR but was originally intended to be called Triana, after Rodrigo de Triana, who first spotted lights on land from the deck of the *Pinta* during the first voyage of Columbus.

The original name was probably only a bow to growing Hispanic influence in the United States and disappeared as the project developed, perhaps out of growing political turmoil about Columbus's legacy. In any event, it suggested that maybe we would like to think of ourselves as equally on the verge of another great Age of Discovery. But whatever our sense of the future, outside of not only NASA and a few historical enclaves, the Columbus discoveries and the European intellectual and religious developments that lay behind them are today at best taken for granted, at worst viewed as the beginning of a sinister Western hegemony over man and nature. The last five centuries, of course, offer the usual human spectacle of great glories mixed with grim atrocities. But we cannot evaluate the voyages of discovery properly without gratitude

---

[288] López de Gómara, *Primera Parte de la Historia General de las Indias*, vol. 22, 156.

for what they achieved in themselves and some of the goods to which they gave rise. In the fifteenth century, the discoveries were rightly regarded as close to a miracle, especially because of the way the century had begun.

The early 1400s were marked by profound religious, political, economic, and even environmental turmoil. At one point in the first decade of the century, there were simultaneously three claimants to the papal throne and three to the crown of the Holy Roman Empire. And the large-scale institutional crises were only a small part of the story. Europe was still suffering from the devastation wrought at the height of the Black Death over half a century earlier and in smaller waves thereafter. Overall, something like 40 percent of the population disappeared in the mid-fourteenth century, in some regions even more. (Even larger percentages would fall to disease in the New World.) Land lay fallow for lack of workers, villages were deserted, poverty spread. As many modern environmentalists have devoutly wished, nature took its vengeance as human population decreased.

Wolves multiplied and returned, even appearing on the streets of capital cities. Human predators — in the form of brigands — made travel unsafe over wide areas. The consequences of the retreat of civilization spurred Henry V, fabled victor of Agincourt, to offer rewards for the elimination of both types of pests. Though the beauty of landscapes emerged as never before in contemporary painting and literature, it was not a century that indulged itself in easy sentimentality about the goodness of unimproved nature, human or otherwise. On the contrary, natural hardships spurred the fifteenth century to nearly unparalleled achievements.

But if the internal situation were not enough, Europe was also being squeezed by forces from outside. In 1453, the Ottoman Turks finally succeeded in taking Byzantium. Turkish troops had already been fighting as far into the Balkans as Belgrade a few years earlier.

Columbus and the Crisis of the West

Otranto, in the heel of Italy, fell to them in 1480 for a time. We might have expected the Christian powers to lay aside rivalries momentarily and defend themselves from an alien culture and religion. But the main Atlantic nation-states—England, France, and Spain—were still only beginning to take shape. The rest of Western Europe was broken, despite the theoretical claims of the emperor, into a crazy quilt of competing small powers. So no coordinated effort occurred, though Pius II and other popes called for a crusade. Pius even wrote to Sultan Muhammad II, conqueror of Constantinople, inviting him to convert to Christianity. Whether this letter was intended seriously or as a mere pretext for further action, it failed. Neither "European" nor "Christian" interests were sufficiently united to galvanize the effort. The pope died in 1464 at the eastern Italian port of Ancona waiting for his people to rally behind him.

A crusade to retake the Holy Land was sometimes a mere pipe dream, sometimes a serious proposal during the course of the century. Ferdinand of Spain listened frequently to such plans but refrained from doing much. (Machiavelli praises him in *The Prince* as one of those rulers who shrewdly take pains to appear good without necessarily being so.) Charles VIII of France invaded Italy in 1494 but also had in mind an attempt to retake Constantinople and restore the Eastern Christian Empire. Earlier, Henry V, on his way to Agincourt, proclaimed his intentions not only to assume the French throne but to "build again the walls of Jerusalem." Western Europe had a persistent if vague sense of responsibility to defend Christianity from Islamic military threats and a deeper need to recover the parts of Christendom lost to Muslim conquest, even if the good intentions were thwarted by intra-European conflicts.

Had Islam continued its advance, much of Europe might have then resembled the cultures we now associate with the Middle East. The Americas might have been largely Muslim countries as opposed to largely Christian ones. Islam was more advanced than Europe in 1492, but in the paradoxical ways of culture, its very superiority contributed to its being surpassed. Muslims do not seem to have taken much interest in Western technical developments in navigation, and even well-placed countries such as Morocco were never moved to brave the high seas in search of new lands. European technological innovation and military advance may have been born of necessity, given the superiority of outside cultures and the conflicts and rivalries among European nations.

This reminds us of something often overlooked in most contemporary historical surveys. The "Eurocentric" forces, of which we now hear so much criticism, were something quite different in the fifteenth century. What we today call "Europeans" thought of themselves as part of Christendom, and a Christendom that desperately needed to return to some of its founding truths. Similarly, they did not regard themselves as the bearers of the highest culture. Ancient Greece and Rome, they knew, had lived at a higher level, which is why the Renaissance felt the need to recover and imitate classical models. The fabled wealth of the distant Orient and the clearly superior civilization of nearby Islam did not allow Christendom to think itself culturally advanced or, more significantly, to turn in on itself, as did self-satisfied empires of the time, such as China. Contemporary European maps—the ones all the early mariners consulted in the Age of Discovery—bear witness to their central belief: Jerusalem, not Europe, was the center of the world.

But this very sense of threat and inferiority, combined with the unsettled social diversity of Europe at the time, gave Europeans a rich and dynamic restlessness. Not surprisingly, the rise toward a renewed Europe began in the places least affected by the population implosion and, therefore, more prosperous: what we today call the Low Countries and, above all, Northern Italy. Renascences, as Erwin Panofsky has demonstrated, had been occurring in Europe since the twelfth century.[289] But the one that took place in Northern Italy in the fifteenth century—the one we call *the* Renaissance—produced multiple and wide-ranging consequences.

Pope Pius II was in many ways emblematic of the mid-century. A cultivated humanist born in Siena in 1405 with the imposing name Aeneas Sylvius Piccolomini, he initially came under the spell of Saint Bernardino, who preached a strictly observant reformed Franciscan life. But he shortly became attracted to the exciting life of the Renaissance Italian humanists, which is to say libertinism and literary pursuits. He shifted parties among papal contenders, pursuing his own ambitions for many years, wrote a popular history (*Historia rerum ubique gestarum*—a book Columbus studied) that gathered together wide-ranging facts and fictions about foreign lands, and even became imperial poet and secretary to the Holy Roman Emperor Frederick III. But compared with the squabbling popes and antipopes who preceded him and the colorful escapades of the Borgias, Pius had his virtues. He was learned and hardworking, enjoyed nature, sought reform, and could have made a difference in Europe had his office enjoyed the respect it once had and was to have again later. The religious renaissance, however, like the cultural, scientific, and artistic one with which we are more familiar, had to come from other sources.

Renaissance achievements found multiple and overlapping uses in a Europe in ferment. The geometry developed by the Florentine Paolo Toscanelli allowed Filippo Brunelleschi, over the objections of a commission of Florentine experts, to dare construction of the unsupported dome that crowns the magnificent Florentine Duomo. Just a few decades later, an intellectually curious Genoese mariner corresponded with Toscanelli in preparation for his attempts to

[289] Erwin Panofsky, *Renaissance and Renascences* (New York: Routledge, 2018).

convince another panel of experts in Spain that it was possible to sail west to the Indies. It was an age when, for various reasons, people had the faith to attempt things beyond what was previously thought possible.

Columbus's religious side seems to have grown out of a religious renaissance that occurred in fifteenth-century Europe. The *devotio moderna*, beginning with Gerard Groote and the Brethren of the Common Life, spread among both religious and laypeople, calling for a return to a more personal religion modeled on the evangelical virtues of the early Church. Its best-known writer was Thomas à Kempis, whose *Imitation of Christ* (ca. 1427) has influenced numerous individuals and movements, Catholic and Protestant, over the centuries. As late as the middle of the sixteenth century, Ignatius of Loyola, for example, the founder of the Jesuits, made it the first book he read when he decided to begin a serious religious life. The *devotio moderna* shaped figures as diverse as Nicholas of Cusa and Erasmus. In many ways, it paralleled the impulses behind the secular Renaissance in its living reappropriation of the religious past as the basis for the future.

Less known, however, is the Observant or Observantine current within the fifteenth century, first among the Franciscans, but later among other orders and lay groups. In fact, one of the major religious disputes for monasteries at the time was the need to choose between strict Observant and nonreformed Conventual rules. (Martin Luther began his religious life in an Observant Augustinian community.) The Franciscans numbered among their members figures such as Saint Bernardino of Siena, Saint James of the Marches, and Saint John Capistrano. Their efforts, too, looked to a religious renaissance by way of return to the more austere and humble ways of early Christianity. Mixed in with that more austere life, there were occasionally garbled versions of the millennial speculations of Joachim of Fiore, a twelfth-century Cistercian abbot, for whom a new age of the Holy Spirit and the final age of the world seemed not far distant.

We have no indisputable evidence that Columbus was a third-order Franciscan Observantine, but his way of dress in his final years in Spain appears to have been similar to theirs. When he traveled through Spain, he stayed at Franciscan monasteries rather than the homes of noblemen. Uncertainties about Columbus's early history and the history of the Observants in Spain prevent any greater precision, but it is clear that, mixed in with his other motives, he early on had absorbed some of the millennial currents of his time. Specifically, he seems to have believed that one reason to open the Western route to the Orient was to enable the gospel finally to be preached to all nations, a prerequisite to the end of the world and the triumphal Second Coming of Christ that some Joachimites predicted would occur in the middle of the sixteenth century.

Significantly, Columbus also seems to have believed something not found in any of Joachim's writings: that Joachim had predicted that a king of Spain would liberate the Holy Land. Though Columbus had a personal reason to keep Ferdinand and Isabella interested in the enterprise of the Indies, he also often urged them to undertake a crusade. The fact that Spain reconquered the kingdom of Granada only at the beginning of 1492 gave Spaniards a sense greater than that of most other Europeans of the need to resist Muslim incursions. In less savory forms, this sense contributed to the Inquisition's injustices to Spanish Muslims and Jews, who were expelled from Spain on the very day Columbus set sail. Columbus's urgings went unheeded, but we have good evidence of his sincerity. For the last decade of his life, the various wills he made altered different clauses, but one remained constant: he directed the executors of his estate to set up a fund in Genoa's Bank of Saint George to help pay for the liberation of Jerusalem. Whatever other motives we may attribute to him, there is no question that on spiritual matters he put his money where his mouth was.

Today, the usual way of characterizing the behavior of the Europeans at this early stage is to fault them for not having the kind of sensitivity to "the other" that a modern anthropologist or ethnologist would bring to such situations. Overlooked in this condemnation is the fact that it was precisely out of these tumultuous conflicts that the West began to learn how to understand different cultures as objectively as possible in their own terms. Columbus himself astutely noted differences between the various subgroupings of Taínos as well as their distinctiveness from other tribes. And even when he was driven to harsh action—against both Indians and Spaniards—it was not out of mere desire for power.

This raises the question, however, of larger intentions and the world impact of fifteenth-century European culture. The atrocities committed by Spain, England, Holland, and other European powers as they spread out over the globe in ensuing centuries are clear enough. No one today defends them. Less known, however, are the currents within that culture that have led to the very universal principles by which, in retrospect, we criticize that behavior today. The information coming from the New World stimulated Francisco de Vitoria, a Dominican theologian at the University of Salamanca in Spain, to develop principles of natural law that, in standard histories, are rightly given credit as the origin of modern international law. To read Vitoria on the Indies is to encounter an atmosphere closer to the U.N. Universal Declaration of Human Rights than to sinister Eurocentrism.

Conquest aside, the question of even peaceful evangelizing remains very much with us. Today, many people, even Christians, believe it somehow improper to evangelize. The injunction to preach the gospel to all nations, dear to Columbus's heart, seems an embarrassment, not least because of the ways the command has been misused. But some of the earlier missionaries tried a kind of inculturation that recognized what was good in the native practices and tried to build a symbolic bridge between them and the Christian faith. The Franciscans in New Spain and the Jesuits in Canada, for example, tried this approach. Not a few of them found martyrdom.

For all our sense of superiority to this now half-millennium-old story, we still face some of the same questions that emerged in the fifteenth century. We still have not found an adequate way to do justice to the claims of both universal principle and particular communities. We have what Václav Havel has called a "thin veneer of global civilization," mostly consisting of CNN, Coca-Cola, blue jeans, rock music, and perhaps the beginning glimmer of something approaching a global agreement on how we should treat one another and the planet.

But that minimal unity conceals deeper conflicts involving not only resistance to superficiality but the survival of particular communities of meaning. We say, for example, that we have an equal respect for all cultures—until we come up against religious castes and sexism, clitorectomies and deliberate persecution. Then we believe that universal principles may take precedence. But whose universal principles? A Malaysian prime minister has instructed the Western nations that, contrary to international assumptions, "Western values are Western values: Asian values are universal values." It may take another five hundred years to decide whether that is so, or whether the opposition it assumes between East and West will even persist.

All of this may seem a long way from the fifteenth century. But it is not mere historical fantasy to see in that beginning some of the global issues that are now inescapably on the agenda for the new millennium. Christianity and Islam, the two major proselytizing faiths in the world, are still seeking a *modus vivendi*. The global culture initiated by Columbus will always be inescapably European in origin and, probably, in basic shape. We chose long ago not to stay peacefully at home and build those otherwise quite wonderful contraptions called cuckoo clocks. That decision brought (and brings) many challenges, but the very struggle should remind us of the glorious and ultimately providential destiny of the ongoing global journey that began in the fifteenth century.

Selected Bibliography

Aiton, A.S. *Antonio de Mendoza: First Viceroy of New Spain*. New York: Russell & Russell, 1927.

Albanese, Catherine L. *Nature Religion in America: From the Algonkian Indians to the New Age*. Chicago: University of Chicago Press, 1990.

Anawalt, Patricia Rieff, and Frances F. Berdan. "The Codex Mendoza." *Scientific American* (June 1992).

Anderson, John J. *Popular History of the United States*. New York: Clark & Maynard, 1880.

Arens, W. *The Man-Eating Myth: Anthropology and Anthropophagy*. New York: Oxford University Press, 1979.

Ausubel, Jesse H. "The Liberation of the Environment." *Daedalus* 125, no. 3 (Summer 1996).

Axtell, James. *The Invasion Within: The Contest of Cultures in Colonial North America*. New York: Oxford University Press, 1985.

Bacon, Francis. *Francis Bacon*. Edited by Arthur Johnston. New York: Schocken, 1965.

Barzini, Luigi. *The Europeans*. New York: Penguin Books, 1984.

Barzun, Jacques. *The Culture We Deserve*. Middletown, Conn.: Wesleyan University Press, 1989.

Bataillon, Marcel. "The Idea of the Discovery of America among the Spaniards of the Sixteenth Century." In *Spain in the Fifteenth Century*, edited by Roger Highfield. New York: Harper & Row, 1972.

Bernal, Martin. *Black Athena: The Afroasiatic Roots of Classical Civilization*. New Brunswick, N.J.: Rutgers University Press, 1991.

Columbus and the Crisis of the West

Bethell, Leslie, ed. *The Cambridge History of Latin America*. New York: Cambridge University Press, 1984.

Bolívar, Simón. *Selected Listings*. Edited by Harold A. Bierck Jr. New York: Colonial Press, 1951.

Boorstin, Daniel. *The Discoverers*. New York: Vintage, 1985.

Borah, Woodrow W. *Justice by Insurance: The General Indian Court of Colonial Mexico and the Legal Aides of the Half-Real*. Berkeley: University of California Press, 1983.

Bourne, Russell. *The Red King's Rebellion: Racial Politics in New England 1675–1678*. New York: Oxford University Press, 1990.

Brading, D. A. *Mexican Phoenix: Our Lady of Guadalupe: Image and Tradition across Five Centuries*. New York: Cambridge University Press, 2001.

Brague, Rémi. *Eccentric Culture: A Theory of Western Civilization*. Translated by Samuel Lester. South Bend, Ind.: St. Augustine's Press, 2006.

Brasser, T. J. "Early Indian-European Contacts." In *Handbook of North American Indians*, edited by Bruce G. Trigger, vol. 15. Washington, D.C.: Smithsonian Institution Press, 1978.

Brown, Joseph Epes. *The Spiritual Legacy of the American Indian*. New York: Crossroad, 1982.

Burke, Peter. "Did Europe Exist Before 1700?," *History of European Ideas* 1, no. 1 (1980).

Canby, Vincent. "Saving the Huron Indians: A Disaster for Both Sides." Review of *Black Robe*, directed by Bruce Beresford. *New York Times*, 30 October 1991.

Carrasco, David. *Religions of Mesoamerica*. San Francisco: Harper & Row, 1990.

Cespedes, Guillermo. *Latin America: The Early Years*. New York: Knopf, 1974.

Chesterton, G. K. *Illustrated London News*, 23 April 1927. In *Collected Works*, vol. 34. San Francisco: Ignatius Press, 1986.

Chiari, Joseph. *Christopher Columbus*. New York: Gordian, 1979.

Clifton, James A., ed. *The Invented Indian: Cultural Fictions and Government Policies*. New Brunswick, N.J.: Transaction Books, 1990.

Selected Bibliography

Collins, John James. *Native American Religions: A Geographical Survey.* Native American Studies, vol. 1. Lewiston, Maine: Edwin Mueller Press, 1991.

Colon, Cristobal. *Libra de las profecías.* Translated and edited by F. Morales Pedron. Madrid: Collecion Tabula Americae, 1984.

Columbus, Christopher. *Libra de las profecías.* Translated and edited by Delno C. West and August Kling. Gainesville: University of Florida Press, 1991.

———. *The Log of Christopher Columbus.* Translated by Robert H. Fuson. Camden, Maine: International Marine Publishing, 1992.

Coe, Michael D., and Stephen D. Houston, *The Maya.* 9th ed. New York: Thames & Hudson, 2015.

Correa, Tom. "The Last Tribe to Get the Black Hills." *The American Cowboy Chronicles* (blog), April 18, 2015. http://www.americancowboychronicles.com/2015/04/the-last-tribe-to-get-black-hills.html.

Crosby, Alfred W. *The Columbian Exchange: Biological and Cultural Consequences of 1492.* Westport, Conn.: Greenwood Press, 1973. ·

The Daily Californian, 14 January 1992.

d'Angelo, Robin. *White Fragility: Why It's So Hard for White People to Talk about Racism.* New York: Penguin Random House, 2018.

Davidson, Jordan. "In Racist Screed, NYT's 1619 Project Founder Calls 'White Race' 'Barbaric Devils,' 'Bloodsuckers,' Columbus 'No Different Than Hitler.'" *Federalist,* June 25, 2020. https://thefederalist.com/2020/06/25/in-racist-screed-nyts-1619-project-founder-calls-white-race-barbaric-devils-bloodsuckers-no-different-than-hitler/.

Davis, Dave D. "Rumor of Cannibals." *Archaeology* 45, no. 1 (January/February 1992).

Delaney, Carol. *Columbus and the Quest for Jerusalem: How Religion Drove the Voyages That Led to America.* New York: Free Press, 2011.

de Lollis, C., et al., eds. *Raccolta di documenti e studi pubblicati dalla Reale Commisione Colombiana.* 14 vols. Rome: 1982–1986.

De Vorsey, Louis, Jr. *Keys to the Encounter: A Library of Congress Resource Guide for the Study of the Age of Discovery.* Washington, D.C.: Library of Congress, 1991.

Díaz del Castillo, Bernal. *History of New Spain*. Translated and edited by J. M. Cohen. New York: Penguin Books, 1983.

———. *History of New Spain*. Translated by Maurice Keating. New York: National Travel Club, 1927.

Dobyns, Henry F. *Their Number Become Thinned: Native American Population Dynamics in Eastern North America*. Knoxville: University of Tennessee Press, 1983.

Dubois, E. T. "Leon Eloy, Paul Claudel, and the Revaluation of the Significance of Columbus." In *Currents of Thought in French Literature*. New York: Barnes & Noble, 1966.

Egan, Timothy. "Chief's 1854 Lament Linked to Ecological Script of 1971." *New York Times*, 21 April 1992.

Eliade, Mircea. *Cosmos and History: The Myth of the Eternal Return*. New York: Harper Torchbooks, 1959.

Eliot, T. S. *Collected Poems, 1909–1935*. New York: Harcourt, Brace & World, 1962.

Elliott, Jan. *Exhibiting Ideology*. Review of *First Encounters*. New York: Racial Justice Working Group, Prophetic Justice Unit of the National Council of the Churches of Christ, 1990.

Elliott, J. H. *Imperial Spain, 1469–1710*. New York: Penguin Books, 1963.

———. *The Old World and the New, 1492–1650*. Cambridge, U.K.: Cambridge University Press, 1970.

———. "The Rediscovery of America." *New York Review of Books*, June 24, 1993. https://www.nybooks.com/articles/1993/06/24/the-rediscovery -of-america/.

Fagan, Brian M. *Kingdoms of Gold, Kingdoms of Jade: The Americas before Columbus*. London: Thames and Hudson, 1991.

Falcoff, Mark. "Was 1492 a Mistake?: Did Columbus Go Too Far?" *American Enterprise* 3, no. 1 (January/February 1992).

Fenton, William N. "Northern Iroquoian Culture Patterns." In *Handbook of North American Indians*, edited by Bruce G. Trigger, vol. 15. Washington, D.C.: Smithsonian Institution Press, 1978.

Fernández-Armesto, Felipe. *Columbus*. New York: Oxford University Press, 1991.

———. *Ferdinand and Isabella*. New York: Taplinger, 1975.

———. "In Defense of Columbus: The Trouble with Eden." *Economist*, 21 December 1991–3 January 1992.

Fernández Mendez, Eugenio. *Art and Mythology of the Taíno Indians of the Greater West Indies*. San Juan: Ediciones "El Cerni," 1972.

———. "1491: American before Columbus." *National Geographic* 180, no. 4 (October 1991).

1492 and All That: Political Manipulations of History. Washington, D.C.: Ethics & Public Policy Center, 1992.

Geertz, Clifford. *The Interpretation of Cultures*. New York: Basic Books, 1973.

Gerace, Donald T., comp. *First San Salvador Conference: Columbus and His World*. San Salvador Island: Bahamian Field Station, 1987.

Gibbon, Edward. *The Decline and Fall of the Roman Empire*. Vol. 2. Edited by J. B. Bury. London: Methuen, 1900.

Gibson, Charles. *The Black Legend: Anti-Spanish Attitudes in the Old World and the New*. New York: Knopf, 1971.

Gill, Sam. *Native American Religions: An Introduction*. Belmont: Cal.: Wadsworth, 1982.

Girard, René. *Violence and the Sacred*. Translated by Patrick Gregory. Baltimore: Johns Hopkins University Press, 1979.

Graves, Robert. *The Greek Myths*. Middlesex, U.K.: Penguin Books, 1964.

Greenblatt, Stephen. *Marvelous Possessions: The Wonder of the New World*. Chicago: University of Chicago Press, 1991.

Guier, Jorge Enrique. *Derecho precolombino*. San José, Costa Rica: Libro Libre, 1991.

Hale, John R. *The Age of Exploration*. New York: Time, 1967.

———. *Renaissance Europe: 1480–1520*. Berkeley: University of California Press, 1977.

Hanke, Lewis. *All Mankind Is One: A Study of the Disputation between Bartolomí de Las Casas and Juan Ginés Sepúlveda in 1550 on the Intellectual and Religious Capacity of the American Indians*. DeKalb: Northern Illinois University Press, 1974.

———. *Aristotle and the American Indians: A Study in Race Prejudice in the Modem World*. Bloomington: Indiana University Press, 1975.

———. *Bartolomé de Las Casas, Historian*. Gainesville: University of Florida Press, 1952.

Harari, Yuval Noah. *Sapiens: A Brief History of Humankind*. New York: Harper Perennial, 2015.

Hay, Denys. *Europe: The Emergence of an Idea*. Edinburgh: Edinburgh University Press, 1957.

Henige, David. *In Search of Columbus: The Sources for the First Voyage*. Tucson: University of Arizona Press, 1991.

Highfield, Roger, ed. *Spain in the Fifteenth Century: 1369–1516*. New York: Harper & Row, 1972.

Highwater, Jamake. *The Primal Mind: Vision and Reality in Indian America*. New York: Harper & Row, 1981.

Holland, Tom. *Dominion: How the Christian Revolution Remade the World*. New York: Basic Books, 2019.

Holmes, George, ed. *Oxford Illustrated History of Medieval Europe*. New York: Oxford University Press, 1990.

Hultkrantz, Åke. *Belief and Worship in Native North America*. Edited by Christopher Vecsey. Syracuse, N.Y.: Syracuse University Press, 1981.

———. *Native Religions of North America*. San Francisco: Harper & Row, 1987.

Hutchins, Robert Maynard, and Mortimer Adler, eds. "East and West." In *Great Books of the Western World*, vol. 1, *The Great Conversation*. Chicago: Encyclopedia Britannica, 1952.

Irving, Washington. *A History of the Life and Voyages of Christopher Columbus*. Philadelphia: Carey, Lea & Blanchard, 1837.

———. *A History of the Life and Voyages of Christopher Columbus*. Edited by James W. Tuttleton. Boston: Twayne, 1987.

Jane, Cecil, ed. *The Four Voyages of Columbus* ("A History in Eight Documents, including five by Christopher Columbus, in the original Spanish with English translations"). New York: Dover Publications, 1988. Reprint of the original 1929 and 1933 volumes of the Hakluyt Society.

Jennings, Francis. *The Ambiguous Iroquois Empire: The Covenant Chain of Indian Tribes with English Colonies from Its Beginning to the Lancaster Treaty of 1744*. New York: W. W. Norton, 1984.

Josephy, Alvin M., Jr., ed. *America in 1492: The World of the Indian Peoples before the Arrival of Columbus.* New York: Knopf, 1992.

――――. *The Indian Heritage of America.* New York: Bantam Books, 1968.

Keegan, William F. "Beached in the Bahamas." *Archaeology* 45, no. 1 (January/February 1992).

Kehoe, Alice B. *North American Indians: A Comprehensive Account.* Englewood Cliffs, N.J.: Prentice-Hall, 1981.

Kellaway, William. *The New England Company, 1649–1776: Missionary Society to the American Indian.* London: Longmans, 1961.

Kenton, Edna, ed. *The Jesuit Relations and Allied Documents.* New York: A. Boni and C. Boni, 1925.

Knox, Bernard. *The Oldest Dead White European Males, and Other Reflections on the Classics.* New York: W. W. Norton, 1993.

――――. "The Oldest Dead White European Males." *New Republic,* 25 May 1992.

Koning, Hans. "Don't Celebrate 1492 — Mourn It." *New York Times,* 14 August 1990.

――――. "Teach the Truth about Columbus." *Washington Post,* 3 September 1991.

Krauthammer, Charles. "Hail Columbus, Dead White Male." *Time,* 27 May 1991.

LaDuke, Winona. "We Are Still Here." *Sojourners* 20, no. 8 (October 1991).

Las Casas, Bartolomé de. *Historia de las Indias.* 3 vols. Mexico City: Fondo de cultura economica, 1951.

――――. *History of the Indies.* Translated and edited by Andrée Collard. New York: Harper & Row, 1971.

――――. *De unico vocationis modo.* In *Classics of Western Spirituality.* New York: Paulist Press, 1992.

――――. *A Short Account of the Destruction of the Indies.* Translated by Nigel Griffin. New York: Penguin Classics, 1999.

Lefkowitz, Mary R. *Not Out of Africa.* New York: Basic Books, 1996.

Lefkowitz, Mary R., and Guy MacLean Rogers, eds. *Black Athena Revisited.* Chapel Hill: University of North Carolina Press, 1996.

Columbus and the Crisis of the West

León-Portilla, Miguel. *Aztec Thought and Culture*. Translated by Jack Emory Davis. Norman: University of Oklahoma Press, 1990.

Leo, John. "P.C. Follies." *U.S. News & World Report*, 27 January 1992.

Leo XIII, *Quarto abeunte saeculo*. In *The Papal Encyclicals*, edited by Claudia Carlen, vol. 2, 1878–1903. Raleigh, N.C.: McGrath Publishing, 1981.

Levenson, Jay A., ed. *Circa 1492: Art in the Age of Exploration*. Washington, D.C.: National Gallery of Art, 1991.

López de Gómara, Francisco. *Primera Parte de la Historia General de las Indias*. Vol. 22. Madrid: Biblioteca de Autores Espanoles, 1852.

Marbury-Lewis, David. *Millennium: Tribal Wisdom and the Modern World*. PBS, 11 May 1992.

McAllister, Bill. "Columbus Jubilee Panel Gets Few Answers." *Washington Post*, 22 November 1992.

MacLeish, William H. "1492 America: The Land Columbus Never Saw." *Smithsonian* 22, no. 8 (1991).

Mann, Charles C. *1491: New Revelations of the Americas before Columbus*. 2nd ed. New York: Knopf Doubleday Publishing Group, 2011.

Martin, Joel S. *Sacred Revolt: The Muskogees Struggle for a New World*. Boston: Beacon Press, 1991.

Martinez, Demetria. "Bishop Challenges Knights to Drop Columbus." *National Catholic Reporter*, 25 August 1991.

Masters, Kim. "Some Might Call It Art ..." *Washington Post*, 9 February 1992.

Maxwell, James A., ed. *America's Fascinating Indian Heritage: Their Customs, Art, History and How They Lived*. Pleasantville, N.Y.: Reader's Digest Association, 1978.

Maxwell, Kenneth. "The Mystery of Chico Mendes." *New York Review of Books*, 28 March 1991.

———. "The Tragedy of the Amazon." *New York Review of Books*, 7 March 1991.

McClay, Wilfred M. "Of Statues and Symbolic Murder." *First Things*, 26 June 2020, https://www.firstthings.com/web-exclusives/2020/06/of-statues-and-symbolic-murder.

Moore, James T., *Indian and Jesuit: A Seventeenth-Century Encounter*. Chicago: Loyola University Press, 1982.

More, Thomas. *Utopia*. Translated by Paul Turner. New York: Penguin Books, 1961.

Morison, Samuel Eliot, *Admiral of the Ocean Sea*. 2 vols. Boston: Little, Brown, 1942.

———. *Christopher Columbus, Mariner*. New York: New American Library, 1956.

———. *The European Discovery of America: The Northern Voyages*. New York: Oxford University Press, 1971.

———, ed. and trans. *Journals and Other Documents on the Life and Voyages of Christopher Columbus*. New York: Heritage, 1963.

Muldoon, James. "The Columbus Quincentennial: Should Christians Celebrate It?" *America*, 27 October 1990.

Nash, Gary B., *Red, White, and Black: The Peoples of Early America*. Englewood Cliffs, N.J.: Prentice-Hall, 1974.

National Conference of Catholic Bishops (U.S.). "Heritage and Hope: Evangelization in America." Pastoral letter. Reprinted in *Origins* 20 (6 December 1990).

National Council for the Social Studies. *The Columbian Quincentenary: An Educational Opportunity*. October 1991.

National Council of the Churches of Christ in the USA. *A Faithful Response to the 500th Anniversary of the Arrival of Christopher Columbus*. Resolution adopted by the Governing Board, New York, 17 May 1990.

Newsweek, Special Issue, Fall/Winter 1991.

New World Encyclopedia, s.v. "Samory," https://www.newworldencyclopedia.org/entry/Samory.

1992/Kairos USA. "A Call to the Work of Repentance." *Sojourners* 20, no. 8 (October 1991).

Noble, David W. *The Eternal Adam and the New World Garden: The Central Myth in the American Novel Since 1830*. New York: Grosset & Dunlap, 1968.

Columbus and the Crisis of the West

O'Gorman, Edmundo. *The Invention of America: An Inquiry into the Historical Nature of the New World and the Meaning of Its History*. Bloomington: Indiana University Press, 1961.

Pagden, Anthony. *The Fall of Natural Man: The American Indian and the Origins of Comparative Ethnology*. Cambridge, U.K.: Cambridge University Press, 1982.

Panofsky, Erwin. *Renaissance and Renascences*. New York: Routledge, 2018.

Paredes, Mario. "A Hispanic Reaction to the NCC." Northeast Hispanic Catholic Center, New York, 25 July 1991. Reprinted in *Origins* 20 (16 August 1990).

Parkman, Francis. *The Jesuits in North America*. In *France and England in North America*, by Francis Parkman, vol. 1. New York: Library of America, 1983.

———. *La Salle and the Discovery of the Great West*. In *France and England in North America*, by Francis Parkman, vol. 1. New York: Library of America, 1983.

Paz, Octavio. *Collected Poems, 1957–1987*. New York: New Directions, 1987.

———. *The Poems of Octavio Paz*. New York: New Directions, 2018.

———. "Reflexiones de un intruso." *Vuelta*, January 1987.

Pearce, Roy Harvey. *Savagism and Civilization: A Study of the Indian and the American Mind*. Berkeley: University of California Press, 1988.

Peckham, Howard, and Charles Gibson, eds. *Attitudes of Colonial Powers toward the American Indian*. Salt Lake City: University of Utah Press, 1969.

Phillips, J. R. S. *The Medieval Expansion of Europe*. New York: Oxford University Press, 1988.

Phillips, William D., Jr., and Carla Rahn Phillips. *The Worlds of Christopher Columbus*. New York: Cambridge University Press, 1992.

Pidal, Ramón Menéndez. *El Padre Las Casas. Su doble personalidad*. Madrid: Espasa Calpe, 1963.

Poole, Stafford, Charles H. Lippy, and Robert Choquette, eds. *Christianity Comes to the Americas*. New York: Giniger Books, 1992.

Selected Bibliography

Prucha, Francis Paul. *The Great Father: The United States Government and the American Indian.* 2 vols. Lincoln: University of Nebraska Press, 1984.

Reff, Daniel T. "Anthropological Analysis of Exploration Texts: Cultural Discourse and the Ethnological Import of Fray Marcos de Niza's Journey to Cibola." *American Anthropologist,* no. 93 (September 1991).

Royal, Robert. *The God That Did Not Fail: How Religion Built and Sustains the West.* New York: Encounter Books, 2006.

———. "Plato Does Colorado: Were the Ancient Greeks Modern Gays?" *Crisis,* March 1995.

———. *The Virgin and the Dynamo: The Use and Abuse of Religion in Environmental Debates.* Grand Rapids: William B. Eerdmans, 1999.

Russell, Jeffrey Burton. *Inventing the Flat Earth: Columbus and Modern Historians.* New York: Praeger, 1991.

Said, Edward W. *Culture and Imperialism.* New York: Knopf, 1993.

Sale, Kirkpatrick. *The Conquest of Paradise: Christopher Columbus and the Columbian Legacy.* New York: Knopf, 1990.

Salisbury, Neal. *Manitou and Providence: Indians, Europeans, and the Making of New England, 1500–1643.* New York: Oxford University Press, 1982.

Sanoff, Alvin P. "The Myths of Columbus." Interview with Kirkpatrick Sale. *U.S. News & World Report,* 8 October 1990.

Schama, Simon. "They All Laughed at Christopher Columbus." *New Republic,* 6–13 January 1992.

Schele, Linda, and David Freidel. *A Forest of Kings: The Untold Story of the Ancient Maya.* New York: William Morrow, 1990.

Schlesinger, Arthur M., Jr. "Four Days with Fidel: A Havana Diary." *New York Review of Books,* 26 March 1992.

———. *The Disuniting of America: Reflections on a Multicultural Society.* New York: W. W. Norton, 1992.

Scott, James Brown. *The Spanish Origin of International Law.* Washington: Georgetown University Press, 1928.

———. "Separating the Man from the Myth." *Scholastic Update* 125, no. 2 (September 1991).

Columbus and the Crisis of the West

Silva Tena, Teresa. "El Sacrificio Humana En La *Apologetica Historia*." *Historia Mexicana* 16 (1967).

"The 1619 Project." *New York Times Magazine*, August 14, 2019. https://www.nytimes.com/interactive/2019/08/14/magazine/1619-america-slavery.html.

Smith, Ryan P. "How Native American Slaveholders Complicate the Trail of Tears Narrative." *Smithsonian Magazine*, March 6, 2018. https://www.smithsonianmag.com/smithsonian-institution/how-native-american-slaveholders-complicate-trail-tears-narrative-180968339/.

Sokolov, Raymond. "Stop Knocking Columbus." *Newsweek*, Special Issue, Fall/Winter 1991.

———. *Why We Eat What We Eat*. New York: Summit Books, 1992.

Soustelle, Jacques. *Daily Life of the Aztecs on the Eve of the Spanish Conquest*. Translated by Patrick O'Brien. Palo Alto: Stanford University Press, 1970.

Starr, Kevin. *Continental Ambitions: Roman Catholics in North America: The Colonial Experience*. San Francisco: Ignatius Press, 2016.

Steinfels, Peter. "Beliefs." *New York Times*, 26 October 1991.

Sweet, Leonard I. "Christopher Columbus and the Millennial Vision of the New World." *Catholic Historical Review* 72, no. 3 July 1986.

Taviani, Paolo Emilio. *Columbus: The Great Adventure*. Translated by Luciano F. Farina and Marc A. Beckwith. New York: Orion Books, 1991.

Thernstrom, Stephan. "The Columbus Controversy." *American Educator* 16, no. 1 (Spring 1992).

Thwaite, Reuben Gold, ed. *The Jesuit Relations and Allied Documents*. 73 vols. Cleveland: Burrows Brothers, 1896–1901.

Todorov, Tzvetan. *The Conquest of America: The Question of the Other*. Translated by Richard Howard. New York: Harper & Row, 1985.

Tooker, Elizabeth. "The United States Constitution and the Iroquois League." In *The Invented Indian: Cultural Fictions and Government Policies*, edited by James Clifton. New Brunswick, N.J.: Transaction Books, 1990.

Toynbee, Arnold. "'Asia' and 'Europe': Facts and Fantasies." In Annex to *A Study of History*. Vol. 8. New York: Oxford University Press, 1954.

Selected Bibliography

Trigger, Bruce G., ed. *Handbook of North American Indians.* 16 vols. Washington, D.C.: Smithsonian Institution Press, 1978.

Tuck, Richard. *Natural Rights Theories: Their Origin and Development.* New York: Cambridge University Press, 1971.

Varela, C., ed. *Cristobal Colon: Textos y documentos completos.* Madrid: Alianza, 1984.

Vargas Llosa, Mario. "Questions of Conquest." *Harper's,* December 1990.

Vignaud, Henry. *Études critiques sur la vie de Christophe Colomb avant ses découvertes.* Paris: H. Welter, 1905.

Viola, Herman J., ed. and trans. *After Columbus: The Smithsonian Chronicle of the North American Indians.* Washington: Smithsonian Institution Press, 1991.

Viola, Herman J., and Carolyn Margolis, eds. *Seeds of Change: Five Hundred Years Since Columbus.* Washington: Smithsonian Institution Press, 1991.

Vitoria, Francisco de. *Political Listings.* Edited by Anthony Pagden and Jeremy Lawrence. New York: Cambridge University Press, 1991.

———. *The Rights and Obligations of Indians and Spaniards in the New World.* Edited by Luciano Pereña Vincente. Salamanca and Washington: University of Salamanca and Catholic University of America, 1991.

Washburn, Wilcomb E. "History of Indian-White Relations." In *Handbook of North American Indians,* edited by Bruce G. Trigger, vol. 4. Washington, D.C.: Smithsonian Institution Press, 1978.

———. "The Meaning of 'Discovery' in the Fifteenth and Sixteenth Centuries." *American Historical Review* 68 (October 1962).

———. "Seventeenth-Century Indian Wars." In *Handbook of North American Indians,* edited by Bruce G. Trigger, vol. 15. Washington, D.C.: Smithsonian Institution Press, 1978.

Watts, Pauline Moffitt. "Prophecy and Discovery: On the Spiritual Origins of Christopher Columbus's 'Enterprise of the Indies.'" *American Historical Review* 90 (1985).

Weatherford, Jack. *Indian Givers.* New York: Crown, 1988.

Weissmann, Gerald. *They All Laughed at Christopher Columbus: Tales of Medicine and the Art of Discovery.* New York: Times Books, 1987.

Columbus and the Crisis of the West

"Westward Expansion of the Lakota." In "Sioux," Wikipedia. Last modified July 27, 2020. https://en.wikipedia.org/wiki/Sioux#cite_note-cheyenne-53.

White, Lynn, Jr. "The Historical Roots of Our Ecologic Crisis." *Science* 155 (March 10,1967).

Wilford, John Noble. *The Mysterious History of Columbus.* New York: Knopf, 1991.

Wills, Garry. "Goodbye, Columbus." *New York Review of Books,* 22 November 1990.

———. "Man of the Year." *New York Review of Books,* 21 November 1991.

Winsor, Justin. *Christopher Columbus, and How He Received and Imparted the Spirit of Discovery.* Boston: Houghton Mifflin, 1891.

Woodward, C. Vann. *The Old World's New World.* New York: Oxford University Press, 1991.

Index

Index

Index

The Discoverers (Boorstin),
38-39
District of Columbia, 30, 41-43
The Divine Comedy (Dante), 34,
261
Dobyns, Henry, 48
Dominican Order, 3, 118-19,
122, 124, 270, 287. See also
Vitoria, Francisco de
Douglass, Frederick, 4, 28
Dudley, Liliana Campos, 184
Dulmo, Fernão, 81

Earth Day, 221-22
Eastern Europe, 11, 173
Eastern Woodland Indians, 133,
168, 174
East Indies, 47
E. F. Schumacher Society, 46
Egypt, 7, 10, 194
Egyptians, 257-58
Einstein, Albert, 25
Eliade, Mircea, 154
Eliot, John, 138-39
Eliot, T. S., 90
Elliott, J. H., 13, 108, 166-67,
192
Emancipation Proclamation,
223
encomienda (land grant), 117-18,
192, 195
El Encuentro, 41, 49-50
England, 4, 11, 61, 109, 132,
137-38, 139, 164, 238, 255,
282, 287
Enlightenment, 173, 253, 259,
262, 276

E pluribus unum (motto), 243,
262
Erasmus of Rotterdam, 285
Estreito, João, 81
Eucharist, 136
Eurocentrism, 14, 39, 109-10,
142, 154, 166, 171, 176-77,
189, 201, 205-6, 231-32, 251-
55, 267-68, 283, 287, 289
Europeanization, 142

Fenton, William, 147
Ferdinand V, king of Spain, 10-
11, 35, 68, 77, 82, 87-88, 107,
113, 282
Fernández-Armesto, Felipe, 54,
57, 75, 81
Fernández de Oviedo, Gonzalo, 75
First Nations, 7
First Vatican Council, 31
Five Nations (Iroquois), 225-26
"Flat Error," 32, 33-34, 37-39
Florence, Italy, 89, 176, 284
"1491: America Before
Columbus" (National
Geographic), 198-99
France, 4, 9, 36, 109, 134-35,
139, 164, 282. See also Jesuits
Franciscans, 87, 106, 119, 132,
216, 284, 285, 286, 288. See
also Junípero Serra, Saint
Franklin, Benjamin, 30, 226
Frederick III, Holy Roman
Emperor, 284
French Revolution, 25, 272
Fuentes, Carlos, 194-97, 225
Fuson, Robert H., 68

Index

Marcus Aurelius, 261-62
Margarit, Mosen Pedro, 72
Martin, Joel S., 207
Martín de la Cruz, 125
Marvelous Possessions
   (Greenblatt), 96-97
Marx, Karl, 214
Marxism, 44, 167, 242
Maryland, 137
Massachusetts Bay Colony, 137
Massasoit (Wamponoag chief),
   237-38
materialism, 14
Mayans, 7, 12, 116, 149-50, 152,
   204, 269
McClay, Wilfred, 5-6
McPherson, James M., 27-28
Means, Russell, 43, 188
The Medieval Expansion of Europe
   (Phillips), 93
Mediterranean, 12, 31, 55, 93,
   260
Melville, Herman, 219
Mendes, Chico, 184
Mendoza, Antonio de, 114-15
Menominee, 240
Mesoamerica, 11, 148, 157, 194,
   205, 269; Mesoamerican, 150,
   152, 159, 168. *See also* Aztecs;
   Incas; Mayans; Olmecs;
   Toltecs; *specific countries*
Mesopotamia, 7, 194
Methodists, 7
Mexico, 18, 77, 125-26, 151-52,
   153, 193, 256; Mexicans, 95,
   112-15, 124, 126, 151-52,
   194-95

Mexico City, 11, 155. *See also*
   Tenochtitlán
Middle Ages, 10, 38-39, 91-93,
   95, 118, 253, 258, 262, 263,
   265-66, 274, 279, 281
Middle East, 10, 12. *See also*
   specific countries
missionaries, 3. *See also*
   Dominican Order; Jesuits
The Mission (1986 film) (Joffé),
   132
Mississippi River, 178
Moctezuma, 155, 194-95
Mohammed, 190
Mohawks, 225
Montesinos, Antonio de, 112,
   119
Moors, 87, 112
More, Thomas, Saint, 166
Morison, Samuel Eliot, 36-37,
   52, 190
Mosaic Law, 265
Mound Builders, 224
Mount Rushmore, 8-9
Mozart, Wolfgang Amadeus,
   97-98, 269
Muhammad II, Sultain, 282
Muldoon, James, 108-9
Muskogean Natchez, 207-8
Muslims, 9, 10-11, 15, 91, 114,
   124, 190, 282-83, 286
The Mysterious History of
   Columbus, 94

Nahuatl, v, 125, 268
NASA, 280
Natchez, 207-8, 225

Index

Phillips, J. R. S., 93
Picasso, Pablo, 197
Piccolomini, Aeneas Sylvius
  (Pope Pius II), 86, 282, 284
Piedra de sol (Paz), 152
Pierce, Franklin, 221
Pilgrims, 236-39
Pius II, Pope, 86, 282, 284
Pizarro, Francisco, 126, 195, 270
Plains Indians, 159-60, 183
Plato, 256, 265, 276
Plymouth, Massachusetts, 137
Politics (Aristotle), 121, 255
Polo, Marco, 86, 177
Poole, Stafford, 106
Portugal, 81, 109, 128, 164, 168,
  266
posthuman future, 14
Powhatan (chief), 237
Prairie Potawatomi, 240
pre-Columbian America, 11,
  151-54, 162-63, 178, 256
The Prince (Machiavelli), 88,
  282
Princeton University, 84, 160,
  202-3
progressivism, 13, 14
Protestantism, 31, 34, 133, 137,
  258, 266. *See also specific*
  demoninations
Public Broadcasting Service
  (PBS), 21, 51, 187, 189-90
Pueblos, 172
Puritan/Puritanism, 137-39, 160,
  239

Quakers, 7, 137

Quarto abeunte saeculo (Leo III),
  32
Quincentenary, 5, 19, 26, 40-45,
  69, 105, 160, 179-82, 187-89,
  194, 197, 201, 210, 213, 216,
  219
Quinto Centenario España
  Foundation, 194

racism, 9, 14, 27-28, 40, 141,
  143, 201, 214-15, 227,
  236, 252, 257, 259. *See also*
  whiteness
Reagan, Ronald, 188
Reformation, 13, 25, 32, 48,
  253, 258, 266
Reiter's syndrome, 85
Religions of Mesoamerica
  (Carrasco), 153-54
Renaissance, 22, 25, 92, 94-97,
  166, 169, 171, 253, 259, 262,
  266, 283-84, 285
Resistance 500, 219-21
Restorationists, 241
Rhode Island, 101, 137
Ricard, Robert, 126
Rio Grande River, 148, 159
Rivera, Diego, 151, 154
Rodrigo de Triana, 280
Roman Empire, 7, 49, 253, 258,
  260-65, 270, 283. *See also*
  Holy Roman Empire
Rome, 3, 10, 17, 44, 117, 120,
  239
Ross, John (Cherokee chief), 8
Rousseau, Jean Jacques, 47

Index

About the Author

Robert Royal is the founder and president of the Faith & Reason Institute in Washington, D.C., and editor-in-chief of *The Catholic Thing* (www.thecatholicthing.org), an online publication that appears daily and is translated into five foreign languages. He writes and speak on questions of ethics, culture, religion, and politics. He has appeared on various television and radio stations around the United States, including frequent appearances on EWTN as a special commentator on Church matters, and has lectured in fifteen foreign countries. His most recent book is *A Deeper Vision: The Catholic Intellectual Tradition in the 20th Century*. Other books include *Dante Alighieri, The Catholic Martyrs of the Twentieth Century: A Comprehensive Global History, The Pope's Army*, and *The God That Did Not Fail*. Royal holds a B.A. and an M.A. from Brown University and a Ph.D. in comparative literature from the Catholic University of America and has received fellowships to study in Italy from the Renaissance Society of America and as a Fulbright scholar.

Sophia Institute

Sophia Institute is a nonprofit institution that seeks to nurture the spiritual, moral, and cultural life of souls and to spread the Gospel of Christ in conformity with the authentic teachings of the Roman Catholic Church.

Sophia Institute Press fulfills this mission by offering translations, reprints, and new publications that afford readers a rich source of the enduring wisdom of mankind.

Sophia Institute also operates the popular online resource CatholicExchange.com. *Catholic Exchange* provides world news from a Catholic perspective as well as daily devotionals and articles that will help readers to grow in holiness and live a life consistent with the teachings of the Church.

In 2013, Sophia Institute launched Sophia Institute for Teachers to renew and rebuild Catholic culture through service to Catholic education. With the goal of nurturing the spiritual, moral, and cultural life of souls, and an abiding respect for the role and work of teachers, we strive to provide materials and programs that are at once enlightening to the mind and ennobling to the heart; faithful and complete, as well as useful and practical.

Sophia Institute gratefully recognizes the Solidarity Association for preserving and encouraging the growth of our apostolate over the course of many years. Without their generous and timely support, this book would not be in your hands.

www.SophiaInstitute.com
www.CatholicExchange.com
www.SophiaInstituteforTeachers.org

Sophia Institute Press® is a registered trademark of Sophia Institute.
Sophia Institute is a tax-exempt institution as defined by the
Internal Revenue Code, Section 501(c)(3). Tax ID 22-2548708.